Commitment
to Welfare

Also by Richard Titmuss

RICHARD M. TITMUSS

Commitment
to Welfare

INTRODUCTION
BY
BRIAN ABEL-SMITH

Professor of Social Administration
London School of Economics

London

GEORGE ALLEN & UNWIN LTD
RUSKIN HOUSE   MUSEUM STREET

FIRST PUBLISHED IN 1968
SECOND IMPRESSION 1970
THIRD IMPRESSION 1971
FOURTH IMPRESSION 1973
SECOND EDITION 1976

© *George Allen & Unwin Ltd, 1968, 1976*

ISBN 0 04 361020 X hardback
0 04 361021 8 paperback

PRINTED IN GREAT BRITAIN
BY COX & WYMAN LTD
LONDON, FAKENHAM AND READING

INTRODUCTION

Though it was not written for this purpose, *Commitment to Welfare*, like *Essays on 'the Welfare State'*, has become a basic text book on Social Policy and Administration which students are advised to read, often rather early in their study of the subject. This is because it says so much of fundamental importance in one highly condensed volume. It is, however, a difficult book to pick up and read without knowledge of the historical context of the debate to which Titmuss was contributing, or of the author.

Richard Titmuss was Professor of Social Administration at the London School of Economics between 1950 and his death in 1973. His early career was spent working for a British insurance company. In the late 1930s and early 1940s he wrote during his evenings and week-ends several important books on social conditions and social problems. The reputation of his work resulted in his appointment as official historian of social policy during the war. His remarkable volume *Problems of Social Policy*, published in 1950, led to his entry to London University as head of an academic department, though he had no degree and had never attended a university.

The present book consists of articles and lectures covering the period 1961 to 1967. Though he was teaching throughout this period, he was also a member of a number of Government Committees and Commissions. His active involvement in the making of policy is reflected in some of the themes developed in this book. From 1965 until 1971 he was a member of the Community Relations Commission—a body established to try and improve race relations in view of the steady flow of immigrants to Britain from mainly the West Indies and South-East Asia. He was a member of the Royal Commission on Medical Education 1965–8. This led him to reflect deeply on the role of the doctor in contemporary society, and the training and education which would be needed for doctors who would serve the next generation. It also focused his interest on the international migration of doctors. His interest in medical care had however been stimulated by his statistical investigations before the war, his examination of the provision of health services during the war as social historian, and the two years he spent collaborating with Dr J. N. Morris in the Social Medicine Research Unit before moving to the LSE.

From its establishment in 1966 until his death he was a member and later Deputy Chairman of the Supplementary Benefits Commission, which is responsible throughout Britain for the provision of cash assistance (subject to a test of need) both to those without social insurance benefits and in supplementation of them. The provision of what many other countries call public assistance is in Britain a central government rather than a local government responsibility, but the SBC is an independent agency with considerable discretionary powers not subject to Ministerial directives. Titmuss' involvement in framing policies for the exercise of these powers and in the practical problems of administering a selective cash benefit helped sharpen his interest in the world-wide debate on how far cash should be provided universally (without a test of need), and how far selectively (subject to some test of income, means or needs). His work for the Commission contributed to the thinking behind several of the essays in Part III particularly Chapter X.

Throughout his life he retained an interest in the role of private insurance. This interest is shown in the fundamental discussion of the role of private and public insurance in Chapter XV. This essay, like so many others in this volume, could stimulate a series of Ph.D.s on premium setting by private insurance companies as well as the evolution of social insurance away from the theoretical model of private insurance towards the achievement of more and wider social objectives.

Titmuss had himself been one of the authors of a pension plan for Britain. *National Superannuation* was published by the Labour Party in 1957 and became adopted as its policy. The broad principles of the plan were incorporated in a bill introduced by Richard Crossman as Secretary of State which failed to become law before the fall of the Labour Government in 1970. An amended plan was introduced in the next Labour Government by Mrs Barbara Castle and became law in 1975.

The LSE Department of Social Science (later Social Science and Administration) of which Titmuss became the sole professor in 1950 provided courses in social administration and also professional education for social workers. Its historical development is explained in Chapter IV. There are no comparable academic departments in the universities of continental Europe or the United States. The development of social policy and administration as an academic subject in the British Universities since the Second World War owed much to Titmuss' influence and example. It was therefore fitting that he should address the first meeting of the newly-formed Social Administration Association in 1967. In this lecture published as Chapter I he discusses the scope of the subject and stresses its relationship with the education of social workers.

Throughout his time at the London School of Economics, there were many who argued that universities and the LSE in particular should not be involved in vocational education—particularly of social workers. In the second and third chapters, Titmuss discusses the role of the university as he envisaged it, having come to it himself from outside. He criticizes the narrow role of universities as seen by the government-appointed Committee on Higher Education 1963 (chaired by Lord Robbins, also of the LSE) and defends the vocational role—the need to combine imagination and experience. He criticizes the excessive emphasis on pure research in universities— particularly the German type of research institute which has influenced developments in the United States. One dangerous consequence was in his view the relative neglect of teaching which he saw as one of the underlying reasons for the students' 'revolt' which hit the LSE in 1967, as it hit North America, France and other countries about the same time. A second consequence, in his opinion, was a failure of schools of social work in some countries to enter into major controversies about social change which had limited the role which social workers played. Social workers should not, in his view, confine themselves to individual therapy—helping the client to adapt to a reality 'which the caseworker knows but the client does not'. He thought they had a duty to contribute to the diagnosis of social failings and help to educate society in the need for action. This theme has since been developed by others, though not always with the same moderation and balance. He was careful not to tip the baby out with the bath water. He saw a role for casework as well as for community work and community action.

Many of the lectures in this volume are on broad subjects which had been chosen as themes for conferences—subjects which Titmuss himself had not chosen and probably would not have chosen. Yet he managed to include in such lectures much that was original and possibly timeless, though many of the arguments are highly compressed. He also included a number of points which were specially directed at the particular audience he was addressing at that point of time. Titmuss not only enlarged our understanding of social policy but also influenced it. Thus while part of the lectures are important because of their deep insight into what social policy is about, other parts are important because they helped to shape events. They led people to favour one policy rather than another and helped to build an informed opinion in favour of a specific legislative change. The lectures help us to understand social history but to some extent they are themselves part of social history.

The second part of the book has as its underlying theme the debate which was rumbling in Britain and in some other countries throughout the 1960s about the organisation of social work and social welfare services. Readers coming new to this debate might find it easier to read the essays in this section in the reverse order. The earliest lecture delivered in 1961 and printed as Chapter IX makes the point that community care for the mentally ill was a fiction unless money and manpower were provided to make it a reality. Three years later (Chapter VIII) he returns to the same theme in the context of provision for the elderly and then discusses the organization of community care services. How much time were family doctors and district nurses actually devoting to the elderly in the community? Whose responsibility was it for taking action? Was 'the medical officer of health really equipped to administer, co-ordinate and develop services to meet *social* needs or should these responsibilities be the concern of a social welfare service at local level' (p. 101)? He knew well that if the medical officer of health were to lose these responsibilities it would bring into question the whole future role and function of the MOH as the job would hardly be viable without them. He calls for an authoritative inquiry into responsibility for the administration and deployment of the local health and welfare services. Such an inquiry—the Seebohm Committee—was established a year later.

Speaking in Canada in 1966 (Chapter VI) he points out the disadvantages of providing separate specialized services for particular categories of client which was the broad situation in Britain at that time and makes the case for bringing together in one organisation social work services which care for different types of client. But how broad should such a service be? Should it be confined to the problems of families or should it extend to cover all or nearly all community social needs? It was the wider option which finally emerged in Britain from 1970 with the establishment within local government of Departments of Social Services.

The third section of the book includes his contributions during this period to a wider debate of much longer duration—a debate which has underlaid the development of social policy for well over a century and is by no means concluded, if it will ever be concluded. How much redistribution should there be in society? What role should private insurance and tax concessions play in this redistribution? How far should redistribution by government be selective (if so, by what criteria) and how far should universal benefits be provided? How far should redistribution be in kind or cash? And, if we were to achieve an acceptable redistribution of cash, should people be left to make their own choices on what services they purchased? During the 1960s the colour of the debate was influenced by an important underlying assumption—that western societies were achieving and would continue to achieve relatively rapid economic growth. As people got richer could they be expected to buy their own social services? Would affluence lead to an end to ideological conflict in society? It was also influenced by a technological development—the growing use of the computer. Did this development make it possible to operate selective services in both a more efficient and more acceptable way? Could the income tax system be transformed into the sole agent of redistribution, doing all the giving as well as the taking so that social insurance, public assistance and all other means tested schemes could be abolished?

Once again the reader may find it easier to read the essays in this section in reverse order. Starting with the origins of public service pensions (Chapter XVII), then the development of Titmuss' earlier essay the *Social Division of Welfare*[1] (Chapter XVI) then the relationship between private and public insurance (Chapter XV) before reading one specific application of his principles to cash provisions for children (Chapter XIV). This essay was written after research findings had been given widespread publicity showing the extent of poverty among families with dependent children. He argues for the partial assimilation of child tax allowances and family allowances. Legislation to replace family allowances and child tax allowances with a single child benefit payable to the mother was passed ten years later—in 1975.

Chapters XI to XIII are Titmuss' reply to the new school of liberal economists of which Professor Friedman of Chicago is the best known exponent. Chapter XIII is devoted to the question of whether economic growth can be expected to lead automatically to social growth and make it possible to dismantle the Welfare State. His lecture, delivered to the Fabian Society in 1966 (Chapter XII) concentrates on four questions. Can economic growth by itself solve the problem of poverty? Can private welfare markets solve the problem of discrimination and stigma? Do they offer consumers more choice? Are social services in kind different from goods in the private market? In answer to this last question, he discusses the example of the marketing of human blood which he developed later into a book *The Gift Relationship* (1970) which achieved a wide readership in the United States and made a major impact on blood policy.

On the international level he shows in Chapter XI the consequences of the international migration of doctors which has constituted a major hidden subsidy from the poorer countries to the richer and questions the morality of preaching family planning to developing nations while attracting away the skilled manpower needed for services to provide birth control and death control (p. 128). He then analyses the functions which social service benefits fulfil.

The first lecture in this section (Chapter X) on 'Universal and Selective Social Services' is still regarded by many people as the most penetrating article which has yet been written on this much discussed subject. In it he shows that income tax coding cannot be simply adapted as a means-testing mechanism to replace all others. Nor is this conclusion falsified by the demonstration in 1971 that a system of tax credits was operationally feasible in Britain.* Even this scheme would have only replaced one means test on those at work—the family income supplement scheme which was not yet introduced when Titmuss wrote this essay.

The final part of the book is devoted to medical care. The reader might like to start with the historical essay (Chapter XX) which discusses some of the underlying forces which led to the development of the National Health Service in Britain. The last chapter gives Titmuss' rationale for collective provision of health services and draws attention to the intrinsic weaknesses of a private market operating in health services, illustrating this theme from the experiences of the United States.

The lecture on the role of the family doctor (Chapter XVIII) was originally delivered to a poorly attended meeting of the British Medical Association at a time when there was growing unrest among general practitioners in Britain about their work load, pay and conditions of service which reflected in part an insecurity about their present and future role. Was there a future for the generalist doctor in the face of the growth of medical knowledge and the world-wide trend towards specialization? Titmuss makes the case for the increasing use of auxiliaries and ancillaries—for what is now the accepted policy of primary care teams and for the independent personal doctor to become a community doctor. In his lecture on the growth in the use of pharmaceuticals (Chapter XIX) he analyses the pressures on the doctor to prescribe, and the influences of continuity of care, communication with different social classes and of the organization of medical care.

This stark summary of some of the questions which Titmuss discusses in this book inevitably over-simplifies both the issues and his analyses of them. The book needs to be read more than once to see just how complex some of these questions really are.

B. ABEL-SMITH
October, 1975

* *See* Treasury and DHSS, *Proposals for a Tax Credit System*, HMSO, 1972.

NOTE

1. R. M. Titmuss, *Essays on 'the Welfare State'*, George Allen & Unwin, 1958, Chapter 2.

PREFACE

Of the twenty-one essays included in this book six have not been published and eight have been printed in conference proceedings and journals (some in other countries) which students of the subject are said to have great difficulty in locating. Naturally, they complain about this, and the patience of my secretary, Mrs Angela Vivian, is sometimes over-strained by the flow of requests for offprints, typewritten copies and the like.

Despite, therefore, some hesitations which I share with many of my colleagues about the value of 'collections' I decided to include with the unpublished essays those which have appeared in scattered places and some others which have been printed in pamphlet form and in journals such as *The Lancet* and *Medical Care*. Here I should add that the gentle persuasiveness and help of Mr Charles Furth, of Allen and Unwin, influenced these decisions.

All these essays have been arranged under four subjects, each in chronological order beginning with the last. I am conscious, however, that this division into four parts gives an exaggerated impression of tidiness which I hasten to disavow. The more I try to understand the role of welfare and the human condition the more untidy it all becomes. Hence, I am also conscious of a certain repetitiveness of ideas and illustrations (on occasion even possibly verbatim) which occur in a number of the essays and under different subject headings. I hope there are not too many.

Permission to reprint has kindly been given by the editors of certain journals and I would like to thank them. A reference to the journal in question (or the origin of the lecture) has been added on the first page of each chapter. In certain cases (particularly the unpublished lectures) I have taken the opportunity to revise and expand the contents. In one published article, *Ethics and Economics of Medical Care*, I have added an explanatory postscript about certain events which followed its appearance in *Medical Care* in 1963; I have also included therein further notes and references to sources and more recent materials.

Apart from my talk to students of the Department of Social Administration at the London School of Economics on the occasion of the Department's Jubilee (which I include for sentimental reasons) and two other lectures (Chapters IX and XX) all the rest have been written in the last four years. This would not have been possible without the aid, subjective and objective, of my wife. If the source of ideas counted for authorship some would have to be attributed to her.

Lastly, I want to thank some of my friends and relations for advice and thoughtful criticism on early drafts of particular essays. I am grateful to Professor Brian Abel-Smith, Professor David Donnison, Mr Tony Lynes, Mrs K. McDougall, Professor J. N. Morris, Mr and Mrs Robin Oakley, Mr Michael Reddin, Professor Peter Townsend and Mr Reg Wright. I wish also to acknowledge the help I have received from my secretary, Mrs Vivian, and all the hard work of three people who, at various times, more than fulfilled the role of research assistants—Mr Lynes, Mr Reddin and Miss Sarah West. To my friends in the United States who have furnished me with materials and stimulated me with writings in recent years I owe a special word of thanks— Professor Eveline Burns, Miss Leonore Epstein, Professor Mitchell Ginsberg, Professor Everett Hughes, Professor Alfred Kahn, Dr Ida Merriam, Professor S. M. Miller, Professor Daniel Moynihan, Miss M. Orshansky, Professor Martin Rein, Professor A. Rogow, and Mr Alvin Schorr.

R. M. T.   Acton, August, 1967

CONTENTS

PART I SOCIAL ADMINISTRATION:
TEACHING AND RESEARCH

Chapter 1

THE SUBJECT OF SOCIAL ADMINISTRATION

Seventeen years ago, at about this time in the season, I was struggling to write something of interest about the subject of Social Administration for an inaugural lecture at the London School of Economics and Political Science.[1] From a few notes I still have about that anxious summer I can see that I did not want to claim too much for the subject. Generalists, and those who conceive their subject as having an integrative function in teaching and research, are confronted with a particular occupational hazard in attempting to give reasons for their existence. In the eyes of others, they may seem to be saying, 'Why then the world's mine oyster.' This impression may also be supported at times by the tendency of social administrators to work in areas of thought and action neglected by other social scientists; they become interested in, for example, organization, structure and development relating to the roles of family planners, town planners, architects, lawyers, nurses, doctors and other professional groups, and they start asking economic, social or administrative questions about institutions and systems which might properly be thought, on a strictly departmental view of the social sciences, to be infringing the unwritten rules of academic trespass.

Understandably then, I was cautious in 1950. For a relatively new subject, amorphous and obviously capable of territorial expansion, there were dangers of being accused of trespass in the even broader acres of sociology, economics or public administration. At the same time, there were others in the social sciences, sociologists and economists in particular, who were claiming that their subjects could, given adequate support by society, unlock the doors to rational decision-making in certain areas of social policy and resource allocation. There were, as Professor Sprott subsequently described them,[2] the 'fact-gatherers' (an industrious but rather grubby group); the 'method-men' (a somewhat sinister statistical brigade); the 'sociological bird-watchers' (with muddy boots and rural lisps) and, in the rear, a varied collection of aloof and straggling theorists.

* Lecture delivered at the first meeting of the Social Administration Association, University of Nottingham, July 1967.

13

One could be equally amusing about social administrators; the pragmatic engineers of incremental change (addicted to lonely short-distance running); the politicians in academic disguise (frequenting the murky corridors of power); the income-maintenance men (a particularly earnest lot); the illegitimate social historians, and so on.

There are occasions when teachers should not take themselves and their subjects too seriously. It is good for our students as well as for ourselves. On an occasion like this one, to launch the Social Administration Association, it is perhaps appropriate to strike a self-critical note. Some of us are so busily engaged with the 'ought' as well as the 'why' that we need to remind ourselves from time to time that we are no more than assistant servants in the struggle against irrationality and obscurantism.

Why, then, if we divest ourselves of any illusions of expertize grandeur, do we need a Social Administration Association? Why are we here—have all our journeys been really necessary—at this particular point in time? Let me begin our discussion by offering a few personal reasons; some negative and some, I hope, of a more positive kind.

First, I would like to say something about certain reasons which cannot justify the establishment of this Association. We are not here to found a branch of the Conservative, Labour or Liberal Parties. While the nature of our subject, including as it does the formation and development of social policies, may lead us to be much concerned with the contemporary human condition, it does not follow that we should see ourselves (or others should see us) as advancing any particular political ideology. Our first duty and our last duty is to the truth. It is because I am sceptical of the claims that are sometimes made for a value-free social science that I restate this fundamental allegiance. The values that we hold should be clear to our students; the evidence on all sides should also be clear. It is part of our responsibilities to expose more clearly the value choices that confront societies in the arena of social welfare.

In saying this I would not wish it to be thought that in my view social administrators are more likely to be culpable of misrepresentation, bias and prejudice than political scientists, economists, sociologists, social psychologists, and members of the Social Medicine Association and similar groupings of teachers and research workers. But we do have a particular public image associated perhaps with the work of reformers from Booth to Beveridge. Sometimes it assumes a curious shape. Seventeen years ago—to reminisce again—I was thought by one of my most distinguished professorial colleagues at the London School of Economics to be actively concerned with the training of midwives. I had to confess that I had no competence in that area although I respected the contribution that that profession had made to human progress in rescuing doctors (as well as parents) from obscurantism, and in raising standards of maternal and child health.

Social administration is not alone in having difficulties in its external relationships. Sociology has to bear the cross of being associated both with socialism and social work. Professor Marshall, in his inaugural lecture 'Sociology at the Crossroads' in 1946 found it necessary, while remarking that 'sociology need not be ashamed of wishing to be useful', to comment on the implication that sociology had some connection with socialism.[3] Others, and members of the British Sociological Association, have since expressed anxiety about being seen walking out in the company of social workers. This, of course, is understandable behaviour in the search for professional standards and exclusiveness and the wish to effect a monogamous alliance with a beautiful natural scientist. It becomes even more understandable if there is any validity in Professor Shil's recent comment that 'sociology is becoming a mild surrogate religion . . . replacing prayer as a source of guidance'.[4]

Now I must turn to other reasons which, in my view, do not justify the formation of a Social Administration Association. First, a word about relationships with the social work profession. The decision to establish a Social Administration Association should not be interpreted as a retreat from our traditional connections with the education and training of social workers; nor, on the other hand, does it indicate any move towards a centralizing takeover bid. The seven social work professional bodies represented on the Standing Conference appear to be working actively towards a unified national organization.[5] Should such a merger take place it will clearly have important implications for the future scope and content of undergraduate and professional courses, both general and specific, in institutions of higher education. The study of social administration in most of its ramifications, theoretical and applied, forms an essential part of the education of social workers. This must be continued and strengthened.

In the past, the connections between the subject of social administration and the content of casework courses (or, to employ a medical analogy, the connections between the basic scientific course and clinical teaching) have not been as close or as integrated as they might have been. There is a need to build more bridges if students are to be helped to see the relationships between structure and function, and between the administrative behaviour of human organizations and the roles of professional workers. My colleagues,

David Donnison and Roy Parker, have contributed to this bridge-building,[6] and similar fruitful developments are taking place in other universities and institutions of higher education.

It is one of the aims of the Social Administration Association to provide a forum for discussion and study for those who have teaching and research responsibilities in this field. The formation of the Association should also make it possible to further the discussion of common teaching problems between social administrators and those more directly concerned with the content of social work training. Social workers are not, however, the only professional group whose basic education calls for the study of social policy and administration.

One of the more interesting trends in British society in recent years has been the growing concern about the education, vocational equipment and in-training of those responsible for the administration and management of the social services, and also with the education of many groups of specialist workers—in schools, hospital offices, town planning departments, trade unions, central and local government, and other institutions. It is coming to be recognized that many of these workers require for the better management of their organizations an introduction to the study of social administration. This is not a matter of teaching techniques of management. It is largely a question of providing administrators with a broader and historical understanding of institutions and systems affecting the operations of the social services, and providing it in such a non-specialist way that students are not led to think of themselves as failures in not aiming to be research workers, professional sociologists or BBC 'Panorama' experts.

These problems of *how* to teach social administration in non-specialist as well as specialist ways will receive added force when the Seebohm Committee reports; when the Scottish White Paper on *Social Work and the Community* is implemented; when the Royal Commission on Local Government utters; when Fulton on the Higher Civil Service is written; when the Maud and Mallaby recommendations are digested; when the Diploma in Municipal Administration is reviewed, and so on.

Obviously, there are tasks ahead for social administrators; not only in research and evaluation but in examining the organization, scope and content of teaching for different categories of workers at different levels in different specific and general settings. These tasks would be relatively uncomplicated if we aimed principally or solely at reproducing ourselves; of discovering and training the next generation of Marshes, Joneses, Lafittes, Donnisons, Titmusses, etc.

16

But this, as I see it, is not our aim. Unashamedly, we can say that we have broader, extra-mural, worker education, liberalizing responsibilities and objectives. In this sense, we reject the philosophy of the Robbins Report of 1963 on Higher Education. What fundamentally the Committee recommended was an extension and expansion of élitest education.[7] Learning to think was conceived as the end in itself. Ability to reason and act effectively in a situation was not considered a criterion of academic success or intellectual competence and it was assumed that any element of education directed towards action was necessarily specific and technical and not abstract or imaginative.[8]

This philosophy of higher education was the reverse of that propounded by the late Alexander Carr-Saunders, a former director of the London School of Economics, when he wrote: 'The young are anxious to think about and discuss general questions affecting the human situation; thus general education, as well as specialized preparation for a particular career, is within the ambition of students; it is the task of the university to unite them.'[9]

With due modesty, I suggest we apply this thought to the tasks that lie ahead in the teaching of social administration. In helping to unite the educational and vocational ambitions of students, the mature as well as the immature, the middle-aged as well as the young, we aim— as an Association—to unite all those teachers concerned with the subject in all institutions of higher and further education—and not just those teachers who happen to find themselves in those places we currently call universities. We thus launch the Association not as an exclusive, protective, élitest admiration club, but as a means of building bridges and fostering communications between teachers in different sectors of our hierarchial system of higher education. Our situations and our roles may vary but we have interests in common.

The primary one is teaching; this to me—the advancement of teaching—is the primary aim in the launching of the Social Administration Association. The subject, seen as an integrative, analytical area of study, is difficult to teach well. We all, I am sure, have experiences and memories of dull, descriptive monologues. But these and similar viruses are the cause of much specialized diseased teaching to undergraduates in all the social sciences; in psychology, in economics, and in the endless thematic orchestrations of role theory. Social Administration is thus not peculiar in this respect. It has, in recent years, and in common with social science disciplines, experienced an 'information explosion' in all its branches or subspecializations. This explosion and accumulation of information, empirical studies and untested (and perhaps untestable) hypotheses has exacerbated the problem of how to teach and what, selectively, to teach. As a result, we may at present be over-teaching information and under-teaching the imaginative excitements of unifying perspectives and principles.

But this only adds to my conviction that the primary function of the university is to teach; secondly, and complementarily, to advance knowledge. I do not, therefore, subscribe to what Ashby has described as 'the academic Arian heresy' which holds to the concept of the university as a research institute.[10] This concept, which came to England from Germany in the nineteenth century, has done, and is doing, much harm to the system of higher education in this country. The academic, with his research team, his questionnaires and computers, his governmental and foundation infrastructure of resources, should be left alone—relieved from the 'burden' of teaching—to do his 'useful' research. No longer is it argued that, as a man of leisured erudition, he should be left alone with his useless philosophic doubts.

The case is attractively presented in de Jouvenel's recent book *The Art of Conjecture*.[11] The author seeks to demonstrate the great importance, indeed the social duty of academics, of attempting to make forecasts with maximum coherence and effectiveness:

'the common task of forecasting will cause (the social sciences) to converge again. None of these human disciplines, each fixed on one aspect of human behaviour and relations, can make forecasts in its field without drawing support from the other disciplines. As data are compiled and methods compared, each discipline will undergo an internal transformation arising from the new orientations towards forecasting. In each, research capable of shedding light on the dynamics of change will be of primary importance, and we shall see few talents devoted to pure erudition (that which cannot conceivably affect our decisions).'

Seen in its essentials, this is the case for a technocratic society. It is based on the premise that modern civilizations have repudiated the sacredness of institutions and commitments, and therewith the means of achieving a known future. We are thus faced with more uncertainty and, at the same time, we want things to change more rapidly. Inter-disciplinary forecasting is the answer. There is no room for radical political choices; another way of pronouncing the demise of the political dialogue. Thus, the academic becomes the master forecaster in a technocratic society. In the past, men fought their misery with dreams; now, in an affluent age, they must fight anxiety with slide rules.

I should not, however, involve you today in this controversy. Whatever the implications of this particular thesis for our subject I want to re-affirm the need for useful education as well as useful research; that is to say, for education which furthers the abilities of men and women to reason and act effectively in a variety of vocational situations.

Most of these situations for most of our students, whether they be overseas students or British students, whether they come from developed or developing countries, will be non-market situations. In other words, we are concerned primarily though not exclusively with the imaginative education of men and women who either will be or are employed in the public and voluntary services as administrators, professionals, research workers or in other vocational roles, and who may in the future contribute, politically and in other ways, to the working of democratic institutions. There is nothing very original in this statement; in the year 1316 a college was founded in Cambridge for the special purpose of providing 'Clerks for the King's service'.[12] The interests of our students, educational and vocational, thus determine to some extent how we define, study and teach the subject of social administration.

Our problems, as teachers of social administration, are not so dissimilar from those that faced teachers of the subject of history a hundred years ago when it had barely attained academic status in England. For the first seventeen years of its academical existence, said J. R. Green, writing in 1867, 'history was struggling out of that condition in which it was looked on as no special or definite study, but as part of that general mass of things, which every gentleman should know'.[13] Freeman pronounced that the History School in those years was 'an easy school for rich men'.[14]

This is familiar stuff; who has not heard it said that social administration is no special or definite study but a part of that general mass of things which every earnest young man or woman should know? And that social administration is a soft option—which begs the question whether all subjects can be equally hard options for all students in an equally hard social science world.

Because I have drawn on the experience of the history school in the nineteenth century it must not be concluded that I am predicting an analogous future for the Social Administration School. I feel no need to predict. That part of the general mass of things in the social sciences with which we, as social administrators, are concerned is, I have no doubt, a part that can be studied and taught in the best traditions of academic scholarship and detachment. What matters is how we teach and how we study; if we bring to these tasks that uncommon mixture of intellectual excitement and practical usefulness we need not worry about the status ranking of social administration in the world of the social sciences.

Now I must say something about the unsoluble problem of defining 'Social Administration'. I have not left myself much time in which to do so; that, I think, is all to the good.

It would be possible to begin by embarking on a content analysis of inaugural lectures on the subject in recent years or by examining the variety of definitions of 'Social Policy and Administration' offered in the growing volume of textbooks and essays in Britain and other countries. This could be invidious or boring or both. But at least I can point out that the term 'Social Administration' is a misleading one; we are not experts in office management and social book-keeping, nor are we technicians in man manipulation. One reason for the term we carry around and which creates so much confusion is that the social sciences have consumed, tainted and spoiled collective nouns in the English language at such a rate in recent decades that hardly any other options now remain. In accepting these difficulties, as we must, we can remember Edmund Burke's consolation: 'Custom reconciles us to everything.' And we can also draw some shreds of compensation from the thought that, unlike some who teach in other fields of the social sciences, we do not have continually to look over our shoulders and ask ourselves whether we are behaving, teaching and researching like professional social administrators. There is no such animal.

If, like others before me, I refuse to offer a definitive explanation of the subject I will nevertheless attempt briefly to say something about our interests and our perspectives.[15]

Basically, we are concerned with the study of a range of social needs and the functioning, in conditions of scarcity, of human organizations, traditionally called social services or social welfare systems, to meet these needs. This complex area of social life lies outside or on the fringes of the so-called free market, the mechanisms of price and tests of profitability. Though this area has some of the characteristics of the market-place, for example, all social services are allocative systems and ration demand and supply, there are many other characteristics which relate to the non-economic elements in human relations.

Social administration is thus concerned, for instance, with different types of moral transactions, embodying notions of gift-exchange, of reciprocal obligations, which have developed in modern societies in institutional forms to bring about and maintain social and community relations. Mauss, the French sociologist, depicted, in his book *The Gift*, the growth of social insurance—of what he called 'solicitude in mutuality and co-operation'—as an expression of need and response in group relationships. 'The theme of the gift,' he wrote, 'of freedom and obligation in the gift, of generosity and self-interest in giving, reappear in our own society like the resurrection of a dominant motif long forgotten.'[16]

Many of the services, transactions and transfers, we study, whether they are classified as social, public, occupational, voluntary or fiscal, contain both economic and non-economic elements. It is the objectives of these services, transactions and transfers in relation to social needs, rather than the particular administrative method or institutional device employed to attain objectives, which largely determine our interests in research and study and the categorization of these activities as social services. The study of welfare objectives and of social policy thus lies at the centre of our focus of vision. We may bring to this focus, singly or in combination, the methods, techniques and insights of the historian, the economist, the statistician, the sociologist or, on occasion, some of the perspectives of the philosopher.

Kenneth Boulding, the economist, is one of the few writers that have attempted to answer the question: what distinguishes social policy from economic policy? In the context in which he uses the word, 'policy' embraces not only goal-formulation but administrative processes, historical change, and methods of delivering, measuring and evaluating services and systems.

After despairing, as I do, of finding any clear definition or clean boundaries, he arrives at the conclusion:

'If there is one common thread that unites all aspects of social policy and distinguishes them from merely economic policy, it is the thread of what has elsewhere been called the "integrative system". This includes those aspects of social life that are characterized not so much by exchange in which a quid is got for a quo' (theoretically the basis of private risk insurance) 'as by unilateral transfers that are justified by some kind of appeal to a status or legitimacy, identity, or community. The institutions with which social policy is especially concerned, such as the school, family, church, or, at the other end, the public assistance office, court, prison, or criminal gang, all reflect degrees of integration and community. By and large it is an objective of social policy to build the identity of a person around some community with which he is associated.'[17]

Boulding and Mauss, from different approaches and different disciplines, have thus helped to clarify our perspectives. The grant, or the gift or unilateral transfer—whether it takes the form of cash, time, energy, satisfaction, blood or even life itself—is the distinguishing mark of the social (in policy and administration) just as exchange or bilateral transfer is a mark of the economic. In an extravagant mood, I suppose, we might think of conceptualizing this area as the 'social market' in contradisdinction to the 'economic market'.

What this implies, of course, as Boulding rightly points out, is that social policy has to concern itself with questions of identity and alienation, for alienation threatens or destroys the system of unilateral transfer. It follows that if social administrators share this perspective of concern then they are 'problem-oriented'. But to be 'problem-conscious' in this sense is a far cry from the image of the social administrator as a technical problem-solver seeking solutions to the dilemmas of the earnings rule, adoption regulations and the eleven-plus. As Wright Mills once observed: 'All social scientists, by the fact of their existence, are involved in the struggle between enlightenment and obscurantism.'[18] Social administrators are no exception.

I reach the conclusion, therefore, that social administration as a subject is not a messy conglomeration of the technical *ad hoc*. Its primary areas of unifying interest are centred in those social institutions that foster integration and discourage alienation. In a universe of change, this explains and unites our concern with the 'ends' (the objectives of social policy) and the 'means' (the development and administration of particular public and voluntary organizations).

It also explains why in recent years the subject has in an empirical and confused way been slowly conceptualizing its major fields of research and teaching. These, I suggest, may broadly be categorized as follows:

1. The analysis and description of policy formation and its consequences, intended and unintended.
2. The study of structure, function, organization, planning and administrative processes of institutions and agencies, historical and comparative.
3. The study of social needs and of problems of access to, utilization, and patterns of outcome of services, transactions and transfers.
4. The analysis of the nature, attributes and distribution of social costs and diswelfares.
5. The analysis of distributive and allocative patterns in command-

over-resources-through-time and the particular impact of the social services.
6. The study of the roles and functions of elected representatives, professional workers, administrators and interest groups in the operation and performance of social welfare institutions.
7. The study of the social rights of the citizen as contributor, participant and user of social services.
8. The study of the role of government (local and central) as an allocator of values and of rights to social property as expressed through social and administrative law and other rule-making channels.[19]

If one surveys the interests, the activities and the writings of social administrators in recent years (as Professor Kay Jones has recently attempted for the Social Science Research Council), I think one would find that most of them would fall within one or other of these eight headings. Stated in this extremely generalized form and remembering, of course, that all require to be viewed in the context of 'social administration as the study of social needs', nevertheless, the range seems immodestly broad; but that is not my intention—it is the price of most attempts to generalize. Even so, there is much that I have omitted in this broad appraisal. I have, for example, largely confined my observations to the study of social administration in our own society. Its relevance to other societies and cultures is a matter which should be discussed on another occasion.

Despite all the gaps and ambiguities of which I am very conscious I would like to end on a coherent note. I happen to believe that as a subject, social administration has begun to develop a body of knowledge and a related set of concepts and principles. It is in the process of knowledge-building which is one of the attributes of science. In doing so, it has borrowed heavily from different disciplines in the social sciences, and now faces the tasks of refining, extending and adapting insights, perspectives and methods so as to further our understanding of, and to teach more imaginatively about, the roles and functions of social services in contemporary society.

NOTES

1. 'Social Administration in a Changing Society', *Essays on the 'Welfare State'*, Allen and Unwin, London, 1963
2. Sprott, W. J. H., *Sociology at the Seven Dials*, The Athlone Press, London, 1962.
3. Marshall, T. H., *Sociology at the Crossroads*, Longmans, London, 1947.

4. Shils, E., 'The Ways of Sociology', *Encounter*, Vol. XXVIII, No. 6, June 1967, p. 90.
5. Standing Conference of the Organizations of Social Workers, Annual Report, 1966.
6. See, for example, the former's book *Social Policy and Administration*, National Institute for Social Work Training Series, Allen and Unwin, London, 1965.
7. *Higher Education*, Report of the Committee under the Chairmanship of Lord Robbins, Cmnd 2154, HMSO, London, 1963.
8. For a more detailed criticism see Robinson, E., *New Society*, November 14, 1963, p. 15.
9. Carr-Saunders, A., *English Universities Today*, London School of Economics, 1959, p. 14.
10. Ashby, E., *Technology and the Academics*, Macmillan, London, 1958.
11. Jouvenel, B. de, *The Art of Conjecture*, 1967.
12. Whitehead, A. N., *Aims of Education*, Benn, London, 1929, p. 138.
13. Southern, R. W., *The Shape and Substance of Academic History*, Oxford, 1961, p. 11.
14. *Ibid.*, p. 11.
15. The problem of definition is discussed in, for example, Slack, K. M., *Social Administration and the Citizen*, Michael Joseph, London, 1966. For international interpretations of social service programmes see Pusic, E., *Reappraisal of the United Nations Social Service Programme*, United Nations Economic and Social Council, E/CN.5/AC.12/L.3/Add.1, 1965.
16. Mauss, M., *The Gift*, Cohen and West, London, 1966, pp. 66–7.
17. Boulding, K. E., 'The Boundaries of Social Policy', *Social Work*, Vol. 12, No. 1, January 1967, pp. 3–11.
18. Wright, Mills C., *The Sociological Imagination*, Oxford University Press, 1959, p. 178.
19. Those who find 'social property' an obscure term will find a helpful explanation in Reich, C. A., 'The Law of the Planned Society', *Yale Law Journal*, Vol. 75, No. 8, July 1966.

Chapter II

THE UNIVERSITY AND WELFARE OBJECTIVES*

I seem to remember someone, somewhere, writing or saying, something like this: if all men and women were to talk only about those matters on which they were expert then a deathly silence would descend on the world. Naturally, I would not wish to reduce this distinguished audience to such an unacademic state. There is, however, little danger of that; I am no expert on 'the university', nor can I claim to be expert on the sociology of education or 'campus sociology' (as our American friends sometimes call it), and I have little to contribute on theories of administrative behaviour which may or may not account for the government or misgovernment of universities.

In confessing to this lack of expertise I am, however, somewhat comforted when I remember an essay written by Harold Laski of the London School of Economics many years ago: it was entitled, 'The Limitations of the Expert'.[1] Laski was thinking, I should add, of the dangers to political democracies of the expert in the social sciences; the threat to the common man of substituting a professionalized expertise for political ideologies.

My interest in this subject stems, therefore, not from any expert knowledge, but from a strong belief that one of the purposes of the university in the modern world is to help society to make more informed political choices about economic growth, about social growth and about educational growth. These are all value-loaded propositions and I shall attempt later on to explain their relevance to the many purposes and functions of the university.

Meanwhile, I must say that my only legitimate claim to speak on this subject derives from seventeen years' experience of teaching in the University of London. This experience has included teaching both inside the University and in many extra-mural capacities; of being an examiner and adviser to some twenty other universities in Britain, North America and Africa; of research and writing; and last, but not

* Lecture delivered at the opening of a new building for the Paul Baerwald School of Social Work, Hebrew University, Jerusalem, Israel, April 1967.

25

least, of being (what my friend Dr Katz calls) a 'faculty errand-boy' for many years.

My first introduction to the schizophrenias of academic life came traumatically and in a statistical form. For many weary hours each year all the 40-50 professors of the London School of Economics had to sit round a table and compete for a share in an inadequate annual budget somewhat grudgingly provided, at the taxpayers' expense, by Her Majesty's Treasury. Not only did I come to understand something of the dynamics of small group behaviour but I learnt other things as well. I learnt that it was becoming increasingly difficult for academics in one discipline to assess the value of research and writing in another discipline; that, in this context, quantity therefore mattered more than quality; I learnt that to study black men in central Africa carried greater academic prestige than to teach young people who wanted to 'do good' among black and white men in Britain; I learnt that, academically, one had not grown up unless one had been to the United States; and I also learnt that the university knew little, and seemed to care less, about the consequences of its methods of admitting, teaching and examining students and about their subsequent careers. But perhaps my most traumatic experience was to be presented with a statistical table, compiled on a faculty or departmental basis, which was solemnly headed 'The Burden of Teaching' with appropriate references to (what was called) 'The Student Load'. I have since seen similar tables from all the medical schools in Britain as a member of the Royal Commission on Medical Education.

This concept of 'Burden-Load' reminded me of an analogous notion in the field of public welfare. The relevant government department used to publish annual statistics which referred to 'The Live Load of National (Public) Assistance'. Underlying this symbolically conscious or unconscious use of words there are judgments about waste; waste of time; waste of effort; waste of resources.

Elsewhere I have attempted to elaborate a number of different economic and social models of 'Welfare'; Welfare as a Residual Burden; Welfare as Complementarity; Welfare as an Instrument of Equality.[2] What I have found disturbing in many universities is that teaching should form part of the model of welfare as a residual burden. If men are treated as a burden to others—if this is the role expected of them—then, in time, they will behave as a burden.

As some of you will know, there has been in recent months a student revolt at the London School of Economics; the premier school of the social (or behavioural) sciences in Britain with over a thousand graduate students. It has been a painful experience, and especially humiliating for those faculties who claim some competence in the understanding of human beings in social situations. What has been experienced has represented, in part, a demand for students' rights; a populist demand that has made itself heard in Berkeley and other universities in North America, Europe and, I understand, in Israel as well. In the complex of relationships between the university and society this is not the only disturbing note; since 1960 doctors educated as an élite group in universities have been on strike on sixteen occasions in seven European countries. Although 'socialized' medicine in Britain has not yet experienced a medical strike there have, nevertheless, been threats of strike action and of mass emigration to private practice in the United States.

My time for this lecture would be completely exhausted if I attempted to unravel the extraordinarily complex issues involved in the student revolt at the London School of Economics. But about one of the many causal factors I am reasonably clear. In some subjects and in some faculties there has been a neglect of teaching. Specialization has increased the difficulties of communication. Degrees have become professorial degrees. The conflict between scientific attachments and teaching commitments has spread wider and deeper. In medicine, as in other fields, observers in the United States like Professor Romano are increasingly asking the question: is there a future for the clinician—the personal doctor?[3] Will not in the future the majority of the products of medical schools want to be medical scientists intent solely on advancing knowledge of the *esoterica* of disease?

This basic question of the balance between teaching and research, which is increasingly presenting itself to medical schools in Europe and North America, is a critical one also for the natural, biological and social sciences. Sixty years ago Paulsen, the historian of the German universities, wrote: 'the principle that the scholars and investigators of the nation shall also be the teachers of the youth has triumphed'. But a few lines further on he is quoting the professor who regards the term as a tiresome interruption of the vacation. And, as Sir Eric Ashby has written, who has not heard the university teacher who says: 'my teaching load is so heavy that I can't get down to my own work'. As though the task of teaching undergraduates is not worth dignifying by the title 'my own work'.[4]

Yet, paradoxically, never before in the history of the university, today faced with an information explosion, a population explosion and a financial explosion, has there been a greater need for teaching, and especially those forms of teaching which educate for change, and which educate young people for careers in a variety of technical, administrative and service responsibilities. Moreover, welfare objectives, reflecting society's needs for increased social mobility and for social and ethnic integration, are bringing to the doors of the university young people who require, particularly in their early years, a higher average level of teaching than is provided by untrained staff appointed primarily for their records, or perhaps only for their promise, in the field of research and who, on being appointed, are left without supervision of their teaching.[5]

At the same time, Government and community are asking questions: questions about the costs of universities; questions about the trained manpower needs of society as universities are seen to be consuming their young in research and doctoral programmes; questions about the distribution, multiplication and overlapping of faculties and resources (do we really need twelve completely autonomous medical schools in London, each with their own artificial kidney units and computers or, to take another example, three departments of Chinese studies in neighbouring universities?).

Should the universities respond to these questions and in what ways? For long there has been a tacit assumption in Western Europe that universities are in the untouchable class and beyond criticism, though curiously little is known about how they actually work. Although, in Britain, we have created many new universities in the last ten years and greatly expanded others, remarkably little has been written—beyond platitudes—about the functioning and administration of universities. As Ashby has said, 'We have lacked a distillation of academic wisdom about how universities ought to be managed.'[6]

In his comparative study of the university in Germany and the United States, Professor Ben-David of this university has drawn attention to some of the distinctive and often conflicting functions of universities in general.[7] They are composed, as he and others have pointed out, of a number of virtually independent, departmentalized hierarchies of institutional and personal prestige. Within each hierarchy, the appointed staff, particularly those in senior positions, possess a remarkable amount of freedom to dispose of their own time in their own way. Even during term-time, the academic (at least in Britain) has no regular hours of daily attendance that he must keep; there is none to say to him 'Go' and he goeth; 'Come' and he cometh; in the way he does his work he is free from almost all explicit control. In vacation his freedom to dispose of his time is even more extensive.

These freedoms are, I believe, to a great degree essential to the job as we know it; to teach, to advance knowledge, and to share in the wider purposes of the university. The personal possession of these freedoms, built into powerful hierarchial systems, does seem to me, however, to militate against institutional self-criticism. Intellectual criticism, the life-blood of scientific progress, certainly abounds, but institutional self-criticism and a capacity for internal reform and change appear to be singularly weak. All too often there appears to be a scholarly conspiracy of silence—a tacit agreement not to disagree publicly—about such matters.

The self-perpetuating possession of personal freedom is one reason. The low prestige accorded to administrators and administrative duties is another; why should the professor-god be troubled with accounting problems? The real and genuine difficulties of changing budgetary priorities as between subjects and departments represent a third; for instance, how does one decide to devote a smaller slice of the cake to theology (divinity) and a larger slice to social work or sociology—especially if the professor of theology is a learned man and a personal friend? Then there are the mythologies of the 'golden age' of scholars which still encumber many universities in Europe.

One traditional belief is that in the past universities were not concerned with vocationalism; their purpose was 'the cultivated man'; to function as a nursery for the education of the gentry and the upper-classes in character, poise and self-assurance. But such beliefs neglect the fact that in their medieval origins European universities were an organic part of religious, legal and administrative life. At no time in Europe have universities been restricted to pure abstract learning. The University of Salerno in Italy, the earliest of European universities, was devoted to medicine. In England, at Cambridge, in 1316, a college was founded for the special purpose of providing 'clerks for the King's service'.[8] For centuries universities have devoted themselves to the applied fields by training clergy, doctors, schoolmasters, lawyers, and engineers. Until the Second World War, Oxford and Cambridge concerned themselves with the vocational training of men to administer and run an Empire.

The point I am making, with great brevity, is that by-and-large universities in the past did reflect and did attempt to meet the trained manpower needs of their age. They were not abstracted from society and wholly unresponsive to the needs of their times. The main function of the medieval university was to produce men properly educated for their ultimate professional service to the community. This, as Pickering has said, 'had an immense effect, and perhaps it would not be overstating the case to say a beneficial effect, on the structure of knowledge and the development of science within the universities'.[9]

Another mythology, which Ashby describes as 'the academic Arian heresy', came from Germany in the nineteenth century.[10] It was the concept of the university as a research institute. Whatever the effects of this idea on social institutions in Germany it was imitated by some British academics and became almost a fetish. It devalued the imaginative excitement of learning.

At this point, I find it appropriate to quote a passage from A. N. Whitehead's *Aims of Education:*

'The justification for a university is that it preserves the connection between knowledge and the zest for life, by uniting the young and the old in the imaginative consideration of learning. The university imparts information, but it imparts it imaginatively. At least, this is the function which it should perform for society. A university which fails in this respect has no reason for existence. This atmosphere of excitement, arising from imaginative consideration, transforms knowledge. A fact is no longer a bare fact: it is invested with all its possibilities. It is no longer a burden on the memory: it is energizing as the poet of our dreams, and as the architect of our purposes.'

Whitehead ended this passage by saying:

'The tragedy of the world is that those who are imaginative have but slight experience, and those who are experienced have feeble imaginations. Fools act on imagination without knowledge; pedants act on knowledge without imagination. The task of a university is to weld together imagination and experience.'[11]

This was written in 1929. The whole book is a protest against dead knowledge, that is to say, against inert ideas. If Whitehead were alive today I cannot but think that he would have urged more strongly (at least for British universities) the need for them to develop constructive self-criticising institutional mechanisms.

It is not for me to say precisely how this should be done; that would involve too much consideration of detail. In any event, each university is uniquely different; each should define its own problems of policy, administration, self-criticism and efficiency; each has to resolve—and continue to resolve—the conflict between freedom and efficiency.

Do not let us be frightened by the word 'efficiency'. Universities today represent a great and growing cost to society. In Britain it now costs £10,000 to produce one doctor, and we spend twenty times more in a year on one non-medical undergraduate than on one primary school child. If universities do not develop the habit of cost-consciousness (and there are many ways of inculcating the habit without impairing the essential academic freedoms) then, eventually, Government will intervene where Government should not intervene.

But my definition of 'efficiency' in this context extends far beyond the narrow world of the accountant or the sillier notions of 'productivity' as applied to higher education. It embraces the effective discharge of obligations to society and responsiveness to the welfare objectives of that society. How to be efficient in this sense without doing harm to academic freedom is to me the central problem of the modern university.

What, in general, are these welfare objectives? Before I attempt to answer that question let me first underline the difficulties of generalizing. I cannot speak of the welfare objectives of Israel though I am acutely conscious of some of them. Nor can I particularize about any one country. What I have to say relates broadly to the British scene though some of the points I make may well be relevant to systems of higher education in other countries.

For purposes of discussion I have to be selective, and I therefore consider certain welfare objectives under two broad headings.

1. General Education and Professional Education

Compared with the past, this generation and the next generation needs and is going to need far more personal doctors, school teachers, social workers, nurses, psychiatrists, biologists, architects, town planners, engineers, librarians, technicians and so forth. One elementary reason is that the tasks that have to be done and that face our societies require more and more expertise.

What contribution should the university make to help to meet these welfare needs both within its own faculties and in myriad ways by assisting satellite systems of higher and professional education (the extra-mural role of the university)?

The Robbins Report of 1963 on Higher Education in Britain did not, apart from considering the need for school teachers, really face this challenge.[12] What broadly the Committee recommended was an extension and expansion of élitest education. Learning to think was conceived as the end in itself. Ability to act effectively in a situation was not considered a criterion of academic success or intellectual competence and it was assumed that any element of education directed towards action was necessarily specific and technical and not abstract or imaginative.[13]

31

This philosophy of higher education was the reverse of that propounded by Alexander Carr-Saunders, the late Director of the London School of Economics, when he wrote: 'The young are anxious to think about and discuss general questions affecting the human situation; thus general education, as well as specialized preparation for a particular career, is within the ambition of students; it is the task of the university to unite them.'[14]

The Robbins Report has been heavily attacked on these grounds by many critics for its failure to comprehend the need for both a general and a specialized, vocational education. The Government has, in consequence, adopted a binary system of higher education which involves, *inter alia*, raising technological institutes to the status of universities, and investing proportionately more resources in the technical, vocational sectors and proportionately less in the traditional, élitest sectors.

This policy has, I believe, two broad welfare objectives: the first is to provide more trained manpower and womanpower for the technical and social service needs of society; the second is to give proportionately more young people from working-class homes career opportunities through this binary system of higher education. On this point I come to my second heading.

2. *The Integrative Function of the University*

In discussing the welfare objective of social integration I must first state my own position. It should not be, in my view, the function of the university to legitimate (and thus increase) class and ethnic divisions in society. I say this because I consider that only cultural and political inertia in the past has allowed us to believe that the educational system operated automatically as a force for social mobility. On the contrary, the weight of evidence shows that in most European countries it has been one of the most powerful forces of social conservatism, giving the appearance of legitimacy to social inequalities by treating 'a social attribute as a natural attribute'.[15]

This general finding applies particularly to the higher sectors in educational systems. Recent studies in Britain substantiate this point. It has been shown, for example, that today 45 per cent of children from higher income and professional families are admitted to full-time degree courses at universities and their equivalent, compared with 10 per cent of those from homes where the father is in a clerical job, right down to 4 per cent where he is a skilled worker, and 2 per cent where he is a semi-skilled or unskilled worker.[16]

These differentials are much sharper for girls than for boys, and they are also much sharper in medical faculties than in any other single faculty. It is much harder for working-class children to enter medicine than any other profession.

There are still people who will say that these differences simply reflect the fact that working-class children have less innate ability than middle-class children. But there is now enough scientific evidence to show that this belief—so far as Britain is concerned—is false. For the evidence I would refer you to the Report of the Robbins Committee on Higher Education.

This picture of inequalities in educational opportunities is probably familiar to you. Something like it also obtains in Western Germany, France, and other European countries. What is perhaps less well known is how remarkably persistent the inequalities in Britain have remained over the last ten to twenty years; the years of 'The Welfare State' when it was widely believed that social inequalities were gracefully succumbing to economic growth and the provision of 'socialized medicine' and other social services.

In point of fact, the relative chances of getting to university for working-class and middle-class children have changed little over the last quarter of a century.

The problem of class divisions in society is now for Britain—as it is for Israel—inextricably bound up with the problem of ethnic divisions. In the next ten years the challenge will have to be faced of educational opportunities for the second generation of immigrants to Britain; the children of half-a-million and more Indians, Pakistanis, West Indians and others, most of whose fathers are at present employed as manual workers. If these children experience the same difficulties in achieving higher educational opportunities as white (or pink) working-class children then it will not be surprising if their failure to do so is attributed to racial prejudice.

The conclusion I draw from these studies of British experience is that left to itself the university system will not reduce these differentials. Nor can we rely on any general expansion of the university sector as we have known it in the past to contribute to the reduction of inequalities. They may indeed become sharper if the social determinants of inequality in modern society increasingly shift from the institutions of property to the institutions of cultural transmission.

To effect change on any scale requires special educational policies directed towards equalizing opportunities for higher education. For the universities, these may take many forms. I will briefly mention a few by way of illustration. Some of them, I may add, are in operation on a limited basis in my own Department of Social Administration at the London School of Economics.

Universities may require to make provision on general educational courses and or vocational courses for older students who do not possess minimum university entrance qualifications. For some of these students, I think of this as the 'philosophy of the second chance'. They are people who, for many reasons, missed a step in the educational ladder. During their twenties and their thirties they come to value education; they want to learn and not just acquire a university ticket. We should count this stronger motivation and experience of life in the real world as the equivalent of examination performance in secondary schools. We should never forget that Darwin and Einstein, like Newton, before them were essentially self-taught.

Secondly, we may need to develop within the university or bring within the organizational ambit of the university more specialized, vocational career courses which will attract and cater for children from poorer homes. In short, we need to offer a greater variety of doors into the university.

Thirdly, we may need to develop systems of quotas designed to widen higher educational opportunities; quotas for departments, for faculties and for courses, and quotas for different categories of students. Interestingly, it was only the intervention of the British Government during the Second World War that led the medical schools to institute a quota of 10 per cent for the intake of women students to read for medical qualifications. This interference with academic freedom assuredly benefited society as well as women.

These are but a few of the possible ways in which universities, given the will, might respond to the welfare objectives of the wider society. They suggest the need for the opening of more and alternative doors; the offering of second educational chances; the deliberate planning of admission policies; a willingness to accept more vocational courses; and a readiness to spread the values of the university beyond the confines of the campus boundary.

Such measures may be regarded, I venture to think, as an encroachment on academic freedom. It is important, however, to distinguish here between the freedom of the individual teacher and the freedom of the university as an institution. As to the first, there is and can be no dispute. Every individual member of the university must be completely free to teach and to express his views according to his own intellectual conscience. In institutional terms, however, there are and must be limits to freedom. No university can be free to establish, say, a faculty of veterinary medicine; to buy as many computers as it thinks fit; to concentrate its resources on teaching students from other countries; or to ignore completely the needs of society.

Somewhere, the limits to institutional freedom and the limits to institutional inefficiency have to be drawn. They are, perhaps, most difficult to draw in respect of the pattern of first degree and higher degree courses. In some universities in Britain as in other countries, degrees are too exclusively professorial degrees; the aim is to reproduce one's own kind; to produce professors. Hence the cult of the Ph.D. From society's point of view the danger is (already apparent in some fields in Britain) that we create too many scientists and not enough technologists.[17] The surplus of scientists, medical scientists and Ph.D's in the natural sciences, may well find congenial employment in the United States but at a considerable cost to the exporting country.

Whitehead, whom I must quote again, once wrote 'Any serious fundamental change in the intellectual outlook of human society must necessarily be followed by an educational revolution.'[18] The past half-century has witnessed profound changes in social attitudes to the problems of poverty, ignorance and fear. The twentieth century, in rejecting the nineteenth century's concept of a small élite confronting a vast proletariat, has identified the need for social rights. We have begun to recognize that social growth—the need for integration, the need for more equality of opportunity, the need for freedom from want—deserves as much attention, intellectually as well as in terms of political action, as economic growth.

Yet, the response of the universities to these welfare objectives has been slow and faltering. Without radical changes in outlook and policy they are, I think, in danger of failing in their obligations to society. But this is not irreversible and inevitable; I believe the universities are capable of responding to the need for change. They represent not only 'the corporate realization of man's basic determination to know' (as Karl Jaspers once said) but man's need to serve his fellows. I criticize them today because I believe in them and the values they stand for; there are indeed times when it is right to admonish those whom one loves.

NOTES

1. Laski, H., *Fabian Tract 235*, London, 1931.
2. To be published in a forthcoming study.
3. Romano, J., 'Requiem or Reveille: The Clinician's Choice', *Journal of Medical Education*, July 1963, p. 583.
4. Ashby, E., '. . . And Scholars', London School of Economics, 1965, p. 5. See also *Technology and the Academics*, Macmillan, London, 1958.
5. Rowe, A. P., 'The Problem of Freedom and Efficiency in Universities',

Freedom and Efficiency, Bulletin of the Committee on Science and Freedom, No. 16, Manchester, England, 1960, p. 7.

6. Ashby, E., 'No cosy consensus: reflections on university government', *Universities Quarterly*, December 1966, p. 110.
7. Ben-David, J., and Zloczower, A., 'The Idea of the University and the Academic Market-place', *European Journal of Sociology*, 11, 1961, pp. 303–14.
8. Whitehead, A. N., *Aims of Education*, Benn, London, 1929, p. 138.
9. Pickering, G., 'The Universities and Society: The Problem as seen from the Oldest Technology', *The Lancet*, i, 57, 1965.
10. Ashby, E., *Technology and the Academics, ibid.*, p. 4.
11. Whitehead, A. N., *op. cit.*, pp. 139–40.
12. *Higher Education*, Report of the Committee under the Chairmanship of Lord Robbins, Cmnd 2154, HMSO, London, 1963.
13. For more detailed criticism see Robinson, E., *New Society*, November 14, 1963, p. 15.
14. Carr-Saunders, A., *English Universities Today*, London School of Economics, 1959, p. 14.
15. This is in part a quotation from Bourdieu's contribution to *Le Sens Commun dans le Partage des Bénéfices* (ed. Darras), Editions de Minuit, Paris, 1966.
16. Moser, C. A., 'Inequalities in Educational Opportunities', London School of Economics, Unit for Economic and Statistical Studies on Higher Education, 1965.
17. Secretary of State for Education and Science reported in *The Times*, March 2, 1967.
18. Whitehead, A. N., *op. cit.*

36

THE RELATIONSHIP BETWEEN SCHOOLS OF SOCIAL WORK, SOCIAL RESEARCH AND SOCIAL POLICY*

One of the odd paradoxes of international conferences of this kind is their custom of expecting the impossible from speakers and from those who have, perforce, to listen to them. We are expected to address our thoughts to immensely broad subjects which virtually defy definition in one language and culture let alone fifty; and to explore topics which will have meaning in societies preoccupied, at one end of the spectrum of wealth and poverty, with how to make self-consciousness bearable in human relations and, at the other end, with how to alleviate mass famine and disease. In short, we are expected to generalize about the human condition on a world scale; a task more appropriate, I would have thought, for religious leaders, theologians and politicians than for social workers.

The heart of the paradox lies in the fact that in our daily lives in schools of social work we rarely if ever venture out into such academically hazardous waters. We do not discuss social research, social policy and the role of schools of social work in abstract, universal terms. When we discuss such subjects at all—which I suggest is very seldom—we do so in concrete, specific frameworks. We talk about people's feelings and facial responses in the casework relationship but always in the context of particular clients or groups of clients. When we discuss social policy we do so in terms of particular, defined, problems; the need for cash aid to assist migrant workers to return to their homes; the need for better provision for abandoned children and so forth. When we discuss research—which is today like science an important word only to be uttered in tones of hushed and devout reverence—we have in mind specific, small and tangible projects.

What I am saying is that in our daily round of activities with students, colleagues, clients and agencies we tend to restrict ourselves

* Lecture delivered at the Twelfth International Congress of Schools of Social Work, Athens, Greece, September 1964, and published in *International Social Work*, Vol. VIII, No. 1, January 1965.

to the immediate, the intimate, the precise and the manageable. And ' . . . last year's words belong to last year's language. And next year's words await another voice'.

We behave like Ibsen once did when he turned to village politics for some of the reasons that lead some people to turn to social work; because social action can be more psychologically comforting, and because here is something in the human condition small enough in scale to comprehend and to believe in. And it was also Ibsen, some of you will remember, who made one of his characters say that he did not read much because he found reading 'irrelevant'. Social workers like doctors, can similarly find reading irrelevant confronted, as they generally are, by the urgencies of human misery, and the limitless bounds for exploring interpersonal relations.

Why, then, do we choose such all-embracing global topics (as the one I am now approaching with obvious hesitation) when we come together at international gatherings of this kind? And here I should add that social workers are not peculiar in this respect; psychiatrists, lawyers and sociologists are also addicted to surveying the cosmos.

I suppose one immediate and obvious answer is that it makes a change; that commodity, we are told, is good for the middle classes in all societies; it is a mark of professional and academic progress; and an example to set for the poorer classes who are so reluctant to move out of their accustomed habits and ways of life. We must get on, and we are helped to do so if others lag behind. But there is another and more understandable reason. If the purpose of such conferences as this is to exchange experiences, to broaden horizons, and to discuss uncommon as well as common problems, then we need to avoid a choice of subject which will encourage participants to indulge in competitive national 'success stories'. I must therefore apply the hint to myself and leave on one side an account of the role of my colleagues at the London School of Economics in the areas of social work, social research and social policy.

As I have now reminded you, the subject was chosen for me. I may be permitted, therefore, to examine first the assumptions which it appears to contain.

Much the most important is the assumption that there should be such a relationship: that schools of social work *should* engage in research, and that through the medium of research findings and in other ways the schools *should* influence the social policies of their own countries, governmental and private. In effect, the implication is that it is a mark of a 'good' school—an index or criterion of standards— for research to be part of its functions, and for such research to be so formulated that it may or will contribute to the shaping of policy.

Now these assumptions, implicit in the subject I have been asked to discuss, should not be accepted uncritically. Nor does it follow that schools of social work can only influence policies by prosecuting research. Historically, they have contributed to the shaping of policy in many countries through a variety of methods, formal and informal: by having representatives on committees of inquiry; by bringing pressure to bear on officials and politicians; by using the press and other channels of communication; and by gently persuading important people, sympathetic to the goals of social work, to talk to other important people. The Charity Organization Societies in England and in the United States had certainly developed this delicate art to a high standard in the nineteenth century. The historical evidence that is now available shows that in England the Charity Organization Society exercised a profound influence on poor law policies eighty years ago; much more powerful, though it was conducted in private and without the aid of research, than the efforts of most schools of social work in the world today. But I remain doubtful whether the views expressed in this relationship between important people represented the opinion of those who carried the heat and burden of social work in practice. It is much more likely that policy and administration were influenced by those who were not practitioners: that what they had to say embodied the value judgments of the upper-classes occupying honorific positions at the apex of social work institutions.

The times have changed, and while these processes no doubt continue in many societies it has come to be recognized that they are no longer sufficient nor wholly satisfactory. Both those who are concerned with the making of policy and those who are concerned with its application in practice increasingly require that social policy should be more rationally based on ascertained and tested fact. In other words, it has come to be believed that social policies are more likely to be effective in practice if they are grounded in a basis of fact about reality. This belief has in part been fostered by the great achievements of scientific research in the physical world. It is only natural that workers in the field of social studies should wish to catch a little of the prestige that descends on those who engage in research.

To return, however, to the main point of my discussion. If, to proceed further, we may accept for the purposes in hand the basic assumptions underlying this choice of subject, I want now to examine the nature of the case for undertaking research. I do not wish at this stage to restrict the argument to instrumental research; that is, to research which is wholly directed to influencing policy. Research, as one particular form of intellectual activity in schools of social work and other institutions concerned with the social situation, can have a number of functions and play a variety of roles. Influencing the policies of governments and private agencies is only one.

Why then, in general, is social research undertaken? In part it depends, of course, on what we want to study; on what we are curious to find out; on what theories we want to develop; on what expectations are placed on us by society at large. But aside from these considerations, there are at least four major groups of motives or reasons for prosecuting social research. These I will call—in no order of relative significance—the 'Professional Status Case', the 'Social Policy Case', the 'Ethical Case', and the 'Educational Case'. Of course, they all overlap and get mixed up in reality, but I chose to classify them in this way because one can only discuss one thing at a time.

The Professional Status Case

In the hierarchy of social values contributing to the prestige of a profession the particular activity which we call 'research' stands very high. If, moreover, it can be described as 'pure' rather than 'applied' research the professional groups concerned can almost claim to have entered the ranks of the immortals. At least they have been suitably attired. They have been purified in the waters of 'value-free' science; they are unconcerned with the relevance of their studies to this horrid and mundane world; they have published while others have perished in an inferno of uncertain status, vocational teaching and 'doing-good'.

Satirical and exaggerated though this may be, I am sure that many teachers in schools of social work will appreciate the point. During the last twenty years or so, economists, sociologists, psychologists and other social scientists have understandably desired to emulate the scientists and research workers inhabiting the world of physical and biological phenomena. While this has undoubtedly set higher standards of relative objectivity for the social sciences and has advanced knowledge in many respects the consequences have not all been admirable.

Research and publication have been elevated to the detriment of teaching; research has been seen solely as a means of individual self-advancement sometimes at the expense of defenceless groups who have unethically been made the subject of investigation; methodology has been made compulsorily 'respectable' for all to the point of boredom for the many; the most incurious and unimaginative souls have been led to think that a questionnaire, a random sample of delinquents, and a computer could entirely compensate for the lack

40

of an idea and, finally, policy-makers have been persuaded to post-pone action until research has been undertaken, Ph.D's acquired and the professional reputation of the participants has been suitably enhanced.

Society can be asked to pay a heavy price for scientism induced or begotten by professionalism. Bernard Shaw once said that 'professions are conspiracies against the laity'; scientism can be too. We know that in the field of medicine there has been a proliferation of trials of new drugs in the sacred name of science and professional advancement without adequate ethical safeguards for patients. For the same reasons, we know that psychologists and sociologists have asked children questions about their parents which no social worker, worthy of the name, could possibly condone. There is, in short, a danger that concern for the value and uniqueness of the individual human being may be diminished if the scientific outlook spreads to embrace more and more of human affairs; it is after all in the nature of science to be chiefly preoccupied with groups, trends, laws and generalizations. And it is a characteristic of the less gifted and less perceptive research worker to cordon himself off in a tiny area of specialized study. As most of us realize at some time in our lives, it is a great comfort to acquire 'one small allotment in the vastness of the knowable'[1] where one feels a little more at home and in peace; a little more professionally secure.

Research workers retire to cultivate their ten square inches of social phenomena for much the same reasons as caseworkers continually re-examine their feelings about dominant mothers and passive fathers, and doctors retreat behind the scientific barricades of the hospital. They are all looking for security and neutrality to protect and perfect their professional souls in an increasing complex and changing world.

These may well be dangerous and unjust thoughts: in voicing them I would not wish you to think that I am opposed to the advance of science and rationality in human affairs. On the contrary, I believe that we need more research and more study, theoretical and applied, in the field of the social sciences. Only in such ways, and always seeing research as a servant and not a master, will man be able to obtain some better control over his environment and acquire more freedom to develop his talents and his personality. As Vivekananda has said, 'There is no good work that has not a touch of evil in it. . . . We should engage in such works which bring the largest amount of good and the smallest measure of evil.'[2] Social research should not be excepted from the application of this principle.

Having warned you of what should be avoided in the 'why' and

41

the 'how' of research, I want now to examine the case for more research related to social policy.

The Social Policy Case

The essence of the 'social' case for more research in the field of policy is that it may enlarge human freedoms. This is true insofar as the findings and applications of research substitute fact for assertion; reality for myth; tolerance for prejudice. Social diagnosis is needed as well as individual therapy: the two should go hand-in-hand in schools of social work. To pursue the latter, while neglecting the former is to fall into the error, however unconsciously, of seeing the function of diagnostic casework as (and I quote from Miss Gordon Hamilton's work) 'adaptation to reality'.[3] Two assumptions underlie this conception of the caseworker's function which has appeared in a substantial number of textbooks. The first is that reality is something which the caseworker knows but the client does not; the second is that if adaptation is genuinely to take place reality must genuinely be accepted by the caseworker.

The ultimate logic of this is to make the caseworker a prisoner of the collective *status quo*; consequently, she will have little or nothing to contribute to the shaping of social policy. She will not in fact desire to do so. This is another way of saying, what Professor Lipset, the sociologist, said recently in his book *Political Man*, that we in the West have reached the end of the political dialogue. The caseworker and the sociologist thus both deny in their different ways that reality like love (in Thomas Hardy's words) 'is never stationary'.

The inescapable fact, regardless of whether we like the world as it is today, is that we are all living in a period of startlingly rapid change. In the past, economic and social changes were effected only at the price of immense hardship. The amount and rate of change under way today, and affecting all countries in varying degrees, may in some areas be less crudely evident in strictly economic terms but the consequences as a whole may be no less profound—though more subtly expressed—in generating social frustration and psychological stress. In other respects, economic and industrial changes dominate the problems of societies in transition. In all countries, the question of 'how we live together in society' is made more insistent by the widespread and pervasive effects of technological change. Yet little is known about how all these factors of change are affecting levels of poverty and need, patterns of family living, and community relations. Change, however induced, cannot take place without people being hurt. In consequence, new and different social needs are continually arising, many of which are (or should be) the direct concern of social workers and social welfare programmes.

To identify and meet these needs and to minimize and prevent the hardships caused by change, social policy should be better informed. More and better data about the human condition, constructive and critical, should be at the disposal of policy-makers and administrators. Their particular myths—about poverty and unmet need, about racial prejudice, about social injustice—require to be attacked by community diagnosis. Research can be one weapon—though as I have said by no means the only one—in the challenge to be more intelligent and rational in the process of shaping and applying social welfare measures. Nor is the argument for research in these fields wholly an instrumental one; the findings of such research can be of general educational value in advancing our knowledge of human behaviour in situations of change.

Should schools of social work contribute to this process of community diagnosis and, by so doing, help to educate society in the need for action? For me, there is only one answer to this question. The alternative could mean, in the ultimate analysis, accepting the position that there is little truth in the claim of social work to be more in touch than any other profession with the poor and the unable, and that all it can offer is individual therapy in the context of a social reality wholly determined by others.

The Ethical Case

Ethical problems of confidentiality and the legal rights of clients as citizens continually confront the social worker as they do members of other professions. The day-to-day administration of social policy as well as the detailed formulation of policy itself also involves basic ethical issues. Let me give you one example, illustrating the ethical components of policy, which will, I hope, underline the need for research by schools of social work. Although this particular example is drawn from experience in the United States, there is little doubt that it could be paralleled in most countries in the world which have established some system of public assistance however rudimentary.

In many American States, and in the District of Columbia, it is common practice for authorities to make unannounced inspections of the homes of persons receiving public assistance. Often such searches are made without warrants and in the middle of the night. The purpose of the inspections is to check on recipients' eligibility for assistance. Eligibility, under state or local law (in the United States and many other countries), may be determined by various aspects of a family's circumstances, including the presence or absence of an adult man capable of supporting the family. The demand for entry may carry with it the threat, expressed or implied, that refusal to admit will lead to discontinuance of public assistance. And many of those on public assistance are unable for reasons of poverty, ignorance or fear to protect their own rights as citizens.

Mr Charles Reich, Assistant Professor of Law at Yale University, published last year a study of 'Midnight Welfare Searches'.[4] He came to the conclusion that these invasions of privacy, as commonly practised, represented 'a flagrant violation of the fourth and fourteenth amendments of the Federal Constitution'. 'A not uncommon psychology,' commented Mr Reich, 'leads those who dispense welfare to feel it only just that the beneficiaries give up something in return. To some public officials, opening one's home to inspection evidently seems a reasonable condition to impose on those whose homes are supported by a public agency. In many other ways, subtle and obvious, the recipients of public bounty are made to pay a similar price. They may be asked to observe standards of morality not imposed on the rest of the community.'

Social self-criticism is an essential part of the democratic process, and it is a tribute to Mr Reich that this study in a neglected area of social policy should have been made. In how many other countries, one is led to ask, would not similar studies be justified today?

This question is of special concern to schools of social work because of their responsibilities for teaching and for providing the leadership that is expected of them in relation to professional standards. It raises in particular, however, two basic ethical issues. The first is: should recipients of welfare be discriminated against in respect of certain fundamental rights and have different standards of morality imposed on them? And the second is: should social workers take part, directly or indirectly, willingly or unwillingly, in such practices as those described by Mr Reich?

In recent years, Mrs Audrey Harvey in England and Mr Keith-Lucas and Mr Alvin Schorr in the United States have examined different aspects of these basic issues.[5] The latter, in a paper published in 1962, offered evidence that casework practice had been moving toward more coercive behaviour, thus contradicting one of the central commitments of social work; namely, free advice for clients and the enlargement of self-determination.

Many social workers in the United States and other countries are aware of the public and private pressures which may drive them into situations of moral conflict. The National Association of Social Workers in the United States has protested vigorously about the violation of the civil rights of welfare recipients and has condemned the unethical implications of 'midnight raids'.[6] Social workers in

Washington have published a report on the functioning of the public welfare system and have drawn attention to the punitive aspects of various regulations.[7] In London, groups of social workers have been formed specifically to study the ethical and practical implications of restrictions and restraints in social welfare programmes.

These are illustrations of the role of research and inquiry in areas of basic concern to social work. To explore such questions fully would take me far outside my terms of reference. In any event, this would be difficult because when one examines the literature for a number of countries it is surprising to find how few studies have been made. My purpose in raising them in this general way, however, was to point the need for research, and to suggest that here at least was an area of social policy of vital concern to schools of social work because of its ethical implications for professional standards, as well as its social and psychological implications for those at the receiving end of welfare.

The Educational Case

Finally, I turn to the fourth of my reasons for supposing that schools of social work should engage in research in the social policy area. By now, I have probably already said enough to substantiate the arguments for research on educational grounds. However, there are one or two further points which I may add by way of conclusion.

Education, as distinct from propaganda, is about freedom; it increases awareness of possible choices. To enable clients better to exercise choice is an integral part of the functions of social work and here, it may be said, the social worker as an individual enacts an educational role which is sanctioned as such by society. Furthermore, I would submit that social work as an institution (like medicine and the law) has a broad educational role in relation to public opinion at large to diagnose, explain and inform.

Historically, individual social workers in many countries have contributed to educating the community about the need for social action; that is to say for collective policies, public and voluntary, to change environments and situations and to provide for unmet needs. They have identified and described particular and general problems of poverty, ignorance, neglect, deprivation and injustice. They have done so not primarily for professional reasons but because of a compassionate concern for the welfare of others, and because of their own inner needs to continue to live with a sense of helplessness; it was therefore necessary to call attention—to be articulate about— the greater helplessness of others.

Today, this problem of community education is more complex.

45

Social work, like other 'service' occupations, has become more organized and professionalized and thus subject to codes of neutrality. Moreover, many more social workers today are employees of large organizations or agencies, public and private, and subject, as employees, to regulations enjoining political neutrality. These codes or expectations required by professional and employing bodies call for supposedly objective attitudes which demand (as Professor Everett Hughes has pointed out in another context) 'an apparent neutrality toward those very problems where neutrality makes one appear a potential ally of the enemy'.[8] We may interpret the 'enemy' in this case as those who support the prevailing system of values in society and their attendant social provisions and policies.

To these new problems of community diagnosis and education I must add another. Theoretical and methodological advances in the social sciences in recent decades have meant that the analysis and description of social problems can no longer be conducted by social workers in isolation and with the relatively cruder tools of the past. It is not enough for social workers to talk to social workers; to be effective in this broad educational role they now need allies. In the past, these allies were sought in the higher reaches of the class and power structure; today, they have also to be found in the social sciences.

All these reasons, I suggest, support the case for schools of social work to engage in research and to devote some of their studies to problems of social policy; its formation, application and revision. The trend towards professionalization combined with changes in the contractual relations between social workers and their employers has in particular placed—almost unwillingly—new and heavy responsibilities on schools of social work. As yet, these have been little recognized. But schools of social work are not alone in this respect. More division of labour within professional groupings; more emphasis on technical skills and expertise; more 'bigness' in the organization and distribution of personal service; more explicit codes of neutrality; all these factors are affecting the professions in general, and medicine and social work in particular. They are making it harder for the individual practitioner and his or her professional association or trade union to play a critical, protesting and educational role in society. Thus, some part of this role now devolves—if it devolves anywhere—on teaching institutions. In short, and for our purposes, on schools of social work.

Professor Dorothy Emmet in England has wisely said that the description and definition of a profession 'has a moral element built into it'.[9] To this I would add that if schools of social work are not to

46

be limited to training in techniques they also must now have a functional moral element built into them.

NOTES

1. Gombrich, E. H., *The Tradition of General Knowledge*, London School of Economics, 1962, p. 15.
2. *Thus Spoke Vivekananda* (Madras, Sri Ramakrishna Math, 1955), p. 35.
3. Hamilton, G., *Principles and Techniques in Social Case Work* (Ed., C. Kasius), 1950, p. 89.
4. Reich, C. A., *Yale Law Journal*, Vol. 72, No. 7, 1963, p. 1347.
5. Harvey, A., *Casualties of the Welfare State*, 1960; Keith-Lucas, A., *Decisions About People in Need*, 1957; Schorr, A. L., *Social Work*, Vol. 7, No. 1, 1962, pp. 60–5. See also Mencher, S., *Social Work*, Vol. 8, No. 3, 1963, p. 59, and Keith-Lucas, A., *Social Work*, Vol. 8, No. 3, 1963, p. 66.
6. *Midnight Raids*, A Statement by the National Association of Social Workers Inc., New York, 1964.
7. *The Public Welfare Crisis in the Nation's Capital*, Metropolitan Washington Chapter, National Association of Social Workers, 1963.
8. Hughes Everett, C., 'The Academic Mind: Two Views', *American Sociological Review*, Vol. 24, No. 4, 1959.
9. Emmet, D. L., 'The Notion of a Professional Code', *Crucible*, October 1962, p. 104.

Chapter IV

TIME REMEMBERED*

This is an important and joyful occasion—as jubilees should be. It is a pleasure to welcome you all and especially to say how delighted we are to have Mrs Mostyn Lloyd and Lord Attlee with us.

We are here to commemorate the decision, taken in December 1912, probably in a yellow London fog, probably arranged beforehand by that skilled negotiator Sidney Webb, to establish a Department of Social Science. It was not a move, as some may have thought, to establish in Houghton Street a branch of the Labour Party. It was more like a take-over bid for the Charity Organization Society or, in the struggle for power in the social work world in those days (perhaps a little less muted than it is these days) an attempt by the Society to infiltrate the new London School of Economics and Political Science.

We know from the school's records that on a resolution, properly moved by Mr Martin White and briefly seconded by Mr Sidney Webb, it was unanimously decided to establish a new department to continue 'the work so admirably carried on since 1903 under Mr C. S. Loch of the Charity Organization Society'. One wonders about that little word 'admirably'. Was it a polite way of swallowing, with Edwardian delicacy, the training functions of the cos? Could it have meant that there was dissatisfaction with the existing methods of training upper-middle class girls in the technique of instructing the poor how patiently to manage their poverty? Is it possible that Sidney Webb, abetted by Beatrice, was, Fabian-wise, farsighted enough to dream that, fifty years hence, the staff and students of the Department would descend for a November weekend on Margate to discuss 'Politics and the Social Worker'?

We do not know. The history of the Department has yet to be written. Nor do we know what heart-searching was caused in the offices of the cos when, a few months after this momentous decision, and when the gas lamps could hardly be seen in the fog of Vauxhall

* Privately published in *The Link*, a souvenir booklet produced by the students of the Department of Social Administration in December 1962 to celebrate the Jubilee of the Department (originally called in 1912 the Department of Social Science).

48

Bridge Road, it was learnt that a vaguely sinister figure had been appointed to the staff of the Department in the person of Mr Clement Attlee. In the event, his contribution was certainly not sinister. Unromantically, it was mostly about local government and social work. According to the reminiscences of Edith Eckhard—one of the great figures in the Department's history who occasionally overheard his tutorials through the wooden partitions of those days—it was in the best traditions of academic life. The publication of his book, *The Social Worker*, testified to his belief in the value of combining the teaching of students with the pursuit of truth.

To many academics in the august reaches of the University of London—to say nothing of the London School of Economics—the work of the Department has, however, always been a rather dull affair. For fifty years, staff and students have been discussing poverty—poverty in the Vauxhall Bridge Road, poverty in London, poverty in Britain, and now poverty in Africa, India and the developing countries. We have continued to ignore Bagehot's advice that 'the character of the poor is an unfit topic for continuous art'.

This has meant that for many years both staff and students have lived in that state which Gogol described as 'disinterested servility'. A concern for others; a concern for the human condition; a concern about education rather than training; a concern about the ethics of intervention in the lives of others—personified in the contribution of people like Mostyn Lloyd and Edith Eckhard—dominated concern about academic or professional status. Not until the 1940s were the staff of the Department given equivalent status and equal pay with their colleagues · in the university. Even in 1950, shortly after I arrived, I remember being asked by one of my professorial brothers how my 'good-looking midwives were getting on'. But we have been too busy to lose much academic sleep about such comments. There have been too many other worthwhile things to do; experiments and advances in social work education, new developments in field-work practice, much empirical research work to be done, books to be written, new courses to be pioneered in social casework and for students from overseas, and, all the time, a body of students, acting through the Social Science Society, as a stimulus and a social control. Like Thomas Hardy's remark in one of his novels that 'love is never stationary' so the Department's concern has continuously been to live with uncertainty and never to acquiesce in the 'deep sleep of dons' decided opinion'.

I am reminded of a story told me many years ago of a member of the staff interviewing a candidate for the Social Science Certificate (as it then was). 'And what do you ultimately want to do?' asked the tutor. 'To be myself,' was the soulful reply. 'Come, come, Miss X,' said the tutor, 'I think we can do a little better than that.'

It is not for me to say whether we have done any better since Professor Marshall handed over his responsibilities to me in 1950. If size is anything, we have done better. From a teaching and research staff of two in 1913, the Department grew to thirteen by 1950 and nearly thirty today, and this is without counting Miss Partridge who, statistically, should perhaps be represented by two more. What we have taught and studied here has influenced social work education in many countries of the world as well as our own—I think particularly of Israel, Australia, New Zealand, Ceylon, Ghana, Nigeria, Holland, Norway and Canada. And the books that have come from the Department on social policy and administration are as widely known overseas as at home.

You must forgive me for saying these things, but my dictionary tells me that jubilee means a 'season of rejoicing' and 'a period of special indulgence'.

Professor Marshall has given you in his paper some account of the origins and development of new courses during the 1940s, and the circumstances in which their introduction reflected the needs of a changing society. I would like to carry the story forward a little by placing on record some of the activities of the Department during the past dozen years. There may be some value in doing this at a time when opinion in a number of universities in the country is (to put it mildly) unfriendly to social work education. Partly (or mainly) for reasons of academic status, it is thought there is something derogatory in teaching young people with a practical bent whose vocational ends embrace various forms of social work. This, of course, is no new idea but the advent of the two-year 'Young-husband' social work courses in the technical colleges is providing—and may increasingly do so—a justification for contracting-out. Disengagement from social work education may also enable these universities to disengage further from the life of the communities in which they are situated and which they are presumed to serve. This is not to say that they necessarily mean to do so, but the growing pressure for places in all faculties is confronting the modern university with acute problems of priorities—local, regional, national, professional and so forth.

These are matters which I do not wish to pursue further on this occasion except to develop one general and important point. The record of the Department since the end of the Second World War does, I believe, show that it is possible to teach—indeed, is only possible effectively to teach—a large body of social work students, both at the

50

pre-professional and professional levels, *and* simultaneously to advance the true aims of the university. The evidence for this statement may be briefly summarized under four headings:

Research and the Advancement of Knowledge
The calendar of the school shows for the period 1956–62 a total of 180 articles and books in the list of publications by members of the Department. Since 1950, fifteen major ·vorks based on original research have been published; one social work journal successfully launched; and a series of *Occasional Papers in Social Administration* published. At the time of writing (December 1962), eighteen research projects of varying degrees of significance were in progress. A more detailed research report was recently provided by Dr Abel-Smith in *The Sociological Review* (Research Report for the Department of Social Administration, Vol. 10, No. 3, November 1962).

Academic Freedom
Throughout this period the staff of the Department have never once conceded any of the essential freedoms of the university. We decide which students should be admitted. We decide what they should be taught, how they should be taught, and who should examine them. We take up many of their difficulties over grants, over restrictive medical examinations by prospective employers and professional bodies, and over other attempts to limit the students' freedom of choice. No research grants have ever been accepted in the Department which limit the right to publish or to comment as the author sees fit. These issues of academic freedom may arise only occasionally and unexpectedly, but it is a distinguishing mark of a responsible university faculty always and at once to make a stand on such matters of principle.

Members of a University
Unlike some university schools of social work in a number of countries, the staff of the Department have always contributed to the life and work of the college and the university. They have done so by serving on a large number of committees and boards of studies; by participating in the social life of the school; and by assisting in the duties of other departments and in the general conduct of the academic business of the school. It is accepted that they have loyalties to the university; to the college; to their immediate colleagues; to their students; and to their professional associations. It is their individual responsibility and theirs alone to combine these loyalties.

The Teachers of Tomorrow

A university, if it is to survive, must reproduce itself. It has to help to train the next generation of teachers, research workers and writers. It cannot (or should not) think exclusively in these terms. The vast majority of students, receiving a liberal education and a vocational training, are not destined to enter the ranks of university teachers. We should not teach or examine them with this end in view. But a minority should and indeed must become university teachers. In this sense, a university (or distinctive parts of a university) has obligations to other universities and their related parts. It has to serve the needs of others and society at large as well as its own staffing needs if it is not to become an isolated, self-perpetuating institution, unresponsive to change.

The Department of Social Administration has recognized these obligations and has attempted to meet them. At the present time, there are thirty-five members of the staffs of similar departments in other universities in the United Kingdom who took their professional courses in the Department. This figure represents a considerable proportion of the social work teaching strength in such departments in the United Kingdom. A similar contribution is being made in the provision of fieldwork supervisors for many agencies and for the newer training courses for child care, medical social work, probation and 'generic' social workers. Other ex-students are teaching in social administration posts in various universities and technical colleges in the United Kingdom and overseas; some are engaged in full-time research in various institutions, and many are holding senior educational appointments in a variety of fields, for example, chief welfare officer in one ministry, chief professional adviser to the National Council for Training in Social Work, and chief officers in many voluntary agencies and local authorities concerned with training programmes.

This spreading of teachers, research and supervisory skills has been aided by the development of advanced studies. Some students have taken the M.Sc. (Social Administration) or Ph.D. degrees, others have had special programmes arranged for them by the professional social staff. In the current session, the staff of the Department is responsible for thirty-eight higher degree and research students.

This contribution to the staffing of other departments has not been limited to the United Kingdom. Through the development of the Mental Health Course since 1945; advanced and higher degree studies, and extended studies on other courses such as the Personnel Management Course, a large number of ex-students are now teaching in universities and other institutions of higher education in many

52

countries of the world. The first Dutch and Israeli psychiatric social workers were trained in the Department. The first Juvenile Court Judge in Israel was one of them. For many years we have had social work students (who are now in teaching positions in their own countries) from Norway, Sweden, Denmark, Finland, Australia, and Ceylon and, more recently, from Ghana, South Africa, Hong Kong, Chile, the West Indies and other countries.

In total, over seventy experienced and older people have been sent from overseas countries since 1946 to take the Mental Health Course. A similar contribution in its work for overseas students has been made by the Personnel Management Course in the Department. So many of the ex-students from these and other courses have since distinguished themselves in their own countries that it would be invidious to mention names. But a few examples of the type and range of posts now held is interesting: head of the mental health training programme in Finland; head of the in-training department for civil servants in Costa Rica; the town clerk of a capital city in West Africa; a woman senator in the Government of British Guiana; permanent secretary of a ministry in Greece; several ministers in newly-independent countries; many chief personnel officers in India, Nigeria, Trinidad, Southern Rhodesia, Peru, Malaya and Ghana; and about a dozen holding senior teaching and administrative posts in Holland, Denmark, Norway, Switzerland, Italy, Sweden, Kuwait, India, Malaya, Australia and Canada.

These are only a few examples of the role that the Department has played during the past twelve years in helping to staff social work and social administration faculties in the United Kingdom and similar faculties and social welfare ministries abroad. Many other illustrations of a more diverse kind could be drawn from an analysis of the careers of students who have taken the Overseas Diploma in Social Administration. Since 1948 over 350 students from over thirty countries have been awarded this diploma.[1] The largest contingents have come from Nigeria, India, the West Indies (including British Guiana), Malaya, Ceylon and Ghana. Many have returned as pioneers: the first psychiatric social worker in one African country (after taking the Mental Health Course); the first almoner in another (after taking a course in medical social work); Permanent Secretary to a Ministry of Education and Social Welfare in a third; private secretary to the first Prime Minister in a fourth; ex-students in responsible social welfare and community development posts in Zanzibar, Thailand, Ethiopia, Aden, Sierra Leone, Hong Kong, Mauritius, Jamaica and Cyprus; twenty-five on the staff of the Social Welfare Department in Malaya; and so on.

To contribute to this extent and in these different ways to the needs of other societies as well as our own for educated and professionally trained people would not have been possible had the Department not accepted its place as an integral part of a university. Only by so doing have we been able to benefit from a great deal of teaching help and assistance in many ways provided by various disciplines in the school. One consequence of academic integration has been that we have attracted an increasing flow of senior scholars and students from overseas who have come to study different aspects of the British social services. Many of them have been senior people in professional, administrative, or university posts awarded fellowships or scholarships of one kind or another. In all, over 130 such students have had special programmes of study arranged for them since 1950. They have included twenty-eight Fulbright scholars and fellows, twenty-seven under UN scholarships, and others under the Marshall Aid, Commonwealth, Colombo Plan, Beaverbrook and British Council Schemes. The Department has also to cater for large numbers of overseas visitors who come for consultation and advice. In one academic year, for example, when records were kept (1954–55) twenty-five professors from universities overseas visited the Department.

The Department has sometimes been criticized for continuing to run two-year diploma courses for both UK and overseas students, and for admitting a proportion of older candidates with educational qualifications below those normally accepted among younger people for first degree courses. As we have watched the subsequent careers of both these diploma groups of ex-students we have felt that this policy has been amply justified. It has, of course, meant an increase in total student numbers because we have, at the same time, been expanding our teaching programmes at the level of professional and advanced studies. The Department was the first in Britain to introduce a Mental Health Course (as long ago as 1930); the first with Personnel Management (1945); one of the first with a Child Care Course (1948); the first to pioneer a 'generic' Casework Course (Applied Social Studies in 1954); the first with an M.Sc. in Social Administration (1955); the first non-medical school to run postgraduate courses for general practitioners (in 1961 in collaboration with the British Postgraduate Medical Federation); the first to act as external examiners and advisers to social welfare faculties in universities overseas (1955).

In 1934–38 there were, on average, a total of 170 students of all categories in the Department. By 1949–50 the number had risen to 219. It is now 266. Although comparisons are not strictly possible, because of the problem of classifying the pre-professional students, nevertheless, in terms of *total* student numbers the Department is easily the largest of its kind in Europe and roughly equal in size to the largest in North America. Over the years it has made by far the biggest contribution of any university in Britain to staffing the public and voluntary social services with trained social workers. Today, the Department accounts for 37 per cent of all students in the country completing a professional course.

And now I must bring to an end, on behalf of the staff, this unashamedly self-congratulatory recital. We seldom if ever say these things in public or in private. Thinking about tomorrow allows little time for remembering things past. And we rarely have the opportunity to thank our students for helping to make the Department what it is today and for adding to the renown of the London School of Economics and Political Science. But this is a jubilee occasion and the moment to express our gratitude to the Social Science Society for all that its members have done over the years to welcome new students and to work out continuously, with the staff, a relationship which we believe to be in the best traditions of university life.

Two lessons for the future do, I think, emerge from this brief review of the past. The effectiveness of teaching—the whole complex process of learning and understanding—does depend, for the vast majority of students, on the quality of the relationships established between staff and students. The tutorial is the foundation. On it must be built many devices, individual and collective, for broadening the sense of partnership in a worthwhile enterprise. Within this context, teaching can never be regarded as a 'burden' by staff or students.

The second lesson is that a Department of Social Administration, like other departments or faculties with vocational or specialist interests, must see itself as an integral part of a university, and must contribute to the purposes of a university in the advancement of knowledge. While this knowledge will have many uses, practical and theoretical, its main value will be to make teachers more effective teachers, and to constantly renew, for students, the intellectual challenge of new ideas and new uncertainties.

NOTE

1. Including forty-one who took the UK Diploma. The total includes a number of UK students who wished to prepare themselves for work in low-income countries.

PART II

THE HEALTH AND WELFARE COMPLEX

THE RELATIONSHIP BETWEEN SOCIAL SECURITY PROGRAMMES AND SOCIAL SERVICE BENEFITS: AN OVERVIEW*

As a student for many years of social problems in Britain and other countries I would like to say, at the outset, that I regard it as a high honour to be asked to address this meeting organized by the International Social Security Association. I am here not as a civil servant (though I respect civil servants), not as an official (though I respect and criticize officials as I often do civil servants) and not as an inspector of the type portrayed by Gogol or any other. I am here simply as a teacher of the University of London whose main responsibility is to explain and discuss with young people some-thing of the realities of social life in the second half of the twentieth century; young people who wish to become social workers, adminis-trators in the social services, research workers in the social sciences, or who have a commitment to help the poor in Britain, in Africa and low-income countries in the world. Some of them may have long hair and wear peculiar clothes but I believe that, underneath their search for identity, their hearts and heads are as sound as ever.

Still on this personal note, may I say two other things? First, my fares to Leningrad and my hotel costs here are generously paid by the International Social Security Association; not by the British Government or by any other organization. I can, therefore, say what I like; one of the great privileges of a university teacher, a privilege which should not, I consider, be over-abused. Secondly, I would wish to affirm that I believe in the building of better social security programmes. Social security (or social insurance as of right) is, in my view, one of the great social inventions of the twentieth century. It has done more to relieve misery and to enhance human self-respect than many other alternative instruments of social policy.

I regard it important that I should make my position and my values quite clear at the beginning. I do so with my students. They

* Lecture delivered at the XVIth General Assembly of the International Social Security Association in Leningrad, USSR, May 1967.

have a right to know where I stand; they are then better able to criticize, disagree with me, and formulate their own views in the search for truth.

Now I have another confession to make. Social security programmes throughout the world vary so much and change so often that I find I cannot keep up to date.[1] Of course, this diversity of programmes and of social services expresses and reflects the rich diversities of different economic, political and social systems, cultural patterns and ways of life. This richness of patterns seems to me to be of great human value in itself; something to be safeguarded. We do not all want to be like the Americans, the Russians, the British or the French. As Tolstoy said in *Anna Karenina*, '. . . each unhappy family is unhappy in its own way.'

But insofar as these cultural diversities are reflected in national social policies, they do present difficulties for anyone who is expected to discuss programmes and policies with an international audience. None of us know—or can remember—all the facts. We must, therefore, treat the subject not by discussing the details for this or that country but with the aid of concepts and models, principles and goals, and in terms of categories of benefits, contributions and users. We have to think of classes of benefit, kinds of entitlement, patterns of utilization, and differences in goals or objectives.

Moreover, I believe this is the only way in which we can attempt to handle comparatively and intelligently the problems of change. We are living in an age of rapid change and rising expectations and aspirations—especially among the young. These phenomena are the product of social, political, economic and technological innovation. Social security and social service programmes are particularly exposed to the winds and the risks of change chiefly because of their concern for the insecurities of industrialism. So these programmes have also to change; they have continually to be evaluated, reviewed and reformed. But in what general direction? Should they be allowed to wither away with rising national incomes? Should they be more or less redistributive in intention and effect as between different income groups in the population? Or, put in another way, should they be less universalistic in scope and coverage, and concentrate more selectively on the poor and handicapped groups in childhood, sickness, handicap and old age? Should they, therefore, become more or less conditional on some test of need-eligibility?

To these examples of important questions, which concern policymakers in varying degrees in many countries, has been added recently another question about the relationship between social security programmes (benefits in cash) and the provision and availability of social services (benefits in kind) such as: medical care and the prevention of physical and mental illness and disablement; rehabilitation and retraining services; education and industrial training; housing, child welfare services and the prevention of family breakdown; and a variety of services for dependent groups —children and old people in particular—including school meals, homemaker and home help services, day-centres and nurseries, day hospitals, residential accommodations, and so on.

It is coming to be recognized that there are problems of relationships between social security systems and social services; that there are problems for administrators and citizens of co-ordination; that both systems cannot be considered separately and in isolation; that there are policy issues of priorities and balance in the planned allocation of scarce resources.

Six years ago, at the 14th General Meeting of ISSA in Istanbul, recognition was first given to some of these problems by the Association. Dr Ida Merriam, of the USA, surveyed the field, discussed the eternally difficult matter of defining 'social security' and the 'social services', and stressed the need for more intensive functional studies.[2]

To save repetition, I shall in this paper follow the broad definitions set out in Dr Merriam's Report.[3]

Three years later, at the last General Assembly in Washington, the subject was again on the agenda. The report of an inquiry in 1962 among members of the ISSA, concerning different aspects of relationships between income maintenance and social service programmes, was presented by Dr Merriam and discussed by delegates.[4] This report also referred to the growing interest in this wide and diffuse field by the United Nations, the International Labour Office and other international agencies. Nor should we forget, of course, the World Health Organization. There seems to be no lack of interest and activity.

Let me remind you, at this point, of two particular matters to which attention was drawn in the 1964 Report. First:

'From the many discussions that are now in progress there is emerging, however, a consensus on some issues. There is now widespread acceptance that social security and social service programmes are both necessary parts of a broader social and economic policy aimed at individual and family welfare. Such policy would include also measures to assure full employment and economic growth, a satisfying structure for urban communities, health and education services, transportation and recreational facilities and so on. The specific relationship of social security and social services will vary according to a country's overall social policy at a particular time.'[5]

The second point in the Report I wish to refer to is this.

'In addition to further factual studies, and evaluative studies, what is needed now is more informed discussion of the advantages and disadvantages of alternative practices and types of relationship, the reasons why particular countries have adopted the policies they follow and what their experience may suggest to others.'[6]

I propose to adopt this advice, and take as my general theme 'the advantages and disadvantages of alternative practices and types of relationship'. Whether it will result in 'informed discussion' is not for me to predict. With this as my theme, I shall, however, attempt to develop the subject under two main headings. The first I shall call 'Effectiveness'; here I shall raise questions about programme objectives and the extent to which they are attained.

My second heading, put simply, is this: 'Consumer Knowledge, Consumer Choice, Consumer Rights'. I hasten to add that I do not use the word 'consumer' in the sense employed by those discussing a market economy. I use it as a convenient omnibus term for all or any of the following: beneficiary, contributor, member, applicant, client, patient or case. In short, I mean citizens in their role as citizens; not citizens in their role as officials, bureaucrats, administrators or politicians. So: we have two headings, 'Effectiveness' and the 'Consumer Interest'.

Before, however, we can usefully discuss these two headings we need to analyse the different functions of benefits and services; different methods or ways of delivering services to consumers, and different patterns of access to services and their utilization. Who gets what, why, and who pays? Or, as we say in Britain, 'whose Welfare State and why?'

It is theoretically possible, for example, to classify the benefits or uses of social security and social service programmes in three main categories:

(a) as forms of future investment: compulsory or voluntary investment in the future. This may be individual, collective or both;

(b) as forms of consumption; immediate increments to individual and/or family welfare (as a method of *distributing* income or command over resources);

(c) as forms of compensation to individuals and/or families for disservices or diswelfares caused by society in general.

Now I will provide some illustrations of these three categories. Education as a social service is one example of category (*a*) of welfare investment from which the individual consumer is assumed to benefit in the future, and from which society is also assumed (though perhaps with less justification) to benefit, economically, socially and politically, in the future. This and other forms of welfare investment may be either compulsory (as with primary education and certain types of industrial-technical training) or selective (as with higher education, professional training and, in some countries, tax deductibles for saving among the higher income groups).

Examples of category (*b*), namely, consumption benefits or immediate increments to welfare, are family allowances, pensions in payment, subsidized housing and some types of free or subsidized medical care. These may be provided as 'of right' for everyone in the population or, selectively, after some test of need-eligibility.

Examples of category (*c*), namely, compensation consumptions, are more difficult to specify because one is raising some fundamental questions about the causal agents in society responsible for disservices or diswelfares borne by individuals and families who, it is increasingly recognized, are not at fault. By way of illustration let me mention a few: the victims of involuntary unemployment and the obsolescence of acquired skills; the victims of industrial accidents and diseases and road accidents; the victims of smoke pollution and other hazards of industrialism; the victims of cross-infection in hospitals, medical error, and the side-effects of new drugs which benefit a majority but harm a minority; the victims of ethnic or religious prejudice; the victims of the mistakes we make in our educational systems by wrongly stigmatizing and rejecting people as 'failures', and so on. They represent, in some senses, the people who are compelled to pay—as diswelfares—part of the costs of other people's progress in a dynamic and changing society.

It is one of the major functions of social security and social service programmes to make some provision for these victims of diswelfare; to compensate them in part for income loss and other injuries to life chances. One of the principal reasons for the acceptance of this compensation function is that, scientifically, statistically and legally, it is becoming increasingly difficult in all modern societies—capitalist, socialist or mixed—to identify the causal agents of diswelfare and charge them with the costs.

Thus, if we are humane and recognize the diswelfares in our societies, we thereby extend the functions and enlarge the roles of social security and social service programmes. We shall then, I suggest, be led to ask some further questions. For instance: we shall begin to ask how and in what ways can we prevent or mitigate 'diswelfares'; we shall begin to ask questions about the effectiveness of our programmes—are they just partial or token compensations—simply emergency first-aid services—or do they aim at full restitution and rehabilitation? And we shall also have to ask, recognizing often that cash benefits alone are not enough and that services in kind alone are not enough, what relationships between the two are likely to be most effective, and what forms of co-ordination are more rather than less likely to achieve effectiveness.

To sum up at this point, therefore, I have said that social security and social service provisions may be classified as forms of investment; as forms of increments to welfare; as forms of partial compensation. In real life as distinct from theoretical models there will, of course, be much overlap. But I find these distinctions helpful in thinking about the objectives of social security and social service programmes.

Now I must say a few words about objectives. I hope it is clear from what I have already said that these programmes, whatever their coverage and content in different countries, are not dominated by a single objective. They contain and express many objectives; some in harmony with each other; some in conflict, ideologically, administratively and financially. They conflict because all programmes, and each individual service, operate some system of rationing: however rich the society, we do not know the optimum needs and we cannot provide optimum services in respect of medical care, education, housing, social security and so forth. This being so, it is important to ask questions about objectives because systems of rationing and the choice of priorities will be profoundly influenced by the objectives of these programmes.

I cannot, at this stage, embark on a comprehensive philosophy of welfare but I would like to mention a few of the more important objectives which influence—and have shaped in the past—the development of social security and social service programmes.

1. To raise worker productivity, increase worker mobility, and add to economic growth (this objective has powerfully influenced, for example, the development of wage-related social security benefits).
2. To insure and protect the worker against the risks and hazards of industrialism and partially to reward those who undertake the 'dirty' jobs in our societies (an example here is the earlier age of retirement and higher pensions paid to coal miners in Russia and other countries).
3. To increase or decrease the birthrate.

4. To prevent juvenile delinquency, crime and other forms of culturally determined anti-social behaviour (in this case, a variety of social service programmes operate as forms of social or police control to support the prevailing system of law and order).

5. To prevent sickness and ill-health in the interests of productivity, or because much sickness is economically wasteful, or because sick people are people experiencing suffering and pain.

6. To integrate all citizens into society. This I call the 'integrative objective'; the purposes of which are to further the sense of community and participation; to prevent alienation; and to integrate the members of minority groups, ethnic groups and regional cultures into the total society.

7. Lastly, to increase or decrease inequalities in the distribution of incomes and command-over-resources-over-life set by the economic system. No social security or social service programme, whatever its declared or official objectives, can be utterly neutral in its actual effects on the distribution of incomes. I do not know of any programmes in any country of the world which do not, in their total effects, increase or decrease inequalities in the distribution of incomes and life chances. Some benefit the rich more than the poor; others benefit the poor more than the rich.

These, I am sure you will tell me, are but only a few of the many objectives which may, in different ways, influence the coverage, content and methods of rationing of social security and social service programmes. The relative weight and importance accorded to these and other objectives will depend on the prevailing values in a given society; on the extent to which, as Marcel Mauss, a wise French sociologist, observed, the morality of gift-exchange is embedded in the institutions of a society.[7]

On this note I am led back to consider the advantages and disadvantages of alternative practices and types of relationships between social security and social service programmes. As I said earlier, we can consider these issues under two broad headings, 'Effectiveness' and 'Consumer Interest'.

First, what do we mean by 'effectiveness'? Because human needs are complex and interdependent the concept of 'effectiveness' is difficult to clarify particularly in the area of services in kind. It is broader and goes beyond the notion of efficiency—administrative and/or financial efficiency or cheapness per unit of service—in the operating costs of a programme.

Effectiveness, I suggest, can be interpreted broadly in two ways. It can mean the attempt to maximize the delivery of a range of services, in cash and in kind, to help or encourage individuals or families to modify, resolve or face a series of personal problems which they cannot adequately deal with by recourse to other channels or institutions (such as the family, the market, their personal resources, etc.). The principle of maximization applies particularly, of course, in the case of individuals who are recognized as in need of compensation for disservices caused to them by society. There is here a more explicit social obligation to maximize the provision of services.

A second interpretation of 'effectiveness' relates to the expression or articulation of a need for services. There are some needs which cannot be self-diagnosed; for medical care, for instance, or mental health services or rehabilitation services. There are some needs which, though they are 'felt' needs, are not expressed because of ignorance on the part of the individual that services exist, and that anything can be done to mitigate or remove the need. There are similar needs again which are not expressed because of a fear of bureaucracy and officialdom; because of the stigma attaching to the use of a service—like the old poor law in European countries —or because of a fear of being shamed by a doctor or other professional gatekeeper guarding access to a service and of being accused of unnecessarily troubling professional people.

There are, indeed, many systems of rationing or barriers which operate to deter the expression of need. While, on the one hand, we may want individuals to express their needs so that a range of services may take early and preventive action (to prevent chronic incapacity among the old, for instance), yet, on the other hand, we may want to deter the expression of need for fear of overwhelming a service with demands it cannot adequately meet and, thus, creating dissatisfaction and cynicism among potential consumers. Sometimes we call this abuse or malingering.

In recent years in Britain and other countries a number of research workers have studied these problems of unmet needs and unexpressed needs for services in cash and in kind. Broadly speaking, what they have found is that in relative terms there are more unmet and unexpressed needs among the poor, the badly educated, the old, those living alone and other handicapped groups. Their needs are not expressed and are not met because of ignorance, inertia, fear, difficulties of making contact with the services, failures of co-ordination and co-operation between services, and for other reasons. These are the people—and there are substantial numbers of them in all populations—who are difficult to reach. Yet they are often the people with the greatest needs.

66

By contrast, middle-income groups make more and better use of all services; they are more articulate, and more demanding. They have learnt better in all countries how to find their way around a complicated welfare world.

In terms of maximizing effectiveness, therefore, the real challenge lies in the problem of 'how to reach the difficult to reach' in our societies. And this challenge contains a moral element when those who do not or cannot express their needs are the victims of dis-welfares inflicted by society. There is then a distinctive obligation on society to provide compensatory services in the form of income loss replacement and services in kind.

Now I must turn briefly to my second heading 'Consumer Interest'. Basically, of course, this is linked to the principle of 'effectiveness'. But when we look more closely at programmes and services from the consumer's point of view—and especially the 'hard to reach' and inarticulate consumer—we shall, I think, see that 'Consumer Interest' contains four major elements. I call these (1) Knowledge, (2) Choice, (3) Rights, (4) Participation.

To extend knowledge about the availability and use of pro-grammes and services raises, of course, many questions. It can mean shifting the emphasis from deterrence (and concealed forms of rationing) to making more possible, and encouraging, the con-scious expression of unmet need or inadequately met need by the consumer. This may have far-reaching implications, not only in terms of scarce resources, but for the ways in which programmes and services are structured; how they are administered centrally and locally; and in relation to the education and intraining of administrators, officials in contact with consumers, and professional workers (in my view one of the most neglected areas of social secu-rity and social service policy). The important question is also raised of the extent to which social security programmes should extend knowledge and encourage the use of social services in kind, and *vice versa*.

Second, a word about Choice. The question of offering choices to consumers arises in a number of ways. Choices may be offered, for example, within social security programmes as to alternative ways of calculating and paying social security benefits as of right. Choices may also be offered between benefits in cash and benefits in kind; for example, old people living alone or unmarried mothers on low subsistence standards and in poor housing conditions might prefer the security of residential accommodation to higher assistance payments. Choices may also be offered within services in kind; for example, the alternatives of medical care and welfare services for disabled people in their own homes or in institutions or a combination of both through the provision of day hospitals, night hospitals, home-for-the-weekend hospitals, day and night homemaker services, occupation centres, and so on.

My third heading relates to the question of Consumer Rights. Many need-eligibility programmes are basically designed to keep people out; not to let them in. Moreover, they are often so administered as to induce among consumers a sense of shame, guilt or failure in using a public service. If we wish to maximize the effectiveness of programmes and services and, particularly, to reach the 'hard to reach' in our societies then we have to examine ways and means of shifting the emphasis from the stigma of deterrence to the concept of social rights. This, again, raises questions about not only the structure and relationships of services in cash and in kind, but about how the services are actually delivered by administrators, officials and professional workers. Specifically, we are led to ask questions about the extent, scope and actual use of discretionary powers by officials in the operation of conditional programmes and services. Are such powers used as forms of social control and in respect of what groups? In what ways can or should these powers over people be translated into clearly formulated rules of entitlement or rights?

Lastly, I come to the heading of 'Consumer Participation'. Here there is the question of the extent to which consumers and consumer representatives can and should be involved in the administration and delivery of programmes and services from the top levels of policy, planning and decision-making to the lower levels of access to services, appeal courts and tribunals, and the whole area of complaint procedure and the redress of wrongs. Does more or less consumer participation support the general aim of effectiveness— of maximizing consumer use of programmes and services? To what extent can or should consumer participation exercise an influence on the quality of services provided by administrators, doctors, teachers, social workers and other professional people? And what is the role of the volunteer—whether trade unionist or local citizen —and of the voluntary agency—religious or secular—in encouraging or discouraging the fact and the sense of consumer participation?

These are some of the important questions which are raised when we begin to consider the problems involved in the relationships between social security programmes and social services in kind under the two broad headings of 'Effectiveness' and 'Consumer Interest'.

Few of them in practice, as solutions, are simple to apply; few of them, in fact, can be applied without recognizing that there are advantages and disadvantages in different kinds of relationships; each present different areas of conflict and different clashes of opinion about ends and means.

To impersonalize social security programmes, that is to say, to provide cash benefits as of right with the minimum of forms, rules and regulations can mean a loss of personal contact with consumers either in their own homes or in social security offices. Thus, opportunities may be lost of 'reaching the hard to reach'; of providing knowledge about other services; of diagnosing unmet needs; of maximizing the effectiveness of social policy as a whole. On the other hand, we have to recognize the fundamental importance of providing impersonally and 'as of right' adequate social security benefits; to the consumer this is an essential freedom, the freedom to spend such benefits in any way the individual wishes.

Or take another example of potential conflict; the problem of the conditional use of services. Should income maintenance programmes (or any form of income guarantee) be conditional on the consumers' use of certain services in kind, for example, rehabilitation, retraining and medical care services, because we wish to maximize the effectiveness of all the services involved? Or put in another way: should income maintenance payments be 'wasted' on consumers who may take no steps to change their circumstances, improve their health and ways of life? The conflict here is between the concept of effectiveness and the rights of the consumer to certain services irrespective of their morals and patterns of behaviour.

Ultimately, of course, the answers to these questions concerning the advantages or disadvantages of different forms of relationships between services in cash and in kind will depend on the definition of social policy objectives and on our scale of values. They will depend on the priorities decided on in the allocation of scarce resources; on the relative importance we accord to economic growth and social growth, and on how the scales are weighted between the rights of the individual and the rights of society.

To conclude this introductory paper which has, I fear, been somewhat general and theoretical in nature, I would like to end with a simple, practical illustration of the effects of one particular form of relationship between an income maintenance programme and certain services in kind. We can best teach what we best know, so this illustration is taken, not surprisingly, from experience in my own country.

It relates to the problem of preventing blindness in old age. This is a human problem which I need not enlarge on for this perceptive audience. Humanitarianism can, however, in this case lead to substantial financial savings; insofar as blindness can be prevented, economic resources may be saved on a large scale for many years if old people are helped to go on living in their own homes without the need for institutional care and other services.

Scientific advances in recent years in medicine, surgery and ophthalmology have demonstrated that some of the major causes of blindness, for example, cataract, can be prevented. This is an established scientific fact. But prevention primarily depends on early diagnosis of faulty vision and early access to the appropriate medical and ophthalmological services. This problem of preventive action is particularly difficult to resolve among older men and women; they tend through inertia, fear, ignorance, loneliness and the fateful acceptance of physical limitations, ascribed to ageing, not to take action.

In 1966 the Ministry of Health in London published a forbidding statistical report called *The Incidence and Causes of Blindness in England and Wales 1948–62*.[8] It was written by Professor Arnold Sorsby, Britain's most distinguished ophthalmologist.

The report showed, for example, that for all ages and both sexes the incidence of blindness caused by cataract declined during 1948–62 by approximately 25 per cent.[9] For men and women aged sixty to sixty-nine the decline was as remarkably high as 54 per cent, and there were even substantial declines over the age of seventy.[10] Advances were also recorded for many of the other causes of blindness.

It would appear that these trends in the prevention of blindness in old age are due, *inter alia*, to two major factors. The first is the availability of free medical and hospital services since the National Health Service—'socialized medicine'—was introduced in Britain in 1948, and a subsequent improvement in the provision of inpatient and outpatient ophthalmological facilities. The second relates to earlier preventive action. It would seem that more elderly people were helped, encouraged and advised to do something about their faulty vision. What is relevant here is the source of reference—the way in which these people were referred—to the local authorities who maintain registers of the blind and the partially sighted. This Report showed that the most important sources of reference were not doctors; not medical sources at all. Lay sources of referral for action accounted for two-thirds of all referrals among those aged over seventy.[11]

Of all lay sources of reference, the National Assistance Board was by far the most important referral agent. The primary statutory function of the Board as a Government Department (now the Supplementary Benefits Commission) is to grant assistance, mainly cash allowances, to those in need after satisfying certain conditions about means. The Board discharges its functions largely through home visiting. In 1965 it paid allowances to some 2 million people in Britain, and its officers carried out $7\frac{1}{2}$ million visits to the homes of people—mainly old people.[12]

Here we have a concrete example of a large group in the population with multiple needs for services in cash and services in kind who are 'hard to reach'. To reach them—to maximize effectiveness —requires, as this example demonstrates, some personal contact primarily in the home of the consumer; some personal relationship —and not a paper relationship—which can be the source of knowledge and information, advice and encouragement. It is also a source of freedom. Blindness prevented is an enlargement of freedom.

There is, I must confess, much more that could be said on the subject of this paper. There are no simple explanations and no simple answers. The principles and the examples I have discussed in this paper could, I am sure, be expanded and improved on by many in this audience with far more experience than I possess. So all I can claim to have done is to have set the stage for further thought and study.

NOTES

1. On variation and change see *Social Security Programs Throughout the World, 1964*, US Dept of Health, Education and Welfare, Social Security Administration, 1965.
2. *Bulletin of the International Social Security Association*, November-December 1961, Nos 11–12, p. 675.
3. On the subject of definitions see also *Social Security Programs Throughout the World, 1964*, US Dept of Health, Education and Welfare, 1965.
4. *Bulletin of the International Social Security Association*, October-December 1964, Nos 10–12, p. 358.
5. *Ibid.*, p. 358.
6. *Ibid.*, p. 361.
7. Mauss, M., *The Gift*, Cohen and West, London, 1966.
8. Reports on Public Health and Medical Subjects, No. 114, HMSO, 1966.
9. *Ibid.*, p. 65.
10. *Ibid.*, p. 37.
11. *Ibid.*, p. 56.
12. *Report of the National Assistance Board for 1965*, Cmnd 3042, HMSO, London, 1966.

71

Chapter VI

THE WELFARE COMPLEX IN A CHANGING SOCIETY*

More than a century ago John Ruskin said, 'Not only is there but one way of doing things rightly, but there is only one way of seeing them, and that is seeing the whole of them.'¹ This is an admirable sentiment to which no one will dissent; at least not at first glance. But although professional people declare their faith in the generic, the whole, the comprehensive and the multidisciplinary—whether they are talking about diagnosis, therapy, social action or planning—they still want to specialize and to define more clearly their own professional, administrative or volunteer roles. They want to be more certain about themselves and their identity in an increasingly complex society. To acquire and cultivate one small allotment of skill and knowledge where one feels somewhat more secure in the vastness of the knowable is a great comfort.

To these internal pressures are added external ones. Professional people want their identity, role and functions to be known to others, for identity and specialization are linked to status. Professional people, whether they be doctors, social workers or teachers, are pre-eminently people with status problems.

Can people be specialists (and thus acquire status) and at the same time see things whole? Does the generalist (who is presumed to see things whole) have a future in society, particularly in the health, welfare and community care fields? Today questions such as these are being asked concerning the future training, roles, functions and relationships of the general medical practitioner (or personal family physician) and the family-oriented social worker. These are, in fact, two of the great unresolved dilemmas—the future of the community doctor and the community social worker. Much less concern is expressed for the future of those who find protection and status in the institution; for example, the physician in the hospital or the caseworker in the child guidance clinic. Paradoxically, the discovery in

* Lecture delivered at the Canadian Social Welfare Conference, Vancouver, Canada, June 1966, and published in *Milbank Memorial Fund Quarterly*, Vol. XLV, No. 1, Pt 1, January 1967.

recent years of the social and psychological needs of patients and clients to receive care in their own homes has coincided with the rise of the institution as the source of status, specialization and professional power.

This trend no doubt accounts in part for the observation of the Hall Commission's report on Canada's health services: 'In a world of specialists, it has become imperative to review and redefine the role of the general practitioner.'[2] Society is confronted with precisely that issue. Does the general practitioner have a future? What is his place in the organizational structure of health and welfare services?

The question of the future functions and field of work of the general practitioner is a far wider one than of his relationships with the hospital and of co-ordination with physical medicine specialties.[3] If he is concerned with the mental as well as the physical, with social diagnosis as well as medical diagnosis, then the more complex issue arises of his relationships with a network of personal social and welfare services: services for the deprived child and the unmarried mother; child guidance and the social services of the school; the probation (or correction) services for young people and adults; special services for the educationally deprived, the mentally subnormal and other handicapped groups; transitional hostels and community care services for the mentally ill; rehabilitation and retraining services for the physically handicapped and an extensive and varied range of domiciliary, residential and welfare services for the aged. Many of these services—public, voluntary and a mixture of both elements—have not only expanded greatly in recent years, but have been changing in form and function. With the growth, for example, of the day hospital movement, the therapeutic mental institution and a variety of transitional (or half-way) accommodations to cater to the health and welfare needs of special groups, the policy maker, as well as the social statistician, has great difficulty in defining correctly what is and what is not a 'hospital'.

This blurring of the hitherto sharp lines of demarcation between home care and institutional care, between physical disability and mental disability, between educationally backward children and so-called 'delinquent' children, and between health needs and welfare needs, is all part of a general movement toward more effective service for the public and toward a more holistic interpretation and operational definition of the principles of primary, secondary and tertiary prevention.[4] On a broader plane, society is moving toward a symbiosis which sees the physician, the teacher and the social worker as social service professionals with common objectives.

The accepted purpose of the health service is to treat the individual who has some malfunction in such manner as to restore him to health, and that must involve the individual's mental, emotional and social functions as well as his physical functions.

The accepted purpose of the educational *process*, of which the educational *service* is only one part, is to promote and stimulate every individual's mental, physical and emotional capacities.

The accepted purpose of social work (and the welfare services) is to help the individual who is inadequate or disturbed to develop his ability so that he may play his part in society in such a way that both he and society are tolerably satisfied.

The health, education and social work (personal welfare) services are thus all concerned with the individual and the family, and all concerned with his mental, physical and social development. They all have in common a concern for prevention, early case-finding and early mobilization of a network of specialized services with responsibilities for therapy and treatment.

This movement in the philosophy and goals of the health, education and personal welfare services, expressed in recent developments in the aims and functions of the services themselves, does present the professional worker, as well as the administrator, with relatively greater problems of communication, co-ordination and collaboration. If the patient or client is not to be fragmented, then more co-ordination is required, thus more channels of communication and more processes of formal and informal collaboration are needed, and more easily recognizable points of access and information are required in the interests of the often bewildered and confused citizen. A new element has to be added to the professional's role in the community: the capacity to be a co-operative 'enabler'. The solo entrepreneurial clinical or casework role is no longer adequate by itself in many cases; someone has to enable (or to mobilize) a variety of services and agencies to come into play in the interests of the total needs of the individual and his or her family.

This is not a static situation, but is, in fact, a rapidly moving picture with changes in political and professional thinking about ends and means, and with changes in the responsibilities and goals of a large variety of social organizations and agencies.

What are the effects of these new ideas and of reformulated principles of policy and action on the existing organizational structures of the health and welfare services? Can the present structures and administrative patterns absorb and put into practice the new thinking about people and their needs at the level of community action? More co-ordination and collaboration is essential if these needs are to be effectively met. Questions must be asked about the barriers which existing organizational structures create to prevent more co-ordination and collaboration. One should, therefore, ask questions about the structures and systems in which these services operate. To what extent do they encourage and enable, or discourage and prevent more effective co-ordination and collaboration?

Modern man has been said to be man in organizations. The work of Weber, Parsons, Simon and many others, and the empirical studies of such writers as Blau and Scott,[5] have greatly extended the knowledge of the principles and problems of organizational life. Social units (which are called formal organizations) are character-ized by explicit goals, elaborate systems of rules and regulations, formal status structures, and, often, clearly marked lines of autho-rity and communication. The particular form they may take in the social welfare field has recently been analysed by Donnison.[6] By their nature and constitutions, organizations tend to assume iden-tities of their own which may make them independent of or imper-vious to the public they are presumed to serve. Although this tendency may be less true of the public service model than of the philanthropic model in the welfare field (because of lay democratic control), nevertheless all such organizations resist change from within. These models appear to have a built-in opposition to the internal development of a self-criticizing function. In the univer-sities, or at least the British universities, this is known as 'the con-spiracy of silence'. Change in goals and functions is difficult to bring about without external criticism.

One form in which the professional protest manifests itself in the health and welfare field has been described by Blau and Scott[7] and Gouldner,[8] among others. Their studies showed that organizations which were thought by professionals to be unsatisfactory and which failed to offer career prospects and opportunities for professional advancement experienced a high rate of staff turnover. More move-ment was noted from employer to employer and from agency to agency among these organizations, and the spirit of loyalty to the organization was weak. Hughes analysed the phenomenon of the 'itinerant' professional who, being 'more fully committed and more alert to the new developments, will move from place to place seek-ing ever more interesting, prestigeful and, perhaps, more profitable positions'.[9]

The problem of the 'itinerant' professional is a serious one. It particularly concerns teachers, social workers, physicians and many professional and sub-professional groups upon whom the health, education and welfare services depend. High rates of staff turnover and shortages of professional skills are most apparent in poorly housed, working-class areas and in districts which contain substantial proportions of immigrants. This particular factor, which in large measure determines continuity of care, makes co-ordination and collaboration much more difficult, if not impossible. Yet in these areas, the slums of modern society, high quality services are most needed if levels of living and opportunity are to be improved for the poorer sections of the population, and if the new immigrants from overseas are to be peacefully and tolerantly absorbed into society.

Because it impinges so much on the problems of co-ordinating services, the issue of 'itinerant professionalism' raises again the question of the structure of organizations and agencies. It does so especially in those areas of the country which are poorly served with professional skills, and are underprivileged in the whole of their social infrastructure, public and private—hospitals, mental institutions, clinics, schools, social centres and agencies, clubs and so forth.

This is only one of the many factors which, in recent years, have stimulated discussion in Britain about the effectiveness of the existing structures and patterns of administration of the local health and welfare services. These are mainly, although not wholly, the statutory responsibility of elected local authorities of cities, towns and counties. These authorities have statutory duties and powers (sometimes in association with voluntary bodies) to provide and promote community care services—either in private homes or in hostels and other small, specialized institutions—for the mentally ill and subnormal; for the elderly, the chronically ill and handicapped living at home; and for the blind, deaf or mute, and those substantially and permanently handicapped by illness, injury or congenital deformity.[10]

Other statutes require these local authorities to provide for children in care and their families.[11] More recent British legislation in the shape of the Children and Young Persons Act, 1963, gave greatly extended powers to these authorities to *prevent* child neglect, delinquency and family break-up. In the health field, these authorities are responsible for maternity and child welfare, the school health services, home nursing and a health visiting service, home help services, chiropody treatment and a wide range of public health measures.

The general practitioner services are administered locally by separate bodies (Executive Councils) appointed by the Minister of Health and which have some local authority representation. The

76

primary reason for this separation is that, when the National Health Service was introduced, the medical profession refused to be associated with elected local government authorities. This was also one of the chief reasons why the idea of the health centre (visualized as a major instrument of co-ordination) has materialized in only a few areas. Most of the medical profession, although welcoming the idea in theory, failed to endorse it in practice.

The probation service for juveniles and adults, which has expanded substantially in the last few years, is another local service which is administered separately and is not under the direct jurisdiction of elected local authorities.

This brief account of the local structures of health and welfare administration (which is necessary to understand the problems of co-ordination) does no more than indicate a pattern of great complexity. Large numbers of voluntary organizations, local and national, also operate in many general and specialized fields of community organization, child care, welfare of the aged, the blind, the deaf and other handicapped groups—sometimes in co-operation with the local authorities, sometimes not.

The major problems of co-ordination—affecting case-finding, diagnosis, advice, treatment and care—arise, however, in the public sector. Though voluntary organizations play a significant role in certain sectors, community care in Britain is now a public responsibility. That was made clear by the publication of the Government's ten-year plan in the health and welfare field.[12] This plan, together with another ten-year plan for hospital development,[13] envisaged, first, a relatively rapid decline in the role of the large institutions for the mentally ill and for the elderly chronically ill, and, second, a great expansion in the provision of community care services of all types.

Planning, however, is only one step. Implementation is another and co-ordination and evaluation yet another. Effectively translating these plans into practice depends on a number of key factors in addition to finance. Because social care to support and strengthen family life in the home and the community depends on the work of educated and trained staff, one of the key factors is the recruitment, training and provision of adequate career channels for physicians, psychologists, social workers, welfare workers, health visitors, home nurses, teachers and physiotherapists for small, specially built hostels, day hospitals, children's institutions, occupational centres and a variety of community agencies. It is a manpower problem involving many detailed aspects of recruitment, training and professional advancement.

A second key factor is the quality of administration, a factor which many countries have tended to neglect. Perhaps too much emphasis has been placed on casework skills and not enough on administrative and 'enabling' skills. The lessons of experience in Britain in recent years have shown that, to make a clear distinction between casework on the one hand, and administration on the other, is not possible in all circumstances.

The work of the National Assistance Board (prior to 1948 'public assistance') is an example of the importance of combining administrative and social work skills, backed by imaginative in-training schemes and the careful selection of interviewing and visiting officers. In 1948, Britain abolished the poor law and centralized the organization and financing of national assistance; cash aid, after an inquiry into means, for those in need—the elderly, widows, unmarried mothers, the long-term ill and other groups. Since 1948, the Board has steadily decentralized the administration of this branch of social security, and now operates it for some two million persons (mostly pensioners) as a 'citizen's right', not as a charity.[14] Its information pamphlet for the public now begins with the words 'What are my rights?' In decentralizing this service the Board has, over the years, extended its welfare functions and now provides, on a national scale, a regular visiting service for hundreds of thousands of lonely and elderly people. As a Minister said in Parliament, 'Here is the foundation of an agency to which any citizen could turn in time of trouble or difficulty, of sickness, bereavement, incapacity or personal plight, a service which could call upon and co-ordinate other services to meet the needs of the particular situation.'[15]

Concrete demonstrations of effective co-ordination in the welfare field do not often appear in the literature of social research. A striking example may be found, however, in the National Assistance Board's aid to elderly citizens. A report by Sorsby[16] shows that, in its first fifteen years, the National Health Service provided a 50 per cent increase for both free inpatient work and free outpatient facilities in ophthalmology, and that during these years the incidence of blindness from cataract declined 25 per cent or more, with reductions also recorded for many of the other causes of blindness.

Though, as Sorsby comments, no direct cause and effect relationship between these two developments can be established, they are difficult to separate in one's mind. No similar substantial declines in the incidence of blindness among the total population have been recorded for any other country. Sorsby's report, therefore, may well be one of the few statistical and objective pieces of evidence in support of the proposition that a free system of medical care can improve health and prevent disability especially for the middle-aged and elderly. The incidence of cataract among the age group of seventy and older declined about 30 per cent in twelve years.[17]

This is prevention in practice. What economic savings have accrued in the form of reduced demands for long-term care in hospitals, in institutions for the aged and blind and for community services, to say nothing of the prevention of human misery, would be difficult to compute.

One other conclusion relates to the matter of the referral of elderly people with visual problems and needs for services of various kinds and for voluntary registration on the national registers for the partially sighted and the blind. By far the highest source of reference for the older age groups—the numerically overwhelming section of the blind population—was the National Assistance Board, not the general practitioner.[18] This shows that to Freidson's ideas of lay referral systems and professional referral systems must be added a third—public welfare referral systems.[19] One lesson to be drawn from this example is that an effective welfare referral system can contribute to the application, in practice, of the idea of prevention.

In considering the problems of structure and co-ordination, the functions of the Board in providing a regular and continuous visiting service, acting as an enabling and mobilizing agent and co-operating with other community services must be taken into account along with the work of other local organizations.

The Board's officers who are in direct contact with members of the public may be described as 'welfare workers'. They are not trained social workers, nor should they be, for much of their work is of routine nature. But when social work aid is needed the Board's officers are often in some difficulty. To which agency or department at the local level should they turn?

At the present time, in most local government areas, trained social workers may be found in the public welfare department, the public health department, the public children's department, the housing department, the education department (all within the same local authority organization), the probation service, the citizen's advice bureau, and a variety of voluntary agencies. Social work skills in the public sector are thus divided and fragmented by administrative and statutory functions. Moreover, because most local departments are relatively small as organized units—due to the size of the population served in each local authority area—only a few trained social workers may be employed in each department. This leads to the ineffective use of trained staff, overlapping functions, difficulties for agencies (such as the National Assistance Board and the general practitioner) in locating the most relevant and accountable referral contact, a lack of adequate professional career opportunities and serious difficulties in sending social and welfare workers and administrators for training, graduate study and refresher courses when the staff unit is small.

In short, local government in Britain is burdened with too many small departments and too much 'balkanized' rivalry in the field of welfare. Attempts to resolve these problems in the 1950s, particularly in relation to the children's services, through the establishment of local 'co-ordinating committees' have not proved successful.[20] Demands for better co-ordination in the health and welfare fields and for more preventive work have increased, and have become increasingly urgent as public opinion has recognized the need for more trained social workers.

Like Canada and the United States, Britain is faced with a serious shortage of social workers at all levels, from the professionally equipped caseworker to the trained welfare worker. The shortage appears (and becomes) more acute because of the growth in public demand for the expansion of existing services and for the development of new services; for example, major reforms in prison after-care services, community care for people discharged from mental hospitals, social work services attached to schools and welfare services for immigrants.

The response to this national call for more trained staff, when viewed in historical perspective, has been impressive. In addition to an increase in the output of university schools of social work, more than twenty new two-year certificate courses in colleges and other institutions of higher education outside the university system have been established in about three years, under the auspices of a National Council for Training in Social Work. This year the enrolment in these courses will rise to more than 300, and this figure will double by 1968–70.[21]

In recent years special fields such as child care have shown considerable improvement in the ratio of trained to untrained staff. For England and Wales as a whole, the proportion of child care staff without any social work qualifications at all has declined to 35 per cent.[22] A study of Ontario Children's Aid societies reported that 74 per cent of social work positions were filled by staff without any social work training.[23] These data may not be comparable, but they indicate in broad terms the magnitude of the problems of trained manpower.

Summary
The themes of this paper must now be brought together. Social
policy in Britain in the personal health, welfare and education fields
is moving toward integrated community services, preventive in
outlook and of high quality for all citizens in all areas irrespective
of means, social class, occupation or ethnic group. Territorial welfare justice is one element in this movement; the most effective
integrated deployment of community services and residential (or
institutional) services is another, along with ease and simplicity of
access and referral for all individuals and families; yet another
is the recognition of the need to locate and attach personal social
work services to publicly 'normal' and acceptable points in the
social system—the general practitioner, the school, the social security system and local government.

Britain's experience in recent years has indicated the necessity of
learning how to use more effectively, and as a unity, the general and
the specialized, community services and institutional services, the
professional expert, the ancillary and the administrator. In the immediate future this may be more difficult to achieve than would the
proliferation of a host of new agencies, projects and instruments of
welfare. But in the long run it is more likely to provide a comprehensive co-ordinated service for the people.

The problem of organizational structure at the local level must,
however, be resolved if a greater degree of co-ordination and collaboration is to be achieved.

Two possible broad routes to structural reform have recently
been proposed in Britain.[24] One takes the form of a local authority
family service department whose functions would include those of
the present children's department, social work and probation services for young offenders under the age of sixteen, the institution
of new family courts and a family advice centre, and, in general,
merging the services for mothers and children to provide a comprehensive family welfare service. Broadly speaking, this proposal is
the expression of two primary influences: the idea of the family as
the treatment unit and the prevention of child neglect and delinquency.

The second proposal is more far-reaching in terms of structural
reorganization. It rejects the idea of a 'family service' and argues
that reform should not be based on biological or sociological
criteria, such as the family, or on one element in the pattern of
needs. Nor should it be oriented to delinquency. Instead, reorganization should proceed from the standpoint of the need for services
at the community level, irrespective of age, family background or

behaviour patterns. Accordingly, this would mean the establishment of departments of social service at the local level. Such departments could embrace all the functions of existing children's departments and welfare departments, probation services for children and young people, and substantial welfare, social service and mental health responsibilities shouldered at present by other departments —chiefly health departments. The top executive of such a department would be a chief social administrator assisted by a chief social worker whose primary responsibility would be to advise professionally on the most effective deployment of all social work and welfare skills in the local public sector.

These two proposals, and a series of variants on the same theme, have stimulated much debate. To different degrees, they both strive to more effectively use trained manpower; to encourage more preventive action; to avoid fragmentation, overlapping and lack of co-ordination; to provide better career structures for social administrators as well as social workers and, in general, to adapt organizational structures to allow and encourage modern ideas of community and mental health care to grow, develop and diversify.

As a result of the public and professional debate, conducted against the background of a rising tide of criticism of the small-scale, ineffective structures of local government, the national Government appointed a committee of inquiry (the Seebohm Committee)[25] in 1965, 'to review the organization and responsibilities of local authority personal social services in England and Wales, and to consider what changes are desirable to secure an effective family service'.[26] A similar inquiry is being undertaken for Scotland.[27]

The Seebohm Committee's field of inquiry includes people of all ages who are the concern of the welfare services, the children's service and social work in health, education and housing departments.

At this stage, speculation about the nature of the Committee's recommendations, which are expected at the end of 1967, would be useless. The Committee probably will not shelve the problems of organizational structure and planning by recommending a series of co-ordinating committees in the health and welfare field. These have been tried in Britain and have failed.

In the ultimate analysis society may have to choose between 'the sense of community' on the one hand, with which is equated small-scale and often ineffectively preventive, poor-quality services, and larger social groupings offering better quality services and more freedom of choice for consumers, but with the recognized dangers of larger bureaucracies and professional power units. In facing this dilemma the question must be asked whether the purpose is to serve people—and many of the clients are defenceless people—or to advance the interests of established organizations and professional groups.

NOTES

1. Ruskin, John, 'The Two Paths', Lecture 2, London, 1859.
2. *Royal Commission on Health Services*, Volume II, Roger Duhamel, Queen's Printer and Controller of Stationery, Ottawa, 1965, p. 259.
3. See, for example, *The Field of Work of the Family Doctor* (the Gillie Report), Central Health Services Council, Ministry of Health, London, HMSO, 1963.
4. For discussion of these models of prevention in the health field, see Morris, J. N., *Uses of Epidemiology*, Livingstone, London, 1964.
5. Blau, P. M., and Scott, W. R., *Formal Organizations*, Chandler Publishing Co., San Francisco, 1962.
6. Donnison, D. V., *Social Policy and Administration*, Allen and Unwin, London, 1965.
7. Blau and Scott, *op. cit.*, pp. 60–6.
8. Gouldner, A. W., 'Cosmopolitans and Locals: Toward Analysis of Latent Social Roles', *Administrative Science Quarterly*, 1, 281–306, and 2, 444–80, 1957–58.
9. Hughes, Everett C., *Men and Their Work*, The Free Press, Glencoe, Illinois, 1958, p. 136.
10. Principally under the National Health Service Acts, the National Assistance Act, 1948, and the Mental Health Act, 1959.
11. The Children's Act, 1948.
12. *The Development of Community Care*, Cmnd 1973, HMSO, London, 1963.
13. *A Hospital Plan for England and Wales*, Cmnd 1604, HMSO, London, 1962.
14. *Report of the National Assistance Board for 1964*, Cmnd 2674, HMSO, London, 1965.
15. House of Commons Debate, *Hansard*, 701, 872–3, November 10, 1964.
16. Sorsby, Arnold, 'The Incidence and Causes of Blindness in England and Wales, 1948–62' in *Reports on Public Health and Medical Subjects*, No. 114, Ministry of Health, HMSO, London, 1966.
17. *Ibid.*, p. 39.
18. *Ibid.*, p. 57.
19. Friedson, E., *Patients' Views of Medical Practice*, The Russell Sage Foundation, New York, 1961.
20. Parker, J., *Local Health and Welfare Services*, Allen and Unwin, London, 1965, p. 50.
21. *First Report of the Council for Training in Social Work, 1962–4*, London, 1965.
22. Watson, S., 'Manpower in the Child Care Service', *Social Work*, July 1964.
23. Canadian Association of Social Workers, Canadian Association of Social Workers Acts, June 1964 (mimeographed); see also Department of Health and Welfare, Statistical Information on Canadian Schools of Social Work, Ottawa, Research and Statistics Division (memo), June 1965.
24. The literature is extensive, but some of the more important contributions include: *Report of the Royal Commission on Local Government in Greater*

London, Cmnd 1164, HMSO, London, 1960; *Report of the Committee on Children and Young Persons* (Ingleby Committee), Cmnd 1191, HMSO, London, 1960; *Child and Young Persons, Scotland* (Kilbrandon Committee), Cmnd 2306, HMSO, London, 1964; *The Child, the Family and the Young Offender* (Home Office White Paper), Cmnd 2742, HMSO, London, 1965; Donnison, D., Jay, P., and Stewart, M., *The Ingleby Report: Three Critical Essays*, Fabian Research Series No. 231, London, 1962; Ruck, S. K., *London Government and the Welfare Services*, Routledge, London, 1963; Labour Party Study Group, *Crime—A Challenge to Us All* (Longford Report), London, 1964; Hastings, S., and Jay, P., *The Family and the Social Services*, Fabian Tract No. 359, London, 1965; Jefferys, M., *An Anatomy of Social Welfare Services*, Joseph, London, 1965; Parker, J., *Local Health and Welfare Services*, Allen and Unwin, London, 1965, and Titmuss, Richard M., 'Social Work and Social Service: A Challenge for Local Government' (see Chapter VII). See also 'Co-operation, Co-ordination and Team-Work' in *Report of the Working Party on Social Workers in the Health and Welfare Services* (the Younghusband Report), HMSO, London, 1959, Chapter 12.

25. The Government has also established a Royal Commission on the future of local government.

26. Seebohm Committee, Public Information Paper B, London, 1966.

27. Subsequently published *Social Work and the Community*, Cmnd 3065, HMSO, London, 1966.

Chapter VII

SOCIAL WORK AND SOCIAL SERVICE: A CHALLENGE FOR LOCAL GOVERNMENT*

Two of the reservations—spoken and unspoken—which many local government councillors and officials have often had about social work and its aims and methods are (if I may summarize briefly): first, is not social work an expensive and, maybe, even an esoteric, fringe benefit? Cannot individuals, with a little commonsense advice, stand on their own feet? Secondly, is there not in the claims sometimes made by social workers a fundamental threat to the notions of local democracy? Are not the locally elected representatives of the people and their locally-based administrators sensitive to the changing needs of their own communities, and able to meet them without the intervention of professionally trained social workers with their insistence on confidentiality and a non-judgmental approach to people in trouble and often at odds with society?

These are important questions. Should they not be asked today? Most professions, including the doctors and the lawyers, may sometimes be regarded as associations for spreading the gospel of self-importance. Social workers cannot, of course, be completely immune from this occupational hazard of professionalism. Discounting, then, some of the more exaggerated claims for the achievements of social work, I must leave to those of you who are still troubled by these questions Miss Goldberg's assessment of the social situation today.[1] In doing so, I would like to add one further consideration.

It is an interesting and often overlooked fact that, during the last twenty years, whenever the British people have identified and investigated a social problem there has followed a national call for more social work and more trained social workers. Consider, for one moment, the history of twenty years of Royal Commissions, central and local committees of inquiry, working parties, conferences and Government task forces concerned with: the mentally ill, the

* Lecture delivered to the Social Workers Conference at the Health Congress, Eastbourne, April 1965, and published in the *Royal Society of Health Journal*, Vol. 86, No. 1, 1966.

schizophrenic discharged from hospital, the mentally subnormal, the maladjusted child, the physically handicapped, the blind and the deaf, industrial rehabilitation and training, the elderly isolates and desolates, the chronically ill and bedridden, the long-stay patient in hospitals and other kinds of residential accommodation, neglected and deprived children, young delinquents and those brought before the juvenile court, youth employment, the after-care of prisoners, the prevention of venereal disease, and the after-care of those who have contracted it, the problems of prostitution, unmarried mothers, unsupported wives, marital breakdown and the role of the courts, drug addiction, alcoholism, homeless families, immigrants from the Commonwealth, and so on.

Whatever else may be said of the British people, I do not think we can be accused of neglecting at least to inquire into some of the more distressing social problems of our age and to investigate the needs of many of the victims of change, social, economic and technological. In each and every case, when these committees have reported they have recommended the employment of more trained social workers. They have not said that local councillors or local government officials with a flair for listening and a sympathetic ear can do the job. Instead, the nation has said 'We want more social workers.' Not unnaturally, there has then been a tendency to think that the problem has been solved; a committee has made recommendations for action; the right answers have been found. The nation's conscience has been quietened. The temperature has been lowered in the knowledge that the necessary action will be taken as local government energetically pursues the challenge of 'community care'.

I do not think it is a philosophical or statistical accident that all these eminent Royal Commissions and committees of inquiry have come to similar conclusions. In their different specialized areas of concern, they have taken evidence, diagnosed the needs of people in different situations, and concluded that for the effective use of services, for effective and humane care, after-care and prevention, trained workers are required in all these varied local settings.

Many of you may say (and, for myself, I think it is very difficult not to do so) that you are not disputing the validity of these recommendations. You accept them. You accept the case for education and training. You are convinced of the need for more social workers, but some of you may be quietly adding, 'Please, Professor Titmuss, will you now tell us how and where we can obtain more trained social workers? We have advertised, and advertised and advertised. . . .'

I agree. There is a great shortage of social workers; child care officers; probation officers; medical social workers; psychiatric social workers and general purpose social workers. Every committee has said so from the *Report of the Committee on Social Workers in the Mental Health Services* in 1951 to the *Younghusband Report* in 1959.[2] In relative terms there is a greater shortage today of trained social workers than of general medical practitioners.

But, to be frank, for many years we saw the need but we did not will the means. Central government and local government were unwilling to find grant-aid for students—and particularly untied grants to allow freedom of choice for students; unwilling to provide more resources to allow university departments to expand training facilities; unwilling in the past to second officers for training; unwilling to provide more practical work training facilities; and unwilling to develop an administrative structure which would provide satisfactory career positions and senior posts for social workers of both sexes. We need more men in social work and we need a career structure with a hierarchy of social work positions alongside administrative positions.

It is only in the last few years that nationally we have begun to recognize that deeds as well as goodwill are required if we are to provide more social workers. We now have a National Council for Social Work Training; many Certificate courses have been started in technical colleges and other institutions of further education; more universities are providing courses; and local government is spending more money on seconding staff for training and in developing 'community care' plans. In short, we have made a start. Further expansion in education and training facilities are, however, urgently required on a very considerable scale if the challenge of 'community care' is to be met in the years ahead.

Meanwhile, it is time that local authorities began seriously to consider two important issues. They are not new ones, but they are acquiring today a greater urgency. One is a practical matter of good management; the other raises more fundamental questions.

Are local authorities quite certain that they are making the most effective use of trained social work staff? How much unnecessary form-filling, record-keeping and report writing is there? Is it essential for committees to be fed (or overfed?) with such a plethora of detail about individual cases? To what extent are social workers undertaking tasks which might be delegated to other and less trained staff? Are social workers at all levels being given the clerical help they need? I am not suggesting here that social workers should be wrapped in cotton-wool and treated as too precious for humdrum tasks; they should take their share of the humdrum like everyone else. It is, moreover, often essential that they should do so because the humdrum may play an important part in preventive social work. What I am advocating is a sensible division of labour in the local 'community care' field which recognizes that specialized skills should be related to specialized functions if specialized services are to operate effectively. Chapter 13 of the *Younghusband Report* (which might profitably be read again by local administrators) had some useful things to say on these practical matters of good management.

Now I come to the more difficult question of administrative and departmental structure; here I am particularly concerned with the distribution of responsibilities in the fields of welfare, child care and health. That all is not well with the present arrangements of many local authorities is evident from the great many things that have been said and written in recent years on the subject of co-ordination, co-operation, teamwork, the role of case conferences and relationships with general medical practitioners.

What I think is being sought in these discussions is not local government tidiness for its own sake but the most flexible administrative structure which will, *inter alia*, make the most effective use of scarce resources (such as trained social workers); reduce overlapping and departmental rivalries; attract and retain more and better recruits into administrative and professional service with local authorities; allow us to absorb and practise in community care the new social and psychological insights (which Miss Goldberg discussed in her paper) and, most important of all, provide clients with a more effective, more flexible and more easily comprehended structure of local action. The best attainable structure of local services will certainly not solve all our problems, but it will at least allow us to think more rationally about them and to work out solutions on a broader front than is possible today in many local authority areas.

In considering this question of structure it is fashionable at the present time to argue the case for Family Service Departments. As I understand it, the core of this new Department would be the Children's Department to which would be transferred certain other responsibilities at present carried in many areas by welfare departments.

I must say I am not happy about this proposal, and for the following reasons. In the first place it is too family-centred and child-centred partly, I suppose, because of our historical preoccupation with social pathology in the form of (what have been called) 'multi-problem families'. While all social work must take account of the primary importance of family relationships, and of helping families as well as individuals, we have to remember that a large number of 'needs' arising in the community are not essentially 'family needs'; mentally ill migrants, elderly widows and widowers, the isolates and childless, unmarried mothers and other categories of people who, in an increasingly mobile society, might well hesitate before turning to a 'Family Department'. What is common to them all is the need for *services* irrespective of age, family background and relationships. If this is accepted then it follows that we require Departments of Social Service at the local level.

Secondly, I suggest that the conception of a Family Service Department is not broad enough. Important welfare responsibilities, both residential and domiciliary, might well remain outside the province of a Family Service Department. By contrast, a Social Service Department could well embrace all the work of Children's Departments and Welfare Departments (or sections) and substantial 'welfare', social service and mental health responsibilities at present carried by other departments—chiefly Health Departments. The research results of a number of studies carried out in recent years which have analysed the 'needs' of clients of these departments all emphasize the importance for the better servicing of 'need' of a broader organizational framework. At present, local government is burdened with too many small departments and too much 'balkanized' rivalry in the field of welfare.

Thirdly, I am doubtful whether a Family Service Department would effectively bring together within one administrative structure all social workers in the employ of a single local authority. This, I suggest, should be the aim of any radical reorganization. We must, as Miss Goldberg's analysis shows, move closer to a regrouped, integrated pattern of services. It would then be possible to envisage a single professional social work hierarchy (needed for career and promotion purposes) working alongside an administrative social service hierarchy—again with improved career and promotion opportunities. For social workers, this larger structure should help to break down artificial and irrelevant specialized loyalties. In the future, social workers must be seen (and must be helped to see themselves) as workers in a unified organization of services and not as the servant of any one discipline with a separate and frag- mented organizational structure. A unified structure could also provide for other agencies (not least a reformed general medical practitioner service) a social work servicing department less depart- mentalized by function and setting.

These, in summary form, are some of the arguments for a structural reorganization which places the emphasis on *social service*
rather than on biological or sociological criteria—like the family—
or on one element in the pattern of needs—like health or rehabilitation. We need departments providing *services*; not departments
organized around categories of client or particular fragments of
need. Moreover, Departments of Social Service should enable local
communities to use not only all social and welfare workers to the
best advantage but would encourage them to mobilize more fully
the work of all voluntary agencies and the energies of local volunteers. We have moved a long way from the notion that the main
job of local government was to *govern* local areas; one of its main
tasks today is to provide accessible social services to meet local
needs and to develop a greater degree of community participation
in the provision of such services. If that overworked term 'Community Care' has any meaning at all then it must have something
to do with the provision of services which are essentially social,
essentially personal and primarily local.

NOTES

1. Goldberg, E. M., *Welfare in the Community*, National Institute for Social
   Work Training, 1966.
2. Cmd 8620, HMSO, London, 1951, and *Report of the Working Party on Social
   Workers in the Local Authority Health and Welfare Services*, HMSO, London,
   1959.

Chapter VIII

PLANNING FOR AGEING AND THE HEALTH AND WELFARE SERVICES*

I trust I shall not be accused of undue political bias in favour of voluntary organizations if I begin by offering my congratulations to the National Old People's Welfare Council. In their choice of title for this conference 'Planning for Ageing' the Council is nothing if not modern. In embracing the notion of planning it cannot now be said, as was often said only a few years ago, that voluntary organizations tend to live, philosophically and intellectually, in a distant romantic age of spontaneous, leaderless, unplanned self-help.

We are, it seems, all planners now. No longer does the man in the Ministry, the man in local government, or the man in the voluntary organization have to entertain any ideological hesitations in articulating the word. He will not be thought to be subverting the concept of free will, the majesty of the law or the independence of the old. Harmoniously and ideologically at peace, we are all now to be busy planning community care for the old.

It is not my intention today to quarrel with this change in the climate of opinion. As a citizen, looking reflectively at the apparent chaos of activity and non-activity at the town hall or local level, I rather welcome it. As an individual, however, I would like to be sure that when my time comes my right to be eccentric in old age will not be eroded by busy, bureaucratic planners. I shall want some rights to some choice of services; not a simple confrontation between, on the one hand, institutional inertia, and, on the other, domiciliary inaction. In other words, I believe that the most important fundamental principle which should guide the planning of services for the old is concerned with the enlargement, or at least the preservation, of the individual's sense of freedom and self-respect. In the world in which we live, by far the largest practical contribution that can be made in applying this principle is to see that many more old people have more spare cash in their pockets, and more in their shopping

* Lecture delivered at the Twelfth National Conference on the Care of the Elderly, Torquay, April 1964, and published in the Conference Report, *Planning for Ageing*, National Council of Social Service, 1964.

baskets, and, as Sir Keith Joseph has said this morning, adequate housing to sustain their self-respect.

Planning, if it means anything at all in relation to the social and economic needs of particular groups in society, means the making of decisions about the allocation of resources and claims on resources in the future as well as the present. If we are to plan for the aged to have a larger share of the national income then we are, in effect, planning for others to have less. What we call 'income maintenance', or in more homely terms, pensions, superannuation and national assistance, thus becomes, if this principle of spare money in one's pocket has priority, the most important single area of decision-making in planning for ageing. No increase in the quantum of community care for the old can compensate for inadequate income and inadequate housing. We may gain in satisfaction from being busy as community carers but the old will lose in self-respect.

I am not here to talk about pensions and national assistance; I am asked to address myself to the issues raised by Britain's first attempt to plan the provision of health and welfare services for the old on a community and national basis. And let me say here, in parenthesis, that we are a long way from being in danger of spending too much on community care to the detriment of existing levels of pensions and assistance benefits. The Ministry of Health's Ten-Year Plan—Sir Bruce Fraser has spoken about it this morning—*Health and Welfare: The Development of Community Care*, published a year ago, makes that abundantly clear.[1] 'Still further development of these services is essential; they are far from having reached their full potential. Without them neither the general practitioner service nor the hospital service can evolve as it should.'

One distinction we can make between the arts of planning and of non-planning (for in this area of social policy both forms of behaviour belong more to art than to science) is in our attitude to facts. If we are to be more intelligent in the formulation of policies and in the administrative provision of services (while accepting that intelligence is not the prerogative of planners) we have to cultivate a greater respect for facts. 'Now, what I want is Facts,' said Mr Gradgrind, in *Hard Times*. To look and plan ahead, we require to know more about the dimensions and categories of need and potential need in the future, locally and nationally. To plan and guide wisely, we have also to pay our respects to the past. We have to ask questions about past trends; about where we have come from; about what we have tried to achieve, and with what success.

'Community care' may be a new concept, a new idea, a sweeter-smelling rose, a more promising health and social hybrid, but it has to grow in the soil we have. That soil is composed of some well-known under-cultivated but deeply weathered particles. To drop the metaphor, we can say that we have to work with the existing structure of central, local and health service government (or something very like it), with administrative and executive tools which may be ill-suited for the tasks in hand, with staffs whose training and skills, I think we would all agree, have been neglected in the past, and with little empires of power and professional self-indulgence in local government, central government and voluntary organizations. As G. K. Chesterton once remarked, 'God expresses himself in many ways, even by local government.' We do not indeed start, as some academic planners sometimes imply, with a clean slate. Reality starts with history.

Obedient to this precept, I want therefore to spend a little time looking back over the past ten years. I begin with some facts about the population of old people just as the Ministry did in its Ten-Year Planning Report. These, for obvious statistical reasons, are restricted to England and Wales; to our friends in Scotland and Northern Ireland, I should say that the general results are very similar.

At the end of 1952, the Registrar General published one of his well-known projections of future populations.[2] He gave estimates for 1962 as well as for longer periods of time ahead. Taking all those aged 65 and over, the population was estimated to increase in the ten years by virtually one million—to nearly six million (5,939,000) by 1962. These and later estimates provoked much alarm about the social and economic costs of an ageing population. Indeed, the nation experienced in the middle 1950s an almost neurotic and fear-ridden phase; the concept of subsistence was formally abandoned; one Government committee recommended that the age of retirement be raised to 68 for men and 63 for women,[3] and the Treasury took action to shift part of the current and future costs of pensions from the taxpayer to those who paid flat-rate and regressive national insurance contributions.

How, in the event, have these estimates of 1952 turned out? Summarizing the results we can say that in 1962 we had 337,000 fewer old people than were estimated ten years earlier, or, roughly, only two-thirds of the expected increase. The Registrar General was closer (or more successful) in estimating the future number of elderly women than elderly men; not because, I should add, of any statistical predilection for ladies but due to different mortality trends between the sexes.

The fact that we have substantially fewer old people today than we expected ten years ago to have is due to higher than expected mortality rates, particularly among men. Death rates among the elderly have not fallen as much as the 1952 estimates implied. The expectation of life at age 65 (and also 75) among men hardly changed at all in these ten years; there was only a minute improvement in the figures. Among women, however, the gains were real and relatively striking. At the age of 75, for example, the expectation of life for women rose by over one year, or by 15 per cent, in the space of ten years.

It is, I suppose, a matter of opinion (and of age) whether this is to be regarded as one of the signal achievements of modern man—or the reverse. Nevertheless, the steadily widening differential between the sexes—especially after the age of 75—has important implications for social policy. For one thing, it means more widows and longer periods of widowhood. One of the interesting demographic facts today is that among women the chance of having a husband by them is nearly as great when they are aged 15–24 as when they are aged 65 and over. According to the Registrar General's current projections for the next ten years (to 1972) nearly 80 per cent of the increased population over 75 will be women, most of whom will have been widowed many years earlier.[4]

To return, however, to the figures for the past ten years. The fact that the number of elderly people increased more slowly than was expected has meant that more progress in the provision of health and welfare services could be reported than would otherwise have been the case. Take, for example, the services provided by home nurses, which I have always regarded as one of the critical components in community care, particularly for those of advancing years. Although we know surprisingly little from a national point of view about the actual changes in the services performed by home nurses it is, I understand, generally accepted that about two-thirds of their visits are paid to elderly people.[5]

Between 1952 and 1962 there was an increase in the total number of home nurses (measured in whole-time equivalents) and the proportion per 1,000 population aged over 65 rose by 8 per cent. But had we had the number of old people estimated in 1952 by the Registrar General there would have been virtually no improvement at all. The progress reported, therefore, was due to higher death rates than had been expected.

Apart, however, from population and mortality trends, what other changes have taken place during the last ten years? To refer again to the work of home nurses, we find that the number of *persons attended* by them fell steadily from 1,177,000 in 1953 to 854,000 in 1962. What does this decline mean? Is there less average need, as the population ages, for the services of the home nurse? Is she becoming more of an adjunct to the general practitioner in giving injections and other medical services for specific groups in the population? It seems that while the home nurse is on average visiting fewer people—old people —she is making more visits per patient. Are these additional visits in place of calls which the general practitioner would otherwise himself have made? Do they mean an improvement in the quality of service rendered to some people in need at the cost, perhaps, of others in need?

Clearly, we require a sustained series of detailed studies of the actual functioning of the basic domiciliary—or community care— services. To what extent is there in progress a redistribution of roles and functions between different workers in the health and welfare field? If there is, can we say whether this redistribution is in the interests of patients or in the interests of workers, or both? How effective are these services in reality for those who receive them? By concentrating more services on particular patients or clients is the area of unmet need widening? Questions such as these were raised by Professor Townsend in his now famous book *The Last Refuge*.[6] What he did by turning the searchlight of precise observation and study on residential institutions now I think requires to be done for the domiciliary health and welfare services.

Any such study would have to pay particular attention to the scope and content of the general practitioner's work. Let me remind you of what the Gillie Report on the field of work of the family doctor had to say last year. 'The family doctor is the one member of the profession who can best mobilize and co-ordinate the health and welfare services in the interests of the individual in the community, and of the community in relation to the individual.' Earlier in the Report the authors had stated that the family doctor—I quote again —'the patient's first line of defence in times of illness, disability and distress', had been, so to speak, at the receiving end of the biological consequences of explosive advances in medical and scientific knowledge during the last twenty years. 'The results', according to this Report, 'in survival of the less physically fit and the aged have added to the scope, but also to the load, of the family doctor's work. This increased load', emphasized the Gillie Report, 'is the central problem in general practice today.'[7]

What evidence is there that the family doctor has been playing an increasing part in the care of the elderly?

With the publication in 1962 of Volume III (*Disease in General Practice*) in the valuable series of studies of general practice by the College of General Practitioners and the General Register Office we are now in a position to assess something of the role of the family doctor in relation to the needs of the elderly since the introduction of the National Health Service.[8] Unfortunately, these studies do not extend beyond the year 1956.

However, by piecing together the results of these studies and of earlier reports from the Ministry of Health and the General Register Office we can discern the broad pattern of changing demands by the elderly on the services of the family doctor for the period 1946–56. We can look, for example, at changes in the medical consultation rates; that is, the yearly number of consultations per person aged over 65.

Before the Health Service came in the combined rate for elderly men and women was approximately 6.3 per year (1946–7), that is, on average, all those over the age of 65 had 6.3 contacts with their family doctor every year. This was about 50 per cent higher than the medical consultation rate for people of all ages over 16. After the National Health Service was introduced, the rate for elderly people rose to about 7 per year (1949–50). Thereafter it began to fall. In 1955–56 (the latest year for which we have any representative figures) the rate for elderly men was 5.9 and for elderly women 6.4. It was then a trifle lower than it had been before the National Health Service was introduced. Similarly, the medical consultation rates for family doctors for people of all ages also declined, and were lower in the middle 1950s than they had been in the first two years of the Health Service.

These trends are, on the face of it, surprising and difficult to interpret. They are more puzzling because of the advent of a free family doctor service for all old people, and because during this period we know that the proportion of over 75s in the population of old people substantially increased, we know that death rates among the elderly were higher than the Registrar General had estimated, and we also know from evidence of research carried out by the Social Medicine Research Unit of the Medical Research Council that disability among men aged 61–63 (as measured by sick absence from work for three months or more amongst men in this age group) steadily increased during the 1950s.[9]

It may be, of course, that in recent years the whole complex pattern of *expressed need* for medical and social care by the elderly has changed, with the advent in various areas of new services, the changing role of out-patients' departments, the greater use of the home nurse for medical or paramedical duties, the rise and rapid spread of the voluntary movement,[10] and other developments. Much of this is, however, conjectural. What we do know is that there has been in recent years a large rise in the use by family doctors of privately organized emergency call services in London and other areas and large cities. It is believed today that over one-half of all family doctors in London make use of such services, and that one privately run organization alone accounts for 60,000 consultations a year.[11] The demands that these emergency medical services meet may not be recorded and counted in family doctor consultation rates, and may not be known to the local health and welfare authorities.

In short, what I am suggesting is that some part of expressed demand for medical and social care by elderly people which formerly was either not made explicit at all or was directly addressed to the family doctor or the local chemist, may now be finding other outlets. If anyone could do all the complicated sums it might well be shown that compared with ten years ago there are today more workers in the broad health and welfare field, public and voluntary, trained and untrained, for old people to talk to; volunteers with meals on wheels, chiropody services, friendly rent collectors, chemists, officials in National Assistance Board offices, old people's clubs, home helps, visitors from a great variety of agencies, and so forth. If this were so it would be an important achievement but we have to remember that less than 5 per cent of old people in the country receive any help from the home help, meals on wheels and home nursing services. To provide a better 'listening and advice' service is surely an essential part of 'community care' for the old, but listening, important though it is in these hurried professional days, is often not enough. Someone has to accept responsibility for action—and often action by others. It is still necessary, therefore, to ask questions about the role of the family doctor in this changing pattern of need and response.

At this point, however, I wish to remind you of the note I struck early in this talk. Constructive thinking and planning for the future development of community care, local and national, must rest on knowledge of the present and the immediate past, and an understanding of the processes already in motion affecting the roles, responsibilities and relationships of many workers providing personal services for the elderly in their own homes and institutions of various kinds. If we wish to support or to change or to do something about the direction of these processes we must first understand where they are now heading, and we must also identify the forces that are propelling them. This approach is particularly needed in the relatively undefined and leaderless field of community care; a field that requires both a lot of generalized workers, public and voluntary, operating from a variety of specialized agencies, and a number of specialized workers operating from generalized and specialized agencies. It is for this reason that I have spent some time looking back at past trends in the family doctor service as it affects the elderly.

What of the future? First, a few words again about population trends. From the most recent projections of the Registrar General, we can say that the health and welfare services may expect, *if* these estimates are anywhere near borne out, just over one million more people aged over 65 in the next ten years.[12] Nearly one-third of this additional population is expected to be aged 75 and over; 7 per cent of the increase (nearly all of them women) will be aged 85 and over. Compared with what we actually experienced in the past ten years, the expected increase in the next ten years will be substantially greater—particularly if we take account of the greater needs of the 'elderly elderly widows'. In other words, the rate of increase in the provision of services will have to accelerate just to stay where we are today, let alone meet the need, as the Ministry have emphasized, to realize the 'full potential' of community care.

This is a challenging task for everyone in this audience. Moreover, with rising standards of living among some sections of the older population, and more geographical mobility in the country generally, we must expect demands for community care to fall much more heavily in some areas than in others. Geographical differences in demand will be further accentuated as the proportion of over-75s in the total elderly population increases substantially.

This underlines the point made in the last annual report of the National Corporation for the Care of Old People; attention was there drawn to the 'apparent failure of many local authorities to relate their plans to their future estimated populations of old people, particularly those over 75.[13] We must expect not only more demand in general for certain old age services but an even greater demand for these services in certain local authority areas. The services and agencies which are likely to be chiefly affected include the following: the general practitioner, the home nurse, the home help for shopping as well as for housework, the night attendant and the bathing attendant, the use of equipment and special aids from local authorities and voluntary agencies, the laundry service, physiotherapy services, the meals service and, by no means the least important, the use of hospitals and other institutions increasingly on a daily, week-end, planned holiday and short-term basis to afford temporary relief for hard-pressed relatives and sons and daughters who may themselves be retirement pensioners or nearing retirement age. We can hardly expect in the future quite the same degree of familial devotion from grandchildren and great-grandchildren as is now given by millions of sons and daughters. In any event, we must expect in the next ten years many more old people (and especially women) aged over 75 who are single or childless, slightly eccentric and unconforming. The proportion may be 25 per cent or even higher,[14] and the number will not be small. It seems likely that by 1972 over one million people in the country will have passed their eightieth birthday, most of them alone with memories of husbands and of husbands who might have been. They will be the survivors of a period in Britain's history when marriage rates were low (much lower than today); when the rate of emigration of men was substantial; when infant death rates were still high and birth rates were falling, and when millions of young husbands and lovers were killed in the First World War. We shall be facing more of the biological and social consequences of that war in the next ten years of 'community care'.

These reflections about the nature and dimensions of the challenge confronting the development of community care for the elderly raise a series of questions concerning the distribution of responsibilities for that development in the future. I am further encouraged to frame these questions after a re-reading of the Ministry of Health's Reports, the Gillie Report, documents and reports sent to me by the National Old People's Welfare Council and certain planning reports on the development of the health and welfare services by individual local authorities—including a number of imaginative reports from the County Council of Lincoln (Lindsey) in respect of the reorganization of their welfare services.

I want, therefore, to think aloud for a few minutes about this problem of responsibilities in the whole field of community care; of who does what in a heterogeneous mass of often undefined circumstances, and who is responsible to whom. It is a much more complicated problem than trying to answer the question: who runs a hospital or who runs a university. There is consequently more danger for the local health and welfare services of situations arising in which the cry is heard 'it is nothing to do with me'. The staffing of the services with more workers whose functions are primarily oral and not manual could make the air noisier with this cry. The 'nothing to do with me' syndrome (which has an affinity with a virus called 'functional specialization') can present itself in situations in which there is (a) ambiguity about the division of responsibility for planning, policy-making and administrative and executive action; (b) ambiguity about who initiates action at the level of individual need and who sees that action is actually taken, and (c) ambiguity about who sees that a series of actions are appropriately co-ordinated at the right time and in the right sequence.

We may all need scapegoats in these situations of ambiguity but it is no use blaming everything on the Ministry of Health or trying to find the answer by proposing a separate ministry for community care; or proposing major changes in the structure of local government and the National Health Service; or by calling once again for the reform of medical education, or by seeking to put all the services and all the workers in one building. Changes in all these areas are no doubt necessary but I venture to think that hitherto we have invested too much spiritual capital in structural goals and buildings (in anatomy) and not enough in this matter of the roles, functions and responsibilities of workers in the field of health and welfare. The one study I know of which did not adopt this anatomical view is Miss K. M. Slack's perceptive report *Councils, Committees and Concern for the Old.*[15] It should be required reading for all those who still believe in the myth of a single focal point, a single authority and a simple solution to the problems of developing the public and voluntary services for the old.

'Community care' is much more a matter of people—of staff—and the texture of their relationships than it is of buildings or equipment; it follows, therefore, that we cannot divorce the care of the elderly from the care of many other dependent groups in the community.

In all this discussion at the present time of who is responsible for what, the family doctor is being cast for the role of co-ordinator, mobilizer, director, stage manager and leader of 'community care'— see pages 9, 13, 21, 29, 37, 39, 48 and 49 of the Gillie Report. Others, however, are seeing the medical officer of health performing this role partly on the grounds that the family doctor is too busy and is trained as a clinician and medical diagnostician. Still others propose that the chief welfare officer and a family welfare service should assume some or most of these responsibilities.

This discussion, essential for the shaping of public opinion, does seem to point to the need for a clearer and more precise definition and allocation of responsibilities over the whole field of the local health and welfare services. It is unsatisfactory for all concerned, including the family doctor, to continue their efforts to improve the services on the assumption that he is willing, able and equipped to undertake this large, idealized and somewhat nebulous role. As I have already pointed out, there is as yet little evidence that in his day-to-day medical work the family doctor is moving, or wishes to move, in this direction.

What do we really mean when we use such terms as leader, co-ordinator, mobilizer, director and planner in the context of community care? Let us remember that we do not make progress by substituting one big word for another, nor do we do so by adding to the number of episodic workers infected with the syndrome 'it is nothing to do with me'.

What does seem to me to be essential is a careful and authoritative inquiry which would aim to define, describe and classify the many different components of responsibility. Such an inquiry would have to take account of responsibilities which relate, first, to the *ascertainment and diagnosis* of social and medical need, secondly, to the *initiation* of action to see that needs are met, and thirdly, to *continuity* of action to see that effective and co-ordinated use is made of the services available. These components relate to existing needs, expressed and unexpressed, and to the use of existing services of all kinds, domiciliary and institutional, public and voluntary. In a sense, we can speak of them as *individualized* service responsibilities. Next, there is the problem of defining more clearly (and again without expecting too much structural tidiness) the division of responsibilities for the *collective provision* and *planning* of services today and over the next ten years. Between both spheres of activity, the individualized service of need and the provision of resources, there should be well defined channels of communication which will allow information to flow easily in both directions. Those who service the individual, whether from public or voluntary agencies, should have easy and flexible access to those who administer and plan the services and *vice versa*. Community care should mean community involvement.

To clarify these somewhat abstract notions, I want to end by asking a few rhetorical and indelicate questions. They are the sort of questions, I think, which a committee of inquiry would have to frame. In terms of relationships, ease of communication between workers, and effective deployment of services, is it functionally better for the family doctor to deal directly with welfare staff or with the medical officer of health? Can the latter (the medical officer of health) defer as easily as welfare staff and social workers to the authority of the family doctor, an authority which derives from the primary responsibility of diagnosing need and initiating action? Is the family doctor equipped, educationally and with the necessary resources, to diagnose social needs and to have this direct relationship with the welfare services? Is the medical officer of health similarly equipped to administer, co-ordinate and develop services to meet *social* needs, or should these responsibilities be the concern of a social welfare service at local level?

These are but a few of the questions which are raised at the local and personal level. There are others at a different level which involve the distribution of responsibilities for policy-making and planning between the Ministry, the local authorities and the hospital authorities. Here again there seems to be a need for a clearer definition of responsibilities.

I will end with a single illustration of this need for a clearer definition of responsibilities but one which seems to me to be critical for the next ten years of community care. Hospital authorities, when planning ahead for new or extended institutional provision, do so on the fundamental assumption that some other authority is (or will be) responsible for seeing that there will be enough trained staff available. They may estimate their needs for doctors and nurses in the years ahead but they do not themselves take action within their own areas to increase the supply of trained staff. Broadly, this responsibility attaches to the Ministry of Health and other authorities.

When we look at the local health and welfare services, however, the position seems to be very different. Who is responsible for seeing from the national point of view that enough trained staff and training facilities will be available over the next ten years, or do we assume that 146 different local authorities (and often each department of each authority as well as many voluntary agencies) have somehow or other to take action to see that additional staff are recruited and trained? Have all these 146 ten-year plans been drawn up on the assumption that staff will be available, or on some other unstated assumption, or have they been drawn up in the context of the very grave shortages of trained staff that exist today? What can we deduce from adding them all up in a grand national total if we do not know what assumptions have been made about the availability of staff, the trend of population, the extent of unmet and unascertained need and so forth?

I realize that like others before me I have asked a lot of questions and answered very few. My justification is that if they are valid questions about the future of the health and welfare services they will stimulate discussion. In any event, I hope that discussion will endorse my plea for an authoritative inquiry into these areas of responsibility for the administration and deployment of the local health and welfare services.

NOTES

1. Cmnd 1973, April 1963.
2. *Registrar General's Quarterly Return*, December 1952.
3. *Report of the Committee on the Economic and Financial Problems of the Provisions for Old Age*, Cmnd 9333, 1954.

4. *Registrar General's Quarterly Return*, December 1962.
5. Cmnd 1973, p. 17.
6. 1962, especially pp. 386–429.
7. *The Field of Work of the Family Doctor*: Report of the Standing Medical Advisory Committee to the Central Health Services Council (the Gillie Report), 1963, pp. 8–10.
8. See Vols I, II and III, *Morbidity Statistics from General Practice*, General Register Office, 1958, 1960 and 1962.
9. Morris, J. N., *Uses of Epidemiology* (second edition), 1964. For sources relating to medical consultation rates see General Register Office, *op. cit.*, *Studies on Medical and Population Subjects*, No. 7 and 9, General Register Office, and Titmuss, R. M., *Essays on the 'Welfare State'*, App. p. 203, 1958.
10. See National Old People's Welfare Council, *Survey of Services for the Elderly provided by Voluntary Organisations*, 1962.
11. *Brit. Med. J.* (1962), ii, Sup. 203.
12. *Registrar General's Quarterly Return*, December 1962, and *Statistical Review for 1961*, Part III, 1964.
13. *Annual Report for Year ended September 1963*, p. 30.
14. See Titmuss, R. M., *Third Congress of the International Association of Gerontology*, 1954.
15. *Occasional Papers in Social Administration*, No. 2, 1960.

Chapter IX

COMMUNITY CARE: FACT OR FICTION?*

It has been one of the more interesting characteristics of the English in recent years to employ idealistic terms to describe certain branches of public policy. The motives are no doubt well-intentioned; the terms so used express, in civilized phrases, the collective aspirations of those who aim to better the human condition. It is necessary to remember, however, that this practice can have unfortunate consequences. Public opinion—in which I include political opinion—may be misled or confused. If English social history is any guide, confusion has often been the mother of complacency. In the public mind, the aspirations of reformers are transmuted, by the touch of a phrase, into hard-won reality. What some hope will one day exist is suddenly thought by many to exist already. All kinds of wild and unlovely weeds are changed, by statutory magic and comforting appellation, into the most attractive flowers that bloom not just in the spring but all the year round.

We are all familiar with that exotic hot-house climbing rose, 'The Welfare State', with its lovely hues of tender pink and blushing red, rampant and rampaging all over the place, often preventing people from 'standing on their own feet' in their own gardens. And what of the everlasting cottage-garden trailer, 'Community Care'? Does it not conjure up a sense of warmth and human kindness, essentially personal and comforting, as loving as the wild flowers so enchantingly described by Lawrence in *Lady Chatterley's Lover*?

I have tried and failed to discover in any precise form the social origins of the term 'Community Care'. In pursuing this search, somewhat idly, I was led to re-read the Report of the Committee on Social Workers in the Mental Health Services (the Mackintosh Report[1]). In three months' time, I would remind you, we shall be celebrating the tenth birthday of the publication of the Report. What progress have we made since 1951 in working out, in terms of

* Lecture delivered at the 1961 Annual Conference of the National Association for Mental Health, London, and published in *Proceedings of the Conference*, and Freeman, H., and Farndale, J. (Ed.), *Trends in the Mental Health Services*, Pergamon Press, London, 1963.

the medical, psychological, social and economic needs of the individual, the concept of community care? What does it mean to local councillors and officials, medical officers of health, general practitioners, mental welfare officers, social workers, disablement resettlement and employment officers, health visitors, probation officers, psychiatrists and many others? Beyond a few brave ventures, scattered up and down the country from Worthing to Nottingham, pioneered by statutory and voluntary bodies, one cannot find much evidence of attempts to hammer out the practice, as distinct from the theory, of community care for the mentally ill and subnormal.

Institutional policies, both before and since the Mental Health Act of 1959, have, on the other hand and without a doubt, assumed that someone knows what it means. More and more people suffering from schizophrenia, depressive illnesses and other mental handicaps have been discharged from hospitals, not cured but symptom-treated and labelled 'relieved'. More and more of the mentally subnormal have been placed under statutory supervision in the community. It is probably true to say that, relative to the numbers in institutions at a given point in time, there are more people with diagnosed mental illness or handicaps of a severe or moderately severe character in the community today than there were in 1951 when the Mackintosh Report was published.

There are many reasons for this trend—some positive, others negative. Institutional life, as it was known in the past by those we find difficulty in tolerating, can be disabling in its effects, emotionally, physically and socially. Numerous Royal Commissions and committees of inquiry have discovered in recent years the virtues of the normal social environment—or as near 'normal' as possible—for old people, for the mentally ill, the educationally subnormal, the handicapped child, the maladjusted, the elderly 'ambulant' and others who need 'care and protection' during some stage in their lives. Yet Government policies in other branches of the social services are punishing or frustrating those who are trying to convert the institution into industrial and social therapeutic communities. Take, for example, the now considerable number of hospitals and institutions in Britain which are attempting to develop valuable schemes of industrial and social rehabilitation for their mental patients. If, however, under many such schemes a patient is encouraged to earn more than £2 a week he will not only have any benefits for a wife and family reduced or entirely stopped, but he will be liable for a tax of 25 per cent or so. The Minister of Health has recently decreed that, in order to allow these patients 'to stand on their own feet', this tax should be raised in the form of higher Health Service and

National Insurance contributions. Therapeutic incentives are proper, it seems, for surtax payers and property speculators but not for the mentally ill, the disabled, the handicapped and many other under-privileged groups.

This is the kind of detail that matters. In a hundred and one ways, this is what doctors and social workers have to think about in the interests of patients and clients. It is at this level of the dynamics of treatment that the concept of community care will be made or marred. If it is to be a reality for many people it must start in the hospital. It must begin with the patients' admission. It must encom-pass all the social services. We may pontificate about the philosophy of community care; we may feel righteous because we have a civi-lized Mental Health Act on the statute book; but unless we are prepared to examine at this level of concrete reality what we mean by community care we are simply indulging in wishful thinking.

To scatter the mentally ill in the community before we have made adequate provision for them is not a solution; in the long-run not even for H.M. Treasury. Considered only in financial terms, any savings from fewer hospital inpatients might well be offset several times by more expenditure on the police forces, on prisons and probation officers; more unemployment benefit masquerading as sickness benefit; more expenditure on drugs; more research to find out why crime is increasing.

The social legislation of 1946 and 1948, which gave to local authorities practically all the legal powers they required to develop community care, has now been on the statute book for thirteen years. The Mackintosh Report, to which I have already referred, pointed out that the social services of local health authorities had been 'profoundly affected by the National Health Service' in respect to the ascertainment, prevention and aftercare of the mentally ill and subnormal. 'It is difficult at this stage,' said the Report, 'to be sure to what extent the proposals for a mental health service put forward by these authorities have been implemented.' Is it unfair to suggest that this plaintive utterance could be repeated today?

Take, for example, the question of trained staff. This is what the Mackintosh Report had to say ten years ago:

'The scope of the mental health services in this country has been greatly enlarged in recent years with the result that there has been a progressive increase in the demand from employing authorities for the services of mental health workers. The representatives of these employing authorities concur with our other witnesses in reporting an acute shortage of *trained* social workers in every branch of the mental health services. One local authority after another has stated that no applications have been received in response to repeated advertisements for psychiatric social workers: some authorities have resorted to making appointments of partly trained or untrained workers, while others have been obliged to leave posts vacant for long periods. The number of social workers who have qualified by completing the mental health course is exceedingly small in relation to the demand; indeed, some authorities report that they are finding difficulty in securing even the services of untrained workers in mental health.'

The Ministry of Health, in its Report for 1950–51, welcomed the Mackintosh recommendations; summarized the findings of a 'Community Care Survey' in 1950 (the Ministry had adopted the term by then); and reported that the workers studied, whether duly authorized officers or others, 'were for the most part keenly interested in their work and anxious for further training to fit them for it'.[2]

Ten years later, and two years after the publication of the Young-husband Report, they are still waiting. Whether they are still as keen on their work I would not venture to say. They are certainly over-worked.

In 1951 eight psychiatric social workers were employed full-time by the 145 local health authorities. In 1959 there were twenty-six, an increase of 2.25 per year. At this rate it will take another fifty-three years (AD 2014) before someone can say that there is an average of one psychiatric social worker to each authority.

Now let us take finance—still one of the best crude criteria of our commitment to community care.

In 1949–50 total expenditure by local authorities in England and Wales on all mental health and mental deficiency services was £1,300,000. In 1959–60 it was approximately £3,500,000.[3] If we allow for price changes, the additional expenditure on capital and current account comes to about £1,225,000 at 1959 prices.[4] If we further allow for the increase in the total population of the country; for the larger increase in the total of mentally ill people *in the community* seeking or needing treatment (judged by turnover, diagnostic and discharge rates), and for the increase in the number of the mentally subnormal under statutory supervision and training, it is probable that we are now spending a smaller amount per head on community care for the mentally ill (as distinct from the mentally subnormal) than we were in 1951. And what we are spending today is substantially less than the sum of £4,900,000 paid out in compensation and expenses in dealing with fowl pest in Great Britain in 1959–60[5].

It may be said, and no doubt the Minister said it yesterday, that the future looks more promising for community care than the past. Local authorities have replied to Ministerial circulars asking them for a 'general statement of subsequent intentions'. These, I would guess, have been vaguely and optimistically converted in the Ministry into estimates of rising expenditure in the next few years. The last ten Annual Reports of the Ministry, for anyone who cares to read them, have set the pattern for statements of general intention. Now we have reached the point when the Ministry believes we should reduce the number of beds in hospitals for mentally ill and subnormal patients. It is suggested that the present proportion of 3,500 beds per million population may be reduced by half over the next fifteen years, and that the number of long-stay patients may be expected to decline steadily to nil.[6]

This implies a quite remarkable degree of optimism concerning the rapidly rising rate of re-admissions; of faith in the capacity and willingness of general practitioners to participate in community care; of trust in the energy and vision of local health and welfare authorities; and of belief in the efficacy of the block grant as a means of developing community care. Or it could mean that our society is increasingly unwilling to accept responsibility, socially and financially, for those who do not recover quickly and those who do not conform to our expectations of medical productivity. To transform the bad old mental hospital into the therapeutic institution will be an expensive process. Let us therefore, runs the argument, get rid of them altogether. At the same time there is a tendency, as Dr Hayward has recently observed,[7] 'to deny the existence of mental illness altogether, and to pretend that mental hospitals belong to the bad wicked past'. 'Are we in fact,' he concluded, 'preparing for a future psychiatric retrogression, in which we have first-class patients in the general hospitals, and second-class and third-class patients somewhere else, more forgotten than they were before?'

If we are expected to take these official statements of intention seriously then I would plead for three acts of policy as an assurance that we really mean business in the immediate development of community care; first, a specific earmarked grant to local authorities for community care services for the mentally ill and subnormal of £10,000,000 for 1961–62; second, central government grants for all social work students and training courses (irrespective of speciality) in the universities and technical colleges and the establishment of courses in fifteen of these colleges by October 1962; third, a Royal Commission on the recruitment and training of doctors with special reference to the need for education in social and psychological medicine.

As the National Association for Mental Health has long recognized, the need for trained and qualified staff in all fields of community care is very great. To aid effectively the work of such staff, we also need more doctors—including general practitioners and public health officers—who are better equipped to understand and deal with the social and psychological aspects of medical care. The reform of medical education has for long been debated. I doubt whether much will be achieved until we have had a Royal Commission. At present, we are drifting into a situation in which, by shifting the emphasis from the institution to the community—a trend which, in principle and with qualifications, we all applaud—we are transferring the care of the mentally ill from trained staff to untrained or ill-equipped staff or no staff at all.

NOTES

1. Cmd 8260 (1951), June.
2. Cmd 8655, Part I, pp. 32–3.
3. Cmd 8655, Part I, p. 71; *Local Health Services Statistics*, published by the Institute of Municipal Treasurers and Accountants and the Society of County Treasurers, 1949–50 and 1959–60.
4. During 1949–59 weekly wage rates rose by about 68 per cent. Allowing for higher salary increases, the percentage would be about 75.
5. Civil Appropriation Accounts for 1959–60 (1961).
6. Report of the Ministry of Health for 1959, Part I, Cmd 1086, p 25; Ministry of Health, Hospital Building Note No. 1, 1961, p. 3.
7. Hayward, S. T. (1961), *Lancet*, i, 387.

PART III

ISSUES OF REDISTRIBUTION IN SOCIAL
POLICY

Chapter X

UNIVERSAL AND SELECTIVE SOCIAL SERVICES*

(1)

The American 'War on Poverty', urgently launched in 1964 under the Economic Opportunity Act, is now seen to be failing; the early idealism is waning, cynicism grows. The reasons are many and complex. The strategy attempted was basically a technical short-cut; a series of programmes to by-pass the established structures of power, governmental, state and local; to reach the poor directly and concentrate resources on them without the support of an infrastructure of social welfare utilized and approved by the non-poor as well as the poor.

What was insufficiently recognized in 1964 was the extent to which many of these programmes would require the poor to define themselves; to stand up and declare themselves poor people, eligible for 'maximum feasible participation' in special poverty programmes. In the Act and, in particular, the regulations under the Act, there is a curious affinity with the New Poor Law Act of 1834 in England. Both endorsed and legitimated prevailing social values, both believed in redemption through work regardless of whether work was available; both were rooted in pathological explanations of poverty. But there was one fundamental difference.

The framers of the New Poor Law deliberately intended the system to operate as an assault on personal dignity and self-respect. Shame was needed to make the system work; many techniques were to hand, the inquisition of the relieving officer being only one. The framers of the American Act vehemently rejected the instrument of shame; in any event, the civil rights movement, 'midnight searches' in the homes of poor people and other indignities of public assistance condemned its use as a servant of policy.

Nevertheless, the 'War on Poverty', despite its radicalism and its unorthodoxies of 'opting out' of the power structure, has not found the answers to the challenge of how to provide benefits in favour of

* Published in the *New Statesman*, September 15, 1967.

the poor without stigma. What makes this problem of redistribution such a formidable challenge today—both in Britain and the USA—is that it is now inextricably mixed up with the challenge of social rights as well as civil rights for 'coloured' citizens. Two standards of service, in quality and methods of administration, one for the black and one for the white, are now seen to be more intolerable to the public conscience than two standards of service for the poor and the non-poor.

The American failure has been due to the belief that poverty was the problem, and that the advance of the poor Negro could be presented as a pro-negro enterprise; it has not been seen as a universalist problem of inequality, social injustice, exclusion. The faults were not political and structural; technical know-how, project innovation, self-help and consumer aggression could eradicate the 'poverty disease' by 1970.

(2)

How to include poor people, and especially poor coloured people, in our societies, and at the same time to channel proportionately more resources in their favour without inducing shame or stigma, remains one of the great challenges for social policy in Britain and the USA. The answers will not be found by creating separate, apartheid-like structures and 'public burden' services for poor people; nor will they be found through short-term 'gimmicks' and slogans or by expecting the computer to solve the problems which human beings have not yet adequately diagnosed.

Those in Britain who are now muddled about the current debate, headlined as 'universalism versus selectivity', should study American experience. They are muddled because of the mixture of ideas in the apparently simple cries 'let us concentrate help on those whose needs are greatest'; 'why provide benefits for those who do not really need them'.

Many people are muddled because there is a case for more selective services and benefits provided, as social rights, on the basis of the *needs* of certain categories, groups and territorial areas (e.g. Plowden's 'educational priority areas')[1] and not on the basis of individual *means*; there is a problem (as there always has been) of priorities in the allocation of scarce resources in the social policy field; there is a case for more redistribution through taxing the middle and upper-middle classes more heavily by making them pay higher contributions for, e.g. medical care and higher education; there is a problem of finding more money for social security, education, health, the welfare services, housing, roads and all sectors of all the public services.

'Selectivity' can mean many different things (which is rarely understood) but to most critics of 'Welfare Statism' it denotes an individual means-test; some inquiry into resources to identify poor people who should be provided with free services or cash benefits; be excused charges, or pay lower charges.

The *Economist* (to cite one school of thought) has been campaigning for more means-tests for years; in 1951 it said that the stigma of the test had gone; that national assistance was too lavish; that it was 'weakening the sense of individual pride and family unity' and discouraging thrift and incentives to work.[2] Now it is arguing that it is not lavish enough. Instead of raising retirement pensions and family allowances more should have been spent on supplementary benefits.[3] The Institute of Economic Affairs (another school) has similarly been campaigning for 'selectivity' since its foundation as a trust in 1957 in order to encourage the growth of private markets in education, medical care and social security. Its latest effort is to reprint an address (*Paying for the Social Services*) by Mr Douglas Houghton in which he advocates the use of a standard income tax means-test 'for a variety of social purposes'.[4] In particular, he suggests prescription charges and charges for hospital treatment. He envisages an extension of the coding system below the point of no tax liability which could be used to determine entitlement to supplementary cash benefit, graduated according to income assessment, and also for rent rebates, rate rebates, school meals, welfare services, health service charges and so on. 'Not only could the structure of PAYE and its ingenious and flexible coding system and tax tables be used to provide an automatic minimum income, it could be adapted to a scheme for payment for state services.' Inland Revenue computers would allocate to everyone a code number based on PAYE assessments. Armed with this number, all would pay according to ability.

(3)

Before considering the practicalities of the computer solution it is necessary to examine more thoroughly the case for more means-tested selective services. The nature, content, scope, characteristics and frequency of a means-test depend to a great extent on its functions and purposes. What are these? This question cannot be answered, however, without considering more specific policy objectives. Means-testing, *as a method*, may in theory be used (to cite a few of its many possible functions):

115

(a) to define for people outside the labour market (whose needs for income maintenance and whose resources are relatively ascertainable and predictable, e.g. old people) the level of income which is to be taken as the minimum for the purposes of income maintenance;
(b) to fix charges or rents for services and to decide who should and who should not pay charges;
(c) to determine those who should receive a 'free' public service or benefit—the rest of the population buying services or benefits in the private market or paying the full cost of the publicly provided service or benefit;
(d) to determine entitlement to the remission (or reduction) of a universal charge (e.g. rate rebates).

Broader social objectives lie behind these functions of determining minimum income levels, fixing charges, remissions, entitlements and so on. The aim may be to deter people from using or 'abusing' a service; to induce a sense of inferiority among those using a public service; to develop two standards of service; to raise more revenue; to help students of poor parents enter universities; to ration resources and so on.

At this point, I do not want to discuss the political values and choices involved except to say this. Socialist social policies are, in my view, totally different in their purposes, philosophy and attitudes to people from Conservative social policies. They are (or should be) pre-eminently about equality, freedom and social integration.

The limited and deliberate intention of this article is to dissect the computer solution; a solution which seems to have muddled quite a lot of well-meaning people. Hence, it is necessary to present a picture (though, admittedly, a small one) which shows something of the administrative, technical and real-life complexities of the issues involved. There can be no return to the simplicity of the poor law (with its inevitable corollary of brutality)—American experience is sufficient warning of that. We have, therefore, painfully to understand that methods of allocating resources (like means-testing and charges) cannot be separately considered from (a) functions, specific purposes and general social objectives and (b) the infinite and infinitely changing circumstances of individuals and families. What follows, therefore, is not easy reading. Ideological reasoning there must be—but superficial administrative proposals cannot be countered with superficial political answers.

(4)

Not only must means-tests differ in content, scope, characteristics and frequency according to their particular functions but, more complex still, they must differ in all these factors according to (a) the kind of service or benefit provided and, to some extent, the causes of the need; (b) the actualities of the need; immediate and temporary, weekly, monthly, yearly, etc.; (c) the characteristics of the consumer (age, sex, marital and household status, dependants, etc.) and (d) the extent to which a variety of economic, social and psychological incentives and disincentives have to be taken into account in the structure and operation of the test. A brief explanation must suffice of some of the reasons for differential treatment in respect of these four categories.

Services in kind and in cash may fulfil, singly or in combination, a large number of functions. They may represent not a benefit at all but a compensation for disservices caused by society and especially those disservices (or social costs) where the causal agent, or agents, cannot be identified, legally held responsible, and charged with the costs. When one examines in detail the social consequences in modern society of technological, industrial, economic and other processes of change it is evident that the problem of compensation is an immense one, and immensely complex. Unless the social costs of these disservices are to lie where they fall (as they did in nineteenth century Britain and as they do to a large extent in the USA today) then we have to find ways and means of compensating people without stigma.

I have discussed this particular function of the social services elsewhere; here I can only give an example.

Consider the serious and growing problem of industrial accidents and diseases. The computer-selectivity proposal linked to a charge for medical care (inpatient and outpatient and general practitioner) would involve $1\frac{1}{4}$ million individuals (new injury claimants each year plus existing disablement pensioners) and their dependants;[5] means-tests to select those who cannot pay, and, later in life, more means-tested selective benefits in respect of income maintenance for the earnings-affected victims of industrial accidents and their wives (widows) and other dependants. Should all these victims of industrial accidents and their families now be charged (as they were in the nineteenth century) with part of the costs, and be means-tested to decide whether the charge should be remitted, and whether and to what extent they should receive additional selective cash benefits? Is this what Mr Gunter wants?

If industrial accidents and diseases are to be excluded (though there is an appallingly difficult medical problem of diagnosis, attribution and checking in distinguishing these medical needs from other medical needs) what about road accidents, medical error, cross-infection in hospitals, and many other categories of accidents and disease? How would one justify and administer charges and means-tests for a variety of services for some groups (e.g. on criteria of *occupational causation*) and not for others?

But the list of claimants for exclusion from charges does not end there. What about the war disabled, war widows and industrial widows, the blind, the mentally retarded, the mentally ill (occupying nearly one-half of all hospital beds), the large number of over-70s in hospital, those who die in hospital, those with infectious diseases, the tubercular, the chronic bronchitic victims of the coal mines and other industries, the unemployed and their families, unmarried mothers, deprived children, fatherless families, and so on and so on? Where in the end does one draw the line among over 5 million inpatient cases and over 35 million outpatient attendances annually and how often? It is possible to make a strong case (most politicians would say a cast-iron case) for exemption from charges for medical care and other services (starting with the war disabled, industrial accidents and the mentally ill) for over forty distinguishable categories or classes in the population. Then, if one is practical, it is necessary in considering inpatient care to take account of length of stay (for all acute cases down to an average of 12.3 days in 1966);[6] the position of other members of the family in all these classes; and the administrative costs of the whole operation of charges, reimbursements, means-tests and the massive burden on employers of supplying and verifying essential data.

This is but one example of how the *cause* of the need giving rise to demands for different services and benefits must be taken into account in considering how and to what extent charges, remissions and means-tests should, in actual practice, differ in content, scope, characteristics and frequency.

But social services fulfil many other different functions apart from compensation and, in each case, different sets of factors have to be considered. For instance, they may represent a form of protection for society; an investment for a future personal or collective gain (e.g. higher education); an immediate and/or deferred increment to personal welfare (e.g. pensions).

If equity is to be served—one of the touchstones of a civilized society—then the content, scope, characteristics and frequency of means-tests and charges must differ according to the type of service to be provided. Different rules must apply to different groups in different circumstances for different types of services. There is no standardized answer.

(5)

Secondly, the time-scale of need introduces another set of differentiating factors. Means-tests and charges cannot be determined in cases of immediate needs (evicted families with unemployed fathers, unmarried mothers, deserted wives, individuals with recurrent spells of sickness and unemployment, and many other categories of emergency needs in changed circumstances) in, say, January 1968, on the basis of the reported earnings (PAYE form P. 60) of one earner only in the tax year April 1966–April 1967. But this is what Mr Douglas Houghton, *The Economist*, the Bow Group (*Policies for Poverty*), the Conservative Political Centre,[7] the Confederation of British Industries,[8] and other theoreticians are, in fact, proposing though their intentions are different.

Thirdly, it should not be necessary to remind these theoreticians that there are no standard families with standard or uniform requirements and resources; not only does family (or household or 'needs unit') composition, its requirements and resources vary greatly in modern society but the majority are in a constant state of flux and change. How would a computerized code number relating to circumstances $1\frac{1}{2}$ to $2\frac{1}{2}$ years ago deal with changes in requirements and resources brought about by birth, children leaving school, marriage and re-marriage, divorce, separation, desertion, death, adoption, illness, disablement, retirement, fires and disasters, institutional care (hospitals, homes for old people, children's institutions and many other forms of institutional care), unemployment, new jobs, new housing and rents, boarders, inheritance, capital appreciation, windfalls and a multitude of change factors altering the composition, responsibilities, requirements and resources of individuals and families?

Let us suppose the impossible; that the PAYE system could be adapted as proposed and computerized by the year 1980. All employers would then have to give to the Inland Revenue at weekly or monthly intervals what they now give once a year (often months after the end of the tax year) a statement of earnings and tax paid by the individual employee, which would have to be married with information on incomes from other sources. It would likewise follow that where the system showed no tax liability for the employee but a title to receive benefits of any kind the employer would be the natural instrument of payment. If he were not, then there would have to be very rapid communication week by week from the employer about each and all employees' earnings to the local office of the Inland Revenue, and thence, if no tax were due, to the paying authority for issue of the benefit. For British industry, this would represent an administrative-cost nightmare. Why have the CBI not thought of this one?

Fourthly, there are fundamental issues of moral values and equity which, in the wider interests of society, must be taken into account in the scope, content, characteristics and frequency of means-tests and charges for services and benefits, and which introduce further reasons for different treatment in different circumstances. Again, in abbreviated fashion, some of these issues may be expressed in the form of questions:

(i) Should men and women who are cohabiting have a financial advantage over husbands and wives?

(ii) Should men who do not work be better off than men who do (the wage-stop problem)?

(iii) Should those with unearned incomes have an advantage over those with earned incomes?

(iv) Should those who give away their capital assets to kin receive more favourable treatment compared with those who do not or who have no such assets?

(v) Should those who save be penalized as compared with those who do not?

(vi) Should wives be encouraged or discouraged, penalized or not for going out to work?

(vii) Should families be encouraged or discouraged from maintaining at home elderly relations, mentally retarded children and other disabled kin?

(viii) Should income tests and charges disregard capital assets, house property, discretionary trusts, education covenants, insurance policies, reversionary interests, fringe benefits, tax-free lump sums, share options, occupational benefits in kind and suchlike?

(ix) Should those who are on strike, or who refuse employment, or who are in prison be treated differently from those who are not in these situations?

(6)

Computers cannot answer these questions. Virtually all types of means-tests designed for individual selective benefits and all schemes for charges with a related right to remission, *involving the population of working ages*, run into these problems of moral values, incentives, and equity. If father gets a wage increase (due perhaps to rising prices), works overtime, moves to a cheaper house, or experiences many other changes in responsibilities and circumstances, at what point does he lose part or all of a family allowance or have to pay a series of charges for various services? Where does the 'cut-off' come and what would 'tapering' involve? Similar problems arise if mother goes to work and incomes are aggregated—as, in equity, they would have to be—but a data marriage of this kind must involve employers and the Inland Revenue in another administrative-cost nightmare.

To consider each of these nine questions in all their diverse ramifications would be tedious. In any event, it should now be clear that the computer code number proposal is not, and never can be, the answer to the problem of child poverty or to any of the other issues raised by the protagonists of selective services, means-tests and charges. Moreover, computermania appears to have blinded many people to the simple fact that the critical form (P 2) on which the present computer case rests is *not* a means-test. It is simply a guide to the employer (for those who have employers) about certain allowances to be set against an individual's earnings for tax deduction purposes. It does not, therefore, relate to wives' earnings, nor to a whole host of circumstances, resources and requirements only some of which have been discussed here.

Even more nonsensical are the proposals put forward in a recent Conservative Political Centre booklet *The New Social Contract*[9] for a reorganization of the income tax and social security system by servicing them through the proposed new Post Office Giro. They do not even begin to understand the administrative, technical, social and psychological issues so briefly surveyed in this article.

(7)

What I find frightening is the extraordinary administrative naivety of those who argue in such terms for 'selectivity'. The superficiality of much of the recent outpourings from the City, the Conservative Political Centre and elsewhere suggests that the writers have made no attempt to understand the complexities involved. If this is indicative of the current level of managerial thinking, cost-consciousness and export marketing then it throws some light on Britain's productivity performance in recent years.

There are alternative ways of finding more money for the social services; reducing subsidies and 'indiscriminate' benefits for the higher income groups, and redistributing more resources in favour of poor areas and particular groups on criteria of need without involving individual means-tests.

Is it not time that the NHS contribution became a graduated contribution? Why not re-introduce Schedule A tax on owner-occupiers?—its disappearance has left us with an indiscriminate social service subsidy if there ever was one. It was abolished by the 'selectivists' in 1963; it has not been mentioned by them since. Charging tax on replacement values, and allowing for depreciation, the removal of this subsidy would bring in over £300 million a year today. Why not raise fees for all university students; stiffen the parental means-test (which at present subsidizes other children at public schools) and abolish other and substantial public school subsidies? The revision and reduction of tax allowances for children and old people is by far the simplest, most equitable and least costly administrative device for preventing 'excessive benefits being paid to those who do not really need them.' Moreover, these and other changes in the structure of taxation would help to diminish the highly regressive incidence of direct and indirect taxation on poorer families. For example, married couples with two children struggling to live on £13 a week pay about one-fifth of their income in total taxation, rates and insurance contributions. Housing allowances on criteria of need as an integrated part of (and not an alternative to) other policies to relieve poverty could also produce savings. And how much longer are we to be burdened with the heavy and wasteful administrative costs (to say nothing of the misuse of computer time) of the chaos of something like 60,000 private pensions schemes?

The purpose of this article was not, however, to discuss the financing of the social services or the reform of taxation. I have tried to be severely practical and to examine some of the hard, inescapable facts and moral dilemmas which must face any government concerned to find the best possible balance between equity, adequacy and administrative efficiency. The fundamental ideological issues of socialist social policies and the private market are not, therefore, discussed here. Had this been my purpose I would have elaborated on my general conclusion. It is this. The challenge that faces us is not the choice between universalist and selective services. The real challenge resides in the question: what particular infrastructure of universalist services is needed in order to provide a framework of values and opportunity bases within and around which can be developed acceptable selective services provided, as social rights, on criteria of the *needs* of specific categories, groups and territorial areas and not dependent on *individual tests of means*? It is in such practical ways which do not involve an assault on human dignity, which are not socially divisive, and which do not lead to the development of two standards of services for two nations that more redistribution can be affected through the social services in favour of those whose needs are greatest.

There can, therefore, be no answer in Britain to the problems of poverty, ethnic integration, and social and educational inequalities without an infrastructure of universalist services. These are the essential foundations. We have to build on them and around them; face the hard, detailed challenge of how precisely to do so, and not run away in search of false gods or worn-out doctrines. Some of the answers have been hammered out and are known in Whitehall; what is now required is the courage to implement them.

NOTES

1. *Children and their Primary Schools* (Plowden Report), Vol. 1, HMSO, London, 1967.
2. *The Economist*, January 20, 1951, pp. 118–19.
3. *The Economist*, April 8th (pp. 109–11), June 24th (pp. 1326–31) and July 29, 1967 (pp. 388–9).
4. Occasional Paper 16, The Institute of Economic Affairs, 1967.
5. *Annual Report of the Ministry of Social Security for 1966*, Cmnd 3338, HMSO, 1967. See also *Annual Reports of H.M. Chief Inspector of Factories for 1966*, Cmnd 3358–9, HMSO, London, 1967.
6. *Annual Report of the Ministry of Health for 1966*, Cmnd 3326, 1967.
7. Sewill, H., *Auntie*, Conservative Political Centre, 1967.
8. Report of CBI Economic Committee summarized in *The Times*, August 4, 1967.
9. Rhys Williams, B., Conservative Political Centre, 1967.

Chapter XI

WELFARE STATE AND WELFARE SOCIETY*

Introduction

I did not choose this title. It was chosen for me. Despite this assistance, I must say that I am no more enamoured today of the indefin-
able abstraction 'The Welfare State' than I was some twenty years
ago when, with the advent of the National Health, National Insurance and other legislative promissories, the term acquired an international as well as a national popularity.

The consequences have not all been intellectually stimulating.
Generalized slogans rarely induce concentration of thought; more
often they prevent us from asking significant questions about reality.
Morally satisfied and intellectually dulled, we sink back into our
presumptive cosy British world of welfare. Meanwhile, outside these
islands (as well as inside) there are critics—economic and political
critics—who are misled into confusing ends and means, and who
are discouraged from undertaking the painful exercise of distinguishing between philosophical tomorrows and the current truths of
reality in a complex British power structure of rationed resources,
and great inequalities in incomes and wealth, opportunities and
freedom of choice.

From what little is known about the reading habits of international bankers and economists, I think it is reasonable to say that
they do not include much in the way of studies on welfare and the
condition of the poor. How then are their views shaped about the
British 'Welfare State'? This we do not know, but at least we can
say that if we mislead ourselves, we shall mislead them. But the
matter does not end there. Models of public welfare can assume
different forms and contain different assumptions about means and
ends. Concepts of welfare can imply very different things to different
people—as we can see from the Study Group Reports to this Conference.

One particular model is the *Public Burden Model of Welfare*. In
general terms, this sees public welfare expenditure—and particu-

* Lecture delivered at the British National Conference on Social Welfare,
London, April 1967, and published in the *Proceedings of the Conference*.

larly expenditure which is redistributive in intent—as a burden; an impediment to growth and economic development. Given this model of the British patient, the diagnosis seems simple. We are spending too much on 'The Welfare State'. Such explanations are, moreover, encouraged by the concept of private economic man embedded in the techniques of national income accounting. An increase in public retirement pensions is seen (as it was seen internationally during the balance of payments crisis in 1964) as an economic burden.[1] A similar increase in spending power among occupational (publicly subsidized private) pensioners is not so seen. Yet both involve additions to consumption demand.

Or take another example: medical care, public and private. It is being argued today that by encouraging the growth of private medical care through a voucher system and by allowing people to contract-out of taxation, the 'burden' of the Health Service would be reduced. The objective it seems is to reduce the assumed 'burden'; thus, those who contract-out diminish the burden. Logically, we should extend to them our gratitude and moral respect for contracting-out of public commitments. But, if Mr Enoch Powell may be accepted as an authority (and I quote from his recent book *Medicine and Politics*[2]), this 'voucher scheme resolves itself merely into a method of increasing state expenditure upon medical care'. In other words, it is a proposal for redistributing more medical resources in favour of private patients. The case for contracting-out must, therefore, be justified on grounds other than the 'welfare burden' argument.

International Aspects of Welfare

If we insist, come what may, on the continued use or misuse and misapplication of the term 'The Welfare State' then we must accept the consequences of international misunderstanding. We cannot assume that observers abroad share, or will share, the social or moral criteria we may apply to welfare; to many of our creditors and currency colleagues in Western Germany, France and the United States, the 'Welfare State' is equated with national irresponsibility and decadence; an easy way of living off foreign loans. To the political scientist as well as the economist these opinions are relevant facts in the same way as (according to some sociologists) social class is what men think it is. These opinions do not, moreover, differ markedly from those expressed in the published statements on welfare during the past fifteen years by bankers, insurance directors, financiers and others in the City of London.[3]

Many of these monetary experts abroad appear to place a different valuation on countries which depend heavily on 'borrowing' human capital as distinct from those which borrow financial capital. For such transactions, no payment is made to the lending country; there are no interest charges, and there is no intention of repaying the loan.

Since 1949 the United States has absorbed (and to some extent deliberately recruited) the import of 100,000 doctors, scientists and engineers from developed and developing countries. In about eighteen years the United States will have saved some $4,000 million by not having to educate and train, or train fully, this vast quantity of human capital.[4] It has spent more on consumption goods; less on public services. It has taxed itself more lightly while imposing heavier taxation on poorer countries. Estimates have been made that this foreign aid to America is as great or greater than the total of American aid to countries abroad since 1949. Moreover, such estimates leave out of account the social and economic effects in Britain (and much more significantly in the poor countries of the world) of having to train more doctors, scientists and engineers, and of having to pay heavily inflated rewards to prevent American recruitment with all their harmful repercussions on incomes, prices and levels of taxation.

In medicine alone, foreign doctors now account for nearly 20 per cent of the annual additions to the American medical profession.[5] The world now provides as much or more medical aid to the United States in terms of dollars as the total cost of all American medical aid, private and public, to foreign countries.[6] A study I have made recently of the columns of the *British Medical Journal* and the *Lancet* from 1951 to 1966 shows that advertisements for British doctors (often accompanied by recruiting campaigns and sometimes actively encouraged by senior British doctors[7]) rose from a yearly average of 134 in 1951 to over 4,000 in 1966.[8] The total number of newly qualified doctors in Britain in 1966 was around 1,700; each of them cost about £10,000 to train, excluding expenditure on student maintenance.[9]

The United States is not alone in attempting to develop its welfare systems (and Medicare) at the expense of poorer countries through the discovery that, today, it is much cheaper and less of a public burden to import doctors, scientists and other qualified workers than to educate and train them. Britain is also relying heavily on the skills of doctors from poorer countries—due in part to the belief less than five to ten years ago among Ministers and leaders of the medical profession that we were in danger of training too many doctors.[10] And, we may add, the belief among liberal economists

126

and sections of the medical profession that Britain was spending too much on the Health Service which was in danger of bankrupting the nation. Even as late as 1962, there were influential voices in the British Medical Association who were speaking of the profession's recent experience of a 'glut of doctors' and the need to avoid medical unemployment in the late 1960s.[11] Guilty as we have been in our treatment of doctors from overseas, and in our failure in the past to train enough health workers for our own national needs, at least it cannot be said that we are deliberately organizing recruitment campaigns in economically poorer countries.

These introductory reflections on some of the international aspects of welfare point, I believe, to three general conclusions. First, they underline the dangers in the use of the term 'The Welfare State'. Second, they remind us that we can no longer consider welfare systems solely within the limited framework of the nation-state; what we do or fail to do in changing systems of welfare affects other countries besides ourselves. Third, to suggest one criterion for the definition of a 'Welfare Society'; namely, a society which openly accepts a policy responsibility for educating and training its own nationals to meet its own needs for doctors, nurses, social workers, scientists, engineers and others. Just as we have recognized the injustices and the waste in the unrestricted free international movement of goods, material and capital, so we must now recognize the need for the richer countries of the world to take action to protect the poorer countries from being denuded of skilled manpower.

To this end, a number of measures could be taken, some unilaterally, some by international agreement. Among the most important would be for the rich countries to decide to spend less on personal consumption goods and more on training young people for the social service professions; to decide to devote more of their resources for genuine international aid to the poorer countries; to decide to ban the deliberate recruitment overseas of skilled manpower; to decide to revise and broaden their immigration policies so that movement between countries is not restricted to the highly educated and trained; and to take other measures too complex to discuss in this paper.

For the rich countries of the world to take action in such ways would represent a few modest steps towards the notion of 'a Welfare World'. Those countries assuming leadership with policies of this nature might then with some justification regard themselves as 'Welfare Societies'.

This principle of community responsibility for the provision of

adequate resources to implement the objectives of national legislation is particularly relevant to the whole field of welfare. The
quantity, territorial distribution and quality of any country's social
services—education, medical care, mental health, welfare, children's
and other personal community services—depends enormously on
the quantity and quality of staff; professional, technical, auxiliary
and administrative. To enact legislation designed to create or
develop services yet not to invest adequately in the training of
doctors, nurses, social workers, teachers, and many other categories
of skilled manpower and womanpower is a denial of this principle
of community responsibility. To rely on the private market and
autonomous professional bodies to fulfil these training needs is
nothing less than a ridiculous illusion. The private national market
has failed lamentably in this country and in the United States to
produce enough doctors, teachers, social workers and nurses. To
resort to the international market to remedy the deficiency of
national social policies can only have tragic consequences for the
poorer countries of the world.

In considering the international aspects of these welfare manpower issues there is one further observation I wish to make before
turning to other Conference themes. It seems to me the height of
collective immorality for the rich countries of the world to preach
to the poorer countries about the economic benefits of family planning while, at the same time, making it more difficult for these
countries to develop family planning programmes by drawing away
the skilled manpower they need for the infrastructure of services
required in which to provide birth control as well as death control
services.

Having delivered myself of these thoughts under the conveniently
broad umbrella-theme of this Conference, I want now to consider
certain other questions of principle in systems of welfare.

Universalist and Selective Social Services

In any discussion today of the future of (what is called) 'The Welfare State' much of the argument revolves round the principles and
objectives of universalist social services and selective social services.
Prominence was given to this issue in Chapters 2 and 4 of the *Guide
to Studies* prepared two years ago for this Conference. Time does
not seem to have eroded the importance of this issue.

I think it is unnecessary, therefore, to remind you in detail of the
many complex questions of principles, goals, methods and assumptions involved in this debate. In regard to some of them—and particularly the question of freedom of choice—I have set out my views

in a recently published lecture *Choice and 'The Welfare State'*.[12]

Briefly, then, I will restate certain of the more general points emphasized in this *Guide*. Consider, first, the nature of the broad principles which helped to shape substantial sections of British welfare legislation in the past, and particularly the principle of universalism embodied in such post-war enactments as the National Health Service Act, the Education Act of 1944, the National Insurance Act and the Family Allowances Act.

One fundamental historical reason for the adoption of this principle was the aim of making services available and accessible to the whole population in such ways as would not involve users in any humiliating loss of status, dignity or self-respect. There should be no sense of inferiority, pauperism, shame or stigma in the use of a publicly provided service; no attribution that one was being or becoming a 'public burden'. Hence the emphasis on the social rights of all citizens to use or not to use as responsible people the services made available by the community in respect of certain needs which the private market and the family were unable or unwilling to provide universally. If these services were not provided for everybody by everybody they would either not be available at all, or only for those who could afford them, and for others on such terms as would involve the infliction of a sense of inferiority and stigma.

Avoidance of stigma was not, of course, the only reason for the development of the twin-concepts of social rights and universalism. Many other forces, social, political and psychological, during a century and more of turmoil, revolution, war and change, contributed to the clarification and acceptance of these notions. The novel idea of prevention—novel, at least, to many in the nineteenth century—was, for example, another powerful engine, driven by the Webbs and many other advocates of change, which reinforced the concepts of social rights and universalism. The idea of prevention —the prevention and breaking of the vicious descending spiral of poverty, disease, neglect, illiteracy and destitution—spelt to the protagonists (and still does so) the critical importance of early and easy access to and use of preventive, remedial and rehabilitative services. Slowly and painfully the lesson was learnt that if such services were to be utilized in time and were to be effective in action in a highly differentiated, unequal and class-saturated society, they had to be delivered through socially approved channels; that is to say, without loss of self-respect by the users and their families.

Prevention was not simply a child of biological and psychological theorists; at least one of the grandparents was a powerful economist with a strongly developed streak of nationalism. As Professor Bentley Gilbert has shown in his recent book, *The Evolution of National Insurance: The Origins of the Welfare State*, national efficiency and welfare were seen as complementary.[13] The sin unforgivable was the waste of human resources; thus, welfare was summoned to prevent waste. Hence the beginnings of four of our present-day universalist social services: retirement pensions, the Health Service, unemployment insurance and the school meals service.

The insistent drumming of the national efficiency movement in those far-off days before the First World War is now largely forgotten. Let me then remind you that the whole welfare debate was a curious mixture of humanitarianism, egalitarianism, productivity (as we would call it today) and old-fashioned imperialism. The strident note of the latter is now, we may thank our stars, silenced. The Goddess of Growth has replaced the God of National Fitness. But can we say that the quest for the other objectives is no longer necessary?

Before discussing such a rhetorical question, we need to examine further the principal of universalism. The principle itself may sound simple but the practice—and by that I mean the present operational pattern of welfare in Britain today—is immensely complex. We can see something of this complexity if we analyse welfare (defined here as all publicly provided and subsidized services, statutory, occupational and fiscal) from a number of different standpoints.

An Analytical Framework
Whatever the nature of the service, activity or function, and whether it be a service in kind, a collective amenity, or a transfer payment in cash or by accountancy, we need to consider (and here I itemize in question-form for the sake of brevity) three central issues:

(*a*) What is the nature of entitlement to use? Is it legal, contractual or contributory, financial, discretionary or professionally determined entitlement?
(*b*) Who is entitled and on what conditions? Is account taken of individual characteristics, family characteristics, group characteristics, territorial characteristics or social-biological characteristics? What, in fact, are the rules of entitlement? Are they specific and contractual—like a right based on age—or are they variable, arbitrary or discretionary?
(*c*) What methods, financial and administrative, are employed in the determination of access, utilization, allocation and payment?

Next we have to reflect on the nature of the service or benefit.

What functions do benefits, in cash, amenity or in kind, aim to fulfil? They may, for example, fulfil any of the following sets of functions, singly or in combination:

(1) As partial compensation for identified disservices caused by society (for example, unemployment, some categories of industrial injuries benefits, war pensions, etc.). And, we may add, the disservices caused by international society as exemplified recently by the oil pollution resulting from the Torrey Canyon disaster costing at least £2 million.[14]

(2) As partial compensation for unidentifiable disservices caused by society (for example, 'benefits' related to programmes of slum clearance, urban blight, smoke pollution control, hospital cross-infection and many other socially created disservices).

(3) As partial compensation for unmerited handicap (for example, language classes for immigrant children, services for the deprived child, children handicapped from birth, etc.).

(4) As a form of protection for society (for example, the probation service, some parts of the mental health services, services for the control of infectious diseases, and so on).

(5) As an investment for a future personal or collective gain (education—professional, technical and industrial—is an obvious example here; so also are certain categories of tax deductibles for self-improvement and certain types of subsidized occupational benefits).

(6) As an immediate and/or deferred increment to personal welfare or, in other words, benefits (utilities) which add to personal command-over-resources either immediately and/or in the future (for example, subsidies to owner-occupiers and council tenants, tax deductibles for interest charges, pensions, supplementary benefits, curative medical care, and so on).

(7) As an element in an integrative objective which is an essential characteristic distinguishing social policy from economic policy. As Kenneth Boulding has said, '. . . social policy is that which is centred in those institutions that create integration and discourage alienation.'[15] It is thus profoundly concerned with questions of personal identity whereas economic policy centres round exchange or bilateral transfer.

This represents little more than an elementary and partial structural map which can assist in the understanding of the welfare complex today. Needless to say, a more sophisticated (inch to the mile) guide is essential for anything approaching a thorough analysis of the actual functioning of welfare benefit systems. I do not, however, propose to refine further this frame of study now, nor can I analyse by these classifications the several hundred distinctive and functionally separate services and benefits actually in operation in Britain today.

Further study would also have to take account of the pattern and operation of means-tested services. It has been estimated by Mr M. J. Reddin, my research assistant, that in England and Wales today local authorities are responsible for administering at least 3,000 means-tests, of which about 1,500 are different from each other.[16] This estimate applies only to services falling within the responsibilities of education, child care, health, housing and welfare departments. It follows that in these fields alone there exist some 1,500 different definitions of poverty or financial hardship, ability to pay and rules for charges, which affect the individual and the family. There must be substantial numbers of poor families with multiple needs and multiple handicaps whose perception today of the realities of welfare is to see only a means-testing world. Who helps them, I wonder, to fill up all those forms?

I mention these social facts, by way of illustration, because they do form part of the operational complex of welfare in 1967. My main purpose, however, in presenting this analytical framework was twofold. First, to underline the difficulties of conceptualizing and categorizing needs, causes, entitlement or gatekeeper functions, utilization patterns, benefits and compensations. Second, to suggest that those students of welfare who are seeing the main problem today in terms of universalism versus selective services are presenting a naive and oversimplified picture of policy choices.

Some of the reasons for this simple and superficial view are, I think, due to the fact that the approach is dominated by the concept or model of welfare as a 'burden'; as a waste of resources in the provision of benefits for those who, it is said, do not need them. The general solution is thus deceptively simple and romantically appealing; abolish all this welfare complexity and concentrate help on those whose needs are greatest.

Quite apart from the theoretical and practical immaturity of this solution, which would restrict the public services to a minority in the population leaving the majority to buy their own education, social security, medical care and other services in a supposedly free market, certain other important questions need to be considered.

As all selective services for this minority would have to apply some test of need—eligibility, on what bases would tests be applied and, even more crucial, where would the lines be drawn for benefits which function as compensation for identified disservices, compensation for unidentifiable disservices, compensation for unmerited handicap, as a form of social protection, as an investment, or as an increment to personal welfare? Can rules of entitlement and access be drawn on purely 'ability to pay' criteria without distinction of cause? And if the causal agents of need cannot be identified or are so diffuse as to defy the wit of law—as they so often are today— then is not the answer 'no compensation and no redress'? In other words, the case for concentrated selective services resolves itself into an argument for allowing the social costs or diswelfares of the economic system to lie where they fall.

The emphasis today on 'welfare' and the 'benefits of welfare' often tends to obscure the fundamental fact that for many consumers the services used are not essentially benefits or increments to welfare at all; they represent partial compensations for disservices, for social costs and social insecurities which are the product of a rapidly changing industrial-urban society. They are part of the price we pay to some people for bearing part of the costs of other people's progress; the obsolescence of skills, redundancies, premature retirements, accidents, many categories of disease and handicap, urban blight and slum clearance, smoke pollution, and a hundred-and-one other socially generated disservices. They are the socially caused diswelfares; the losses involved in aggregate welfare gains.

What is also of major importance today is that modern society is finding it increasingly difficult to identify the causal agent or agencies, and thus to allocate the costs of disservices and charge those who are responsible. It is not just a question of benefit allocation— of whose 'Welfare State'—but also of loss allocation—whose 'Diswelfare State'.

If identification of the agents of diswelfare were possible—if we could legally name and blame the culprits—then, in theory at least, redress could be obtained through the courts by the method of monetary compensation for damages. But multiple causality and the diffusion of disservices—the modern choleras of change—make this solution impossible. We have, therefore, as societies to make other choices; either to provide social services, or to allow the social costs of the system to lie where they fall. The nineteenth century chose the latter—the *laissez faire* solution—because it had neither a germ theory of disease nor a social theory of causality; an answer which can hardly be entertained today by a richer society equipped with more knowledge about the dynamics of change. But knowledge in this context must not, of course, be equated with wisdom.

If this argument can be sustained, we are thus compelled to

return to our analytical framework of the functional concepts of benefit and, within this context, to consider the role of universalist and selective social services. Non-discriminating universalist services are in part the consequence of unidentifiable causality. If disservices are wasteful (to use the economists' concept of 'waste') so welfare has to be 'wasteful'.

The next question that presents itself is this: can we and should we, in providing benefits and compensation (which in practise can rarely be differentially provided), distinguish between 'faults' in the individual (moral, psychological or social) and the 'faults of society'? If all services are provided—irrespective of whether they represent benefits, amenity, social protection or compensation—on a discriminatory, means-test basis, do we not foster both the sense of personal failure and the stigma of a public burden? The fundamental objective of all such tests of eligibility is to keep people out; not to let them in. They must, therefore, be treated as applicants or supplicants; not beneficiaries or consumers.

It is a regrettable but human fact that money (and the lack of it) is linked to personal and family self-respect. This is one element in what has been called the 'stigma of the means test'. Another element is the historical evidence we have that separate discriminatory services for poor people have always tended to be poor quality services; read the history of the panel system under National Health Insurance; read Beveridge on workmen's compensation; Newsom on secondary modern schools; Plowden on standards of primary schools in slum areas; Townsend on Part III accommodations in *The Last Refuge*,[17] and so on.[18]

In the past, poor quality selective services for poor people were the product of a society which saw 'welfare' as a residual; as a public burden. The primary purpose of the system and the method of discrimination was, therefore, deterrence (it was also an effective rationing device). To this end, the most effective instrument was to induce among recipients (children as well as adults) a sense of personal fault, of personal failure, even if the benefit was wholly or partially a compensation for disservices inflicted by society.

The Real Challenge in Welfare

Today, with this heritage, we face the positive challenge of providing selective, high quality services for poor people over a large and complex range of welfare; of positively discriminating on a territorial, group or 'rights' basis in favour of the poor, the handicapped, the deprived, the coloured, the homeless, and the social casualties of our society. Universalism is not, by itself alone, enough: in medical care, in wage-related social security, and in education. This much we have learnt in the past two decades from the facts about inequalities in the distribution of incomes and wealth, and in our failure to close many gaps in differential access to and effective utilization of particular branches of our social services.[19]

If I am right, I think that Britain is beginning to identify the dimensions of this challenge of positive, selective discrimination—in income maintenance, in education, in housing, in medical care and mental health, in child welfare, and in the tolerant integration of immigrants and citizens from overseas; of preventing especially the second generation from becoming (and of seeing themselves as) second-class citizens. We are seeking ways and means, values, methods and techniques, of positive discrimination without the infliction, actual or imagined, of a sense of personal failure and individual fault.

At this point, considering the nature of the search in all its ramifying complexities, I must now state my general conclusion. It is this. The challenge that faces us is not the choice between universalist and selective social services. The real challenge resides in the question: what particular infrastructure of universalist services is needed in order to provide a framework of values and opportunity bases within and around which can be developed socially acceptable selective services aiming to discriminate positively, with the minimum risk of stigma, in favour of those whose needs are greatest.[20]

This, to me, is the fundamental challenge. In different ways and in particular areas it confronts the Supplementary Benefits Commission, the Seebohm Committee, the National Health Service, the Ministry of Housing and Local Government, the National Committee for Commonwealth Immigrants, the policy-making readers of the Newsom Report and the Plowden Report on educational priority areas, the Scottish Report, *Social Work and the Community*, and thousands of social workers and administrators all over the country wrestling with the problems of needs and priorities. In all the main spheres of need, some structure of universalism is an essential pre-requisite to selective positive discrimination; it provides a general system of values and a sense of community; socially approved agencies for clients, patients and consumers, and also for the recruitment, training and deployment of staff at all levels; it sees welfare, not as a burden, but as complementary and as an instrument of change and, finally, it allows positive discriminatory services to be provided as rights for categories of people and for classes of need in terms of priority social areas and other impersonal classifications.

Without this infrastructure of welfare resources and framework of values we should not, I conclude, be able to identify and discuss the next steps in progress towards a 'Welfare Society'.

NOTES

1. See, for example, *The Times*, July 28, 1965, and August 6, 1965; article by H. Heymann, 'Gnomes of Zurich with a London Address', in *The Times*, January 18, 1966, and *The Times*, April 4, 1967 (report by P. Jay, Economics Correspondent), and *The Economist*, editorial 'Into the Wasteland', July 23, 1966, and editorial note on 'Poverty', April 22, 1967.
2. Powell, J. Enoch, *Medicine and Politics*, Pitman, London, 1966, p. 72.
3. See Titmuss, R. M., *Income Distribution and Social Change*, Allen and Unwin, London, 1962.
4. Henderson, G., Institute for Training and Research, *New York Times*, November 6, 1966, p. E 11. See also Perkins, J. A., President of Cornell University and Chairman of the President's Advisory Committee on Foreign Assistance Programmes, *Foreign Affairs*, July 1966; Thomas Brinley, in 'The New Immigration', *The Annals of the American Academy of Political and Social Science*, September 1966; Sutherland, G., *The Political Quarterly*, Vol. 38, No. 1, January-March 1967; Lord Bowden, House of Lords, *Hansard*, December 20, 1966, cols 1971–80; and Grubel, H. G., and Scott, A. D., *Journal of Political Economy*, University of Chicago, 1966, Vol. 14, No. 4, p. 231.
5. West, K. M., 'Foreign Interns and Residents in the United States', *Journal of Medical Education*, December 1965, Vol. 40, pp. 1110–29.
6. 'The dollar value per year of this "foreign aid" to the United States approximately equals the total cost of all of our medical aid, private and public, to foreign nations' (West, K. M., *ibid.*, p. 1127). About three-fourths of all foreign medical trainees in the USA are from developing countries.
7. Gibson, T. C., 'British Physicians on Medical School Faculties in North America', *Brit. Med. J.*, 1967, **i**, 692.
8. Israel, as well as many other countries, is affected by the shortage of doctors in the USA. Of the 265 doctors graduating from Israeli medical schools in 1963–65, nearly 40 per cent left for the USA (statement by Minister of Health quoted in *Haaretz*, March 21, 1967).
9. Hill, K. R., 'Cost of Undergraduate Medical Education in Britain', *British Medical Journal*, 1964, **i**, 300–2.
10. Ministry of Health and Department of Health for Scotland, *Report of the Committee to Consider the Future Numbers of Medical Practitioners and the Appropriate Intake of Medical Students*, HMSO, London, 1957. Seven of this eleven-man Committee were eminent members of the medical profession and the Chairman was an ex-Minister of Health, Sir Henry Willink.
11. In May 1962 a special committee set up by the British Medical Association to consider recruitment to the medical profession concluded in its report that in spite of certain obvious indications of a shortage of doctors it was not prepared to commit itself on the need for more medical students (*The Times*, May 11, 1962). Dr R. G. Gibson, chairman of this committee (and now Chairman of the Council), said two months later that the profession had recently experienced a 'glut of doctors. At present there seemed to be a

shortage, but care must be taken not to create unemployment in the profession a few years from now' (*Brit. Med. J.*, Supp., ii, July 26, 28, 1962).

12. See Chapter 12.
13. Gilbert, B. B., Michael Joseph, 1966.
14. *The Torrey Canyon*, Cmnd 3246, HMSO, London, 1967.
15. Boulding, K. E., 'The Boundaries of Social Policy', *Social Work*, Vol. 12, No. 1, January 1967, p. 7.
16. This study is to be published by Mr Reddin as an *Occasional Paper on Social Administration*.
17. Townsend, P., *The Last Refuge*, Routledge, London, 1964.
18. See also Titmuss, R. M., *Problems of Social Policy*, HMSO, London, 1950.
19. See Townsend, P., *Poverty, Socialism and Labour in Power*, Fabian tract, 371, 1967, and Nicholson, R. J., 'The Distribution of Personal Income', *Lloyds Bank Review*, January 1967, p. 11.
20. For a more specific formulation see Chapter X.

Chapter XII

CHOICE AND 'THE WELFARE STATE'*

For those of us who are still socialists the development of socialist social policies in the next few years will represent one of the cardinal tests on which the Labour Government will be judged—and sternly judged—in the early 1970s. Economic growth, productivity and change are essential; about this there can be no dispute. But as we—as a society—become richer shall we become more equal in social, educational and material terms? What does the rise of 'affluence' spell to the values embodied in the notion of social welfare?

For the purposes of this lecture I have, in asking these questions, to take a long view and disregard our immediate economic and social problems. One assumption I have to make is that over the next ten years (and thereafter) British society will be substantially richer; that, on average, the population of Britain will be living at a higher standard than today. In his pamphlet *Labour's Social Plans†* Professor Abel-Smith dealt with what he called the 'ugly imbalance between private affluence and public squalor', and went on to direct a searching attack on the social policy content of the Government's *National Plan.‡*

He assumed (as I do) that over the period of the National Plan we may expect to be (in company with other highly industrialized countries of the West) a richer society in the 1970s. Now that the Government has begun to lay a sounder basis for a higher rate of growth in the future after inheriting a decade or more of incompetence and dereliction it is, I think, more rather than less likely that our economic targets will be broadly attained.

But, at the present time, economic and industrial policies are involving much hardship for a minority of workers; whether this was or was not inevitable is a matter on which a great deal more could be said, and no doubt will be said. The acid test will come, however, in the next few years; there will be many who will want to

* London Fabian Lecture, November 1966, and published in Fabian Tract 370, 1967.

† Fabian Tract 369.

‡ Cmnd 2764, HMSO, September 1965.

know by the time the life of this Government comes to its natural end whether those who are making sacrifices now in the general interest will be more than justly compensated.

This question of who should bear the social and economic costs of change is relevant to the larger issue of the future role of the social services in a more affluent society. First, however, let us remember the general thesis about 'freedom of choice' now being forcefully presented by various schools of 'liberal' economists in Britain, Western Germany and the United States—notably in the writings of Professor Friedman of Chicago and his friends and followers in London and elsewhere.* Broadly, their argument is that as large-scale industrialized societies get richer the vast majority of their populations will have incomes and assets large enough to satisfy their own social welfare needs in the private market without help from the State. They should have the right and the freedom to decide their own individual resource preferences and priorities and to buy from the private market their own preferred quantities of medical care, education, social security, housing and other services.

Unlike their distinguished predecessors in the nineteenth century, these economic analysts and politicians do not now condemn such instruments of social policy (in the form of social services) as politically irrelevant or mistaken in the past. They were needed then as temporary, *ad hoc* political mechanisms to ameliorate and reduce social conflict; to protect the rights of property, and to avoid resort to violence by the dispossessed and the deprived. This contemporary redefinition of the past role of social policy thus represents it as a form of social control; as a temporary short-term process of State intervention to buttress and legitimate industrial capitalism during its early, faltering but formative years of growth. We are now told that those who in the past were critical of State intervention in the guise of free social services were misguided and short-sighted. The Bourbons of today disavow the Bourbons of yesterday. The times, the concepts, the working classes, and the market have all changed. They have been changed by affluence, by technology, and by the development of more sophisticated, anonymous and flexible mechanisms of the market to meet social needs, to enlarge the freedom of consumer choice, and to provide not only more but better quality medical care, education, social security and housing.

In abbreviated form, these are some of the theories of private social policy and consumer choice now being advanced in Britain[1] and other countries. Like other conceptions of social policy presented in large and all-embracing terms, these theories make a number of

* M. Friedman, *Capitalism and Freedom*, University of Chicago Press, 1962.

basic assumptions about the working of the market, about the nature of social needs, and about the future social and economic characteristics of our societies. These assumptions require examination: the task allotted to me by the Fabian Society in preparing this lecture.

I cannot, however, discuss them all in as much detail as I would like. I propose, therefore, to make more explicit four important assumptions and, in respect of each, to raise some questions and add some comments.

Assumption No. 1—That economic growth without the intervention of comprehensive and deliberately redistributive social policies can, by itself alone, solve the problem of poverty.

None of the evidence for Britain and the United States over the past twenty years during which the average standard of living in real terms rose by 50 per cent or more supports this assumption. The most recent evidence for Britain has been examined by Professors Abel-Smith and Townsend in their study *The Poor and the Poorest.** Had private markets in education, medical care and social security been substituted for public policies during the past twenty years of economic growth their conclusions, in both absolute and relative terms, as to the extent of poverty in Britain today would, I suggest, have been even more striking.

For the United States the evidence is no less conclusive and can be found in the recent studies of Orshansky, Brady, S. M. Miller and Rein, Moynihan, Schorr, Herman Miller and Richard Elman, whose book, *The Poorhouse State: The American Way of Life on Public Assistance,*† provides a grim picture of degradation in the richest country the world has ever known.

Yet, in 1951, the first chairman of the Council of Economic Advisors under the Eisenhower administration said, before his appointment to the Council ' . . . the transformation in the distribution of our national income . . . may already be counted as one of the great social revolutions in history.'‡

Economic growth spelt progress; an evolutionary and inevitable faith that social growth would accompany economic growth. Automatically, therefore, poverty would gracefully succumb to the diffusion of the choices of private market abundance. All this

* Occasional Papers on Social Administration, No. 17, Bell and Sons, 1965.
† Pantheon Books, New York, 1966.
‡ Quoted in H. T. Miller, 'Is the income gap closed? "No"?', *New York Times Magazine*, November 11, 1962.

heralded, as Daniel Bell and others were later to argue, the end of ideological conflict.*

One is led to wonder what liberal economists would have said fifteen to twenty years ago had they had foreknowledge of the growth in American wealth and had they then been asked to comment on the following facts for the year 1966: that one American child in four would be regarded as living in poverty and that three elderly persons in ten would also be living in poverty;† that the United States would be moving towards a more unequal distribution of income, wealth and command-over-resources;‡ that many grey areas would have become ghettos;§ that a nationwide civil rights' challenge of explosive magnitude would have to be faced—a challenge for freedom of choice, for the right to work, for a non-rat infested home,[2] for medical care and against stigma;‖ that, as a nation, the United States would be seriously short of doctors, scientists, teachers, social workers, nurses, welfare aids and professional workers in almost all categories of personal service; and that American agencies would be deliberately recruiting and organizing the import of doctors, nurses and other categories of human capital from less affluent nations of the world.

Britain, we should remember, is also relying heavily on the skills of doctors from poorer countries—due in part to the belief less than five to ten years ago among Conservative Ministers and leaders of the medical profession that we were in danger of training too many doctors.[3] And, we should add, the belief among liberal economists and sections of the medical profession that Britain was spending too much on the Health Service which was in danger of bankrupting the nation.

* D. Bell, *The End of Ideology: on the Exhaustion of Political Ideas in the Fifties*, Collier Books, New York, 1961.

† M. Orshansky in *Social Security Bulletin*, July 1963, January 1965 and July 1965, Social Security Administration, US Department of Health, Education and Welfare.

‡ D. S. Brady, *Age and the Income Distribution*, Research Report No. 8, Social Security Administration, Department of Health, Education and Welfare, 1965. For other evidence of recent trends see S. M. Miller and M. Rein, 'Poverty, Inequality and Policy', in H. S. Becker (ed.), *Social Problems*, John Wiley & Son, New York.

§ See D. R. Hunter, *The Slums: Challenge and Response*, Glencoe Free Press, New York, 1964; H. Gans, *The Urban Villagers*, Glencoe Free Press, New York, 1962; K. E. Taeuber, *Scientific American*, 1965, Vol. 213, No. 2, and K. E. and F. Alma Taeuber, *Negroes in Cities: Residential Segregation and Neighbourhood Change*, Aldine, Chicago, 1965.

‖ *The Negro Family: the Case for National Action*, Office of Policy Planning and Research, US Department of Labour, 1965.

Guilty as we have been and are in our treatment of doctors from overseas, at least it cannot be said that we are deliberately organizing recruitment campaigns in India, Pakistan and other developing countries.

Assumption No. 2: That private markets in welfare can solve the problem of discrimination and stigma.

This assumption takes us to the centre of all speculations about choice in welfare and the conflict between universalist social services and selective means-tested systems for the poor. It is basically the problem of stigma or 'spoiled identity' in Goffman's phrase;* of felt and experienced discrimination and disapproval on grounds of poverty, ethnic group, class, mental fitness and other criteria of 'bad risks' in all the complex processes of selection-rejection in our societies.

How does the private market in education, social security, industrial injuries insurance, rehabilitation, mental health services and medical care, operating on the basis of ability to pay and profitability, treat poor minority groups? All the evidence, particularly from the United States and Canada, suggests that they are categorized as 'bad risks', treated as second-class consumers, and excluded from the middle-class world of welfare. If they are excluded because they cannot pay or are likely to have above-average needs—and are offered second-class standards in a refurbished public assistance or panel system—who can blame them if they come to think that they have been discriminated against on grounds of colour and other criteria of rejection? Civil rights legislation in Britain to police the commercial insurance companies, the British United Provident Association, and the BMA's Independent Medical Services Ltd would be a poor and ineffective substitute for the National Health Service.

Already there is evidence from recently established independent fee-paying medical practices that the 'bad risks' are being excluded, and that the chronic sick are being advised to stay (if they can) with the National Health Service.† They are not offered the choice though they may be able to pay. In point of fact, their ability to choose a local doctor under the Health Service is being narrowed. This is a consequence, I suppose, of what Mr Arthur Seldon of the Institute of Economic Affairs in his most recent essay on 'Choice in Welfare'

* E. Goffman, *Stigma: Notes on the Management of Spoiled Identity*, Prentice Hall, NJ, 1963.

† S. Mencher, *Private Practice and the National Health Service*, pp. 130–6, to be published.

describes as 'a new stirring in medical insurance and a new class of doctors with a grain of entrepreneurial determination to supplement or abandon the NHS and to find salvation in the market'.*

The essential issue here of discrimination is not the problem of choice in private welfare markets for the upper and middle classes but how to channel proportionately more economic and social resources to aid the poor, the handicapped, the educationally deprived and other minority groups, and to compensate them for bearing part of the costs of other people's progress. We cannot now, just because we are getting richer, disengage ourselves from the fundamental challenge of distributing social rights without stigma; too many unfulfilled expectations have been created, and we can no longer fall back on the *rationale* that our economies are too poor to avoid hurting people. Nor can we solve the problems of discrimination and stigma by re-creating poor law or panel systems of welfare in the belief that we should thereby be able to concentrate state help on those whose needs are greatest. Separate state systems for the poor, operating in the context of powerful private welfare markets, tend to become poor standard systems. Insofar as they are able to recruit at all for education, medical care and other services, they tend to recruit the worst rather than the best teachers, doctors, nurses, administrators and other categories of staff upon whom the quality of service so much depends. And if the quality of personal service is low, there will be less freedom of choice and more felt discrimination.

Assumption No. 3: That private markets in welfare would offer consumers more choice.

As I have said, the growth of private markets in medical care, education and other welfare services, based on ability to pay and not on criteria of need, has the effects of limiting and narrowing choice for those who depend on or who prefer to use the public services.

But let us be more specific, remembering that the essential question is: *whose* freedom of choice. Let us consider this question of choice in the one field—private pension schemes—where the insurance market already operates to a substantial extent and where the philosophy of 'free pensions for free men' holds sway.† It is, for example, maintained by the insurance industry that private schemes 'are arrangements made voluntarily by individual employers with their own workers';‡ that they are tailor-made and shaped to meet

* 'Which Way to Welfare', *Lloyds Bank Review*, October 1966.

† A. Seldon, *Pensions in a Free Society*, Institute of Economic Affairs, 1957.

‡ Life Offices' Association, *The Pension Problem: a Statement of Principle and a Review of the Labour Party's Proposals*, 1957, p. 3.

individual (consumer) requirements. This is, *par excellence*, the model of consumer choice in the private welfare market.

What are the facts? For the vast majority of workers covered by such private schemes there is no choice. Private schemes are compulsory. Workers are not offered the choice of deferred pay or higher wages; funded schemes or pay-as-you-go schemes. They are not asked to choose between contributory or non-contributory schemes; between flat-rate systems or earnings related systems. Despite consumer evidence of a widespread wish for the provision of widows' benefits, employees are not asked to choose. There is virtually no consultation with employees or their representatives. They have no control whatsoever over the investment of funds in the hands of private insurance companies which now total some £2,500 millions.* And, most important of all, they are rarely offered on redundancy or if they freely wish to change their jobs the choice of full preservation of pension rights.†

These issues of transferability and the full preservation of pension rights underline strongly the urgency and importance of the Government's current review of social security. We have now been talking for over ten years about the need for freedom of industrial movement, full transferability, and adequate, value-protected pensions as 'of right' in old age; it is time the Government's proposals were made known. But they cannot now help with the immediate problem of the redundant workers in the Midlands and other parts of the country. Have these workers forfeited their full occupational pension expectations? What choices have been concretely offered to them by the private pension market? I have seen no statements or surveys or reports from the insurance industry or from the Institute of Economic Affairs. Surely, here was a situation in which one might have expected the protagonists of private welfare markets to have assembled the facts, and to have demonstrated the superiority of practice as well as theory in the matter of consumer choice. But it looks as though they failed in 1966 as they failed in 1956 when the British Motor Corporation announced on June 27 that 6,000 employees would be sacked on June 29.‡ They were not offered the choice of full preservation of accrued-pension rights.[4]

* W. G. Nursaw, *Principles of Pension Fund Investment*, p. 19, 1966.

† See Report of a Committee of the National Joint Advisory Council, *Preservation of Pension Rights*, Ministry of Labour, HMSO, 1966; the Government Actuary, *Occupational Pension Schemes: A New Survey*, HMSO, 1966, and two forthcoming studies by T. A. Lynes, *Pensions and Democracy*, and *French Pensions*, Occasional Papers on Social Administration.

‡ H. R. Kahn, *Repercussions of Redundancy*, Allen and Unwin, 1965.

Assumption No. 4: That social services in kind, particularly medical care, have no characteristics which differentiate them from goods in the private market.

I propose to consider this last assumption in relation to medical care, and to pursue a little more intensively some of the central issues which I raised in 'Ethics and Economics of Medical Care'.[5] This was written in response to the thesis advanced by certain 'liberal' economists in Britain and the United States who, after applying neo-classical economic theory to Western-type systems of medical care, concluded that 'medical care would appear to have no characteristics which differentiate it sharply from other goods in the market'.[*] It should, therefore, be treated as a personal consumption good indistinguishable in principle from other goods. Consequently, and in terms of political action, private markets in medical care should be substituted for public markets. In support of this conclusion it is argued that the 'delicate, anonymous, continuous and pervasive' mechanism of the private market[†] not only makes more consumer choice possible but provides better services for a more discriminating public. Choice stimulates discrimination which, in turn, enlarges choice.

This thesis is usually presented as applying universally and in terms of the past as well as the present. It is presumed to apply to contemporary India and Tanzania as well as nineteenth-century Britain. It is, therefore, as a theoretical construct 'culture free'. It is also said to be value free. Medical care is a utility and all utilities are good things. But as we cannot measure the satisfactions of utilities— or compare individual satisfactions derived from different utilities— we should rely on 'revealed preferences'. Observable market behaviour will show what an individual chooses. Preference is what individuals prefer; no collective value judgment is consequently said to be involved.

In applying this body of doctrine to medical care we have to consider a large number of characteristics (or factors) which may or may not be said to differentiate medical care from personal consumption goods in the market. I want to concentrate discussion on two of these factors, chiefly because I believe that one of them is central to the whole debate about medical care, and because both of them tend to be either ignored or treated superficially by most writers on the subject. Broadly, they centre around the problems of uncertainty and unpredictability in medical care and, secondly, the difficulty, in theory as well as in practice, of treating medical care as a conceptual entity.

[*] D. S. Lees, *ibid.*, pp. 37–9 and 86–7.　　[†] D. S. Lees, *ibid.*, p. 64.

Consider first the problems of uncertainty which confront the consumer of medical care. Then contrast them with the problems of the consumer of, say, cars; there is clearly a risk to life in both situations if wrong choices are made. It is argued, for example, by Professor Lees and others that the market for consumer durables is affected both by unpredictability of personal demand and consumer ignorance about needs.* The more significant differentiating characteristics in the area of medical care would appear to be (though this is by no means an exhaustive list):

1. Many consumers do not desire medical care.
2. Many consumers do not know they need medical care.
3. Consumers who want medical care do not know in advance how much medical care they need and what it will cost.
4. Consumers do not know and can rarely estimate in advance what particular categories of medical care they are purchasing (such as surgical procedures, diagnostic tests, drugs, and so on).
5. Consumers can seldom learn from experience of previous episodes of medical care consumption (not only do illnesses, or 'needs', vary greatly but utility variability in medical care is generally far greater than is the case with consumer durables).
6. Most consumers cannot assess the value of medical care (before, during or after consumption) as an independent variable. They cannot be sure, therefore, whether they have received 'good' or 'bad' medical care. Moreover, the time-scale needed for assessment may be the total life duration.
7. Most consumers of medical care enter the doctor-patient relationship on an unequal basis; they believe that the doctor or surgeon knows best. Unlike market relationships in the case of consumer durables, they know that this special inequality in knowledge and techniques cannot for all practical purposes be reversed.
8. Medical care can seldom be returned to the seller, exchanged for durable goods or discarded. For many people the consequences of consuming medical care are irreversible.
9. Medical care knowledge is not at present a marketable advertised commodity. Nor can consumers exchange comparable valid information about the consumption of 'good' or 'bad' medical care.
10. Consumers of medical care experience greater difficulties in changing their minds in the course of consuming care than do consumers of durable goods.
11. Consumers of medical care may, knowingly or unknowingly, take part in or be the subject of research, teaching and controlled experiments which may affect the outcome.

* D. S. Lees, *ibid.*, p. 87.

12. The concept of 'normal' or 'average' economic behaviour on the part of adult consumers, built into private enterprise medical care models, cannot be applied automatically to the mentally ill, the mentally retarded, the seriously disabled and other categories of consumer-patients.

13. Similarly, this concept of 'normal' behaviour cannot be applied automatically to immigrant populations or peoples with non-Western cultures and different beliefs and value systems.

These thirteen characteristics are indicative of the many subtle aspects of uncertainty and unpredictability which pervade modern medical care systems. 'I hold', wrote Professor K. J. Arrow, in an article entitled 'Uncertainty and the Welfare Economics of Medical Care', in the *American Economic Review*,* 'that virtually all the special features of this (medical care) industry, in fact, stem from the prevalence of uncertainty.'

To grasp fully the significance of these differentiating character-istics, each one of them should be contrasted with the situation of the consumer of cars or other consumption goods; an exercise which I cheerfully leave to the reader.

I turn now to my second set of questions. Many economists who attempt to apply theories and construct models in this particular area conduct their analyses on the assumption that 'medical care' is (or can be treated as) an entity. Historically, perhaps this may once have been marginally valid when it consisted almost wholly of the personal doctor-patient relationship. Medical cure, we would now say, was more a matter fifty years ago of spontaneous biological response or random chance.

Science, technology and economic growth have now, however, transformed medical care into a group process: a matter of the organized application of an immense range of specialized skills, techniques, resources and systems. If, therefore, we now wish to examine medical care from the standpoint of economic theory we need to break down this vague and generalized concept 'medical care' into precise and distinctive components.

To illustrate the importance of doing so let us consider one example; probably one of the more critical components in curative medicine today, namely, the procurement, processing, matching, distribution, financing and transfusion of whole human blood. Is human blood a consumption good?

With the data now available relating to different blood procure-ment programmes in various countries, organized on private market principles and community welfare principles, it is now possible to

* Vol. LIII, No. 5, December 1963.

consider these economic theories relating to choice and revealed preferences in respect of this particular component of medical care. Consider, first, the thesis that the 'delicate mechanism' of the market works better if left by government to get on with the job: that it is more efficient; provides higher quality services; by allowing choice it generates more demand; and that it results in proportionately higher national expenditures on medical care than socialized systems like the National Health Service. Economists in Britain, West Germany and other countries who advance this thesis support it by drawing on American macro-economic data.

It is appropriate, therefore, to examine the blood transfusion services in New York City and contrast them with the National Blood Transfusion Service in England and Wales. National statistics for the USA are fragmentary and defective in many respects. One reason is the great variety from area to area in the programmes of the American Red Cross, community, hospital and commercial blood banks and services. More information is, however, available for particular cities and areas. It must not be assumed that what obtains in New York is generally applicable in the USA. For a community of some 8 million people, New York uses about 330,000 pints of blood a year.* In England and Wales in 1965 the number of blood donations totalled approximately 1.3 million.† It is variously guessed for the USA as a whole that some six million pints of blood are collected annually.‡

Figures of this order indicate the indispensable and increasingly vital part played by blood transfusion services in modern medicine. The transfer of blood from one human being to another represents one of the greatest therapeutic instruments in the hands of the doctor. It has made possible the saving of life on a scale undreamt of a few decades ago and for conditions which would then have been considered hopeless. The demand for blood increases yearly in every Western country as new uses are developed; as more radical surgical techniques are adopted which are associated with the loss of massive amounts of blood; as road accidents continue to rise; and with the increasingly widespread use of artificial heart-lung machines in open heart surgery (first developed in Britain in 1950) and for numerous other reasons. It is a precious commodity yet in Britain (with a wholly voluntary programme of blood donations) without price. If

* The New York Blood Centre, *Progress Report for 1965*, Community Blood Council of Greater New York, Inc., 1965.
† *Annual Report of the Ministry of Health for 1965*, Cmnd 3039, 1966, Table 75.
‡ American Medical Association, *Directory of Blood Banking and Transfusion Facilities and Services*, Chicago, 1965.

carelessly or wrongfully used it can be more lethal than many drugs. Because of the risks of transmitting the virus of infective hepatitis (homologous serum hepatitis) and other diseases the most rigorous standards are set in Britain in the selection of blood donors, and in the cross-matching, testing and transfusion of blood.

Not only is human blood potentially lethal to the recipient but it has the critical characteristic of '21-day perishability'. Its value rapidly expires. This particular characteristic presents great administrative and technical problems in the operation of blood transfusion services; in the estimation of demand for blood of different groups; in the organization, planning and execution of blood donor programmes; in the technical organization of compatibility tests and cross-matching; and in the distribution of supplies of whole blood in the right quantities and categories, at the right times, and to the right hospitals and the right patients.

After this brief explanation of some of the important factors to bear in mind, I want now to present some information about the present situation in New York. Despite the fact that there are over 150 independent agencies handling blood in New York, some operating on a profit basis and many buying blood from so-called 'professional' donors, there is an acute and chronic shortage of blood.* Operations are postponed daily because of the shortage. 'Professional' donors from 'Skid Row denizens', drug addicts and others who live by selling their blood (at $10 to $25 or more a pint) are often bled more frequently than accepted international standards recommend, and far more frequently than the much higher standard set in Britain.† There is evidence from a number of American cities in which studies have been made that something like 30 to 40 per cent of paid blood donors are unemployed and predominantly unskilled workers. In Chicago, the Blood Donor Service reported a figure of 40.6 per cent for 1965.‡ In 1964, the latest year available, 60 per cent of all donors bled by this service were paid.

The shortage of blood in New York and other cities is in part due to a large amount of wasted blood (resulting from blood-hoarding by hospitals and other agencies) and to the hazardous quality of 'professional' blood. In consequence, blood charges and blood bills remitted to patients are high. Some commercial blood banks in New York import blood from Tennessee, and such banks in the USA have attempted to import blood from England and Australia.

* The New York Blood Centre, *ibid.*, pp. 2–11.

† R. F. Norris, *et al, Transfusion*, 3, pp. 202–9, 1963, and *Medical World News*, March 15, 1963.

‡ Personal correspondence with Medical Director, July-August, 1966.

The New York Academy of Medicine reported in 1956 that the city was relying on 'professional' donors to the extent of about 42 per cent for its blood supplies.* In 1965 the estimated figure was 55 per cent.† 'Professional' donors cannot be expected to be as truthful in clinical history-taking as unpaid volunteers. Studies at the University of Chicago and elsewhere have demonstrated that the chances of the 'professional' donor being a carrier of hepatitis 'are essentially six times greater than those of the volunteer or family donor'.‡ The virus cannot be detected in the laboratory. The patient is the test. The doctor is thus faced with the choice of withholding blood or transfusing blood which may have been obtained from a 'professional' donor—if he knows, which he rarely does, the source of the blood.

In Britain, the situation is incomparably different. There is no shortage of blood. It is freely donated by the community for the community. It is a free gift from the healthy to the sick irrespective of income, class, ethnic group, religion, private patient or public patient. Since the National Health Service was established the quantity of blood issued to hospitals has risen by 265 per cent.§

The question I have raised whether human blood is a trading commodity, a market good like aspirins or cars, or a service rendered by the community for the community, is no idle academic question asked in a philosophical mood. In the last few years it has become in the USA a battleground for lawyers and economists. The costs incurred by respondents in debating this question in one case alone (involving the Federal Trade Commission and a blood bank in Kansas City) have amounted to $250,000.‖ Dr R. L. Mainwaring, President-elect in 1964 of the American Association of Blood Banks, has said that if blood is legally designated as a commodity (thus endorsing commercial practice), 'hospital insurance rates would go sky high. The laboratory director would not be able to rely on anyone else to screen his blood; he would have to do it himself. And, even with perfect cross-matches he could expect that one out of every 200 pints he provided would carry hepatitis virus.'¶

There is much more that I could say (and shall hope to say elsewhere[6]) on these complex issues. But I find no support here for

* *Human Blood in New York City* (privately circulated), New York Academy of Medicine, Committee on Public Health, 1956.
† New York Blood Centre, private communication from Dr A. Kellner, June 1966.
‡ J. Garrott Allen and W. A. Sayman, JAMA, 180: 1079, 1962.
§ *Annual Reports of the Ministry of Health.*
‖ *Transfusion*, 5, 2: 207, March-April, 1963.
¶ *Ibid.*, 4: 68, 1964.

the model of choice in the private market; on criteria of efficiency, of efficacy, of quality, or of safety. No consumer can estimate, in advance, the nature of these and other hazards; few, in any event, will know that they are to be the recipient of someone else's blood. In this private market in New York and other American cities the consumer is not sovereign. He has less choice; he is simultaneously exposed to greater hazards; he pays a far higher price for a more hazardous service; he pays, in addition, for all the waste in the system; and he further pays for an immense and swollen bureaucracy required to administer a complex banking system of credits, deposits, charges, transfers and so forth. Above all, it is a system which neglects and punishes the indigent, the coloured, the dispossessed and the deviant.

The characteristics of uncertainty and unpredictability are the dominating ones in this particular component of medical care. They are the product of scientific advances accentuated, as this study shows, by the application of inapplicable economic theories to the procurement and distribution of human blood.

I draw one other conclusion from this discussion. Socialism is about community as well as equality. It is about what we contribute without price to the community and how we act and live as socialists —and not just about how we debate socialism.

NOTES

1. See, for example, Lees, D. S., 'Health Through Choice', in Harris, R., *Freedom or Free-for-all?*, Hobart Papers, Vol. 3, The Institute of Economic Affairs, 1965, and West, E. G., *Education and the State*, The Institute of Economic Affairs, 1965.
2. 'Welfare recipients in New York who live in rat-infested buildings can receive a so-called "rat allowance" to cover the cost of keeping their lights burning all night long' (Cloward, R. A., and Elman, R. M., 'Poverty, Injustice and the Welfare State', *The Nation*, February 28, 1966).
3. Seven of the eleven-man committee which drew up the Ministry of Health and Department of Health for Scotland's *Report of the Committee to Consider the Future Numbers of Medical Practitioners and the Appropriate Intake of Medical Students* (HMSO, 1957), were eminent members of the medical profession and the chairman was an ex-Minister of Health, Sir Henry Willink. In May 1962 a special committee set up by the British Medical Association to consider recruitment to the medical profession concluded in its report that in spite of certain obvious indications of a shortage of doctors it was not prepared to commit itself on the need for more medical students (*The Times*, May 11, 1962). Dr R. G. Gibson, chairman of this committee (and now Chairman of the Council), said two months later that the profession had recently experienced a 'glut of doctors. At present there seemed to be a

shortage, but care must be taken not to create unemployment in the profession a few years from now' (*Brit. Med. J.*, Supp., **ii**, July 26, 28, 1962).
4. For a discussion of the concept of 'full preservation' see Ministry of Labour, *ibid.*; Lynes, T. A., *ibid.*, and other references in Chapter XV.
5. See Chapter XXI and also criticisms of this study by Professor Lees, Professor Jewkes and others in *Medical Care*, Vol. 1, No. 4, 1963, pp. 234–44, and Lees, D. S., 'Health Through Choice', in *Freedom or Free-for-all?* (Ed., R. Harris), Hobart Papers, Vol. 3, The Institute of Economic Affairs, 1965.
6. The writer has in preparation a book examining the ethics and economics of blood transfusion services in Britain and the USA. The material cited here is only a fragment of all the relevant data. Allen and Unwin hope to publish this book shortly.

Chapter XIII

SOCIAL POLICY AND ECONOMIC PROGRESS*

As large-scale industrialized societies get richer in material terms what is the future for social welfare? Shall we not all, or at any rate the vast majority, have incomes and assets large enough in the future to satisfy our social welfare needs in the private market without help from the State? Should not we have the right to decide our own individual resource preferences and priorities and buy from the private market our own quantities of education, medical care, housing, social security, mental health services, social work support and other services?

Such questions as these are being asked today in Britain; chiefly, I must say, by economists who are more cheerful professionals these days than they used to be when they were specialists in slump and depression, and laid claim to being the pre-eminent 'dismal scientists'. Similar questions are also being asked in Western Germany and in the United States, notably by the distinguished economist Milton Friedman[1] and his followers.

This is not, I would guess, the first time in history that the fundamental issue of the role of the State in the field of social welfare has been debated at the National Conference on Social Welfare; the conflict over individualism and collectivism developed long before the human race decided to invent the social worker. What is relatively new, and startlingly new, in the long history of man's preoccupation with poverty is the fact and the prospect of material abundance. We have only to compare the gross national products of the United States, Canada, Britain, Sweden, France, Western Germany and other industrialized countries in 1945 with the levels achieved in 1965 to realize how much richer as societies we have become in the short space of twenty years. Though there may be in the future as in the recent past periods of relative stagnation, nevertheless, on a long view our societies are steadily getting richer. Barring the utter disaster of international war, we have, therefore, to

* Lecture delivered at the American National Conference on Social Welfare in Chicago, USA, in May 1966, and published in *The Social Welfare Forum* (official proceedings), Columbia University Press, New York, 1966.

prepare ourselves and the next generation for living in very rich societies; rich in the possession of material goods and rich in leisure —or nonwork time. In the next ten years, I am told, the American GNP is expected to rise to a trillion dollars.

What, then, is the future role of social policy? Is it to wither away as social welfare returns to its nineteenth-century residual function of custodial care for a small minority of the population? Are we to assume that the critical social problems of poverty, discrimination, unfreedom and violence that face our societies today will steadily disappear at the behest of economic growth and an expanding private market?

Some economic analysts in Britain noting, in recent years, the rise in national income and wealth have begun to present forcefully the case for the private market in education, medical care and social security.[2] Unlike their distinguished predecessors, they do not condemn these instruments of social policy as politically irrelevant or mistaken in the past. They are needed then as temporary *ad hoc* political mechanisms to ameliorate and reduce social conflict, to protect the rights of property, and to avoid resort to violence by the dispossessed and the deprived. This contemporary redefinition of the past role of social policy thus represents it as a form of social control; as a temporary, short-term process of state intervention to buttress and legitimate industrial capitalism during its early, faltering but formative years of growth. Those, we are now told, who in the past were critical of State intervention in the guise of social policy were misguided and shortsighted. The Bourbons of today disavow the Bourbons of yesterday. The times, the concepts and the market have all changed. They have been changed by affluence, by technology and by the development of more sophisticated, anonymous and flexible mechanisms of the market to meet social needs, to enlarge the freedom of consumer choice and to provide not only more but better education, medical care, housing and social security.

In abbreviated form, these are some of the theories of private social policy now being advanced in Britain and, no doubt, by likeminded analysts in the United States. Paradoxically, at first sight, they have seized upon and welcomed the reformulation of a 'negative income tax' (or tax allowances in reverse) extended to the poor and low-wage earners. For the State to bring about in this way through the fiscal system a minimal degree of income redistribution should lead to a gradual disengagement from the direct provision of public services in kind, such as education, housing and medical care. If the poor are provided with a little more purchasing power their other needs should be treated as consumption goods to be purchased in the private market—so runs the argument.

Like other conceptions of social policy, presented in such large and all-embracing terms, this theory makes a number of assumptions about the future economic characteristics of our societies. These need to be examined; moreover, in the process of doing so we may be helped to redefine the role of social policy in contemporary terms.

One fundamental assumption underlying this theory is that the present pattern of income and wealth differentials, which determine each individual's command over resources through time, will continue—and by implication should continue—in the future. It is accepted, of course, that absolute standards will rise for everyone; that the $3,000 family will become in x years and in real terms the $6,000 family (a doubling of purchasing power); the $100,000 family will become the $200,000 family, and so on. This assumption implies that the invisible resource allocation of the market will bring about, without the intervention of public policies, an equal proportional rise in living standards for all individuals and families. It further implies, as a social good, that the absolute differences should widen; that the gap between these two families in pretax incomes should double from $97,000 at present to $194,000 in the future. While this increase in inequality may, of course, be somewhat diminished by the effects of progressive taxation, there will occur, nevertheless, a great increase in the absolute gap unless taxation becomes far more sharply progressive in its impact than it is at present. Those who advocate this private market theory do not, however, call for a more progressive system of direct taxation. On the contrary, they argue for more tax cuts.

In short, according to this model of economic progress, within which is incorporated a declining role for social welfare, what is central is the promise of a doubling of the standard of living for everyone, including the poor. Poverty, as defined by the values and standards of 1966, will virtually disappear; meanwhile, the absolute differences in income and wealth will widen greatly. Economic models, for all their appearance of neutrality, may also be value-judgment models.

A second fundamental assumption, which follows closely from the first assumption that the competitive market is and will continue to be an efficient and proportionately just allocator of resources, concerns the divergence between social costs and private costs. We know, in general, that the diseconomies and disservices involved in the production and consumption of goods do inflict damage on nonconsumers and third parties—in such forms, for

155

example, as urban blight, slum ghettos, air and river pollution, the destruction of aesthetic amenities, ill-health, industrial injuries, the invasion of privacy, and so on. Many of these damages and disservices to the 'quality of life', which may also involve harm to the values of honesty, self-development, creativity and respect for civil rights, represent noneconomic variables which no statistician or economist has yet been able to quantify in dollars and pounds.

Similarly, while we may recognize the significance to human beings of the disutilities and disservices of technological and scientific changes, nevertheless, we still cannot adequately measure their effects. The social as well as the economic damages wrought by these changes are often borne by those who do not immediately benefit, and they may create new needs for more than one generation. Some of the more obvious and striking examples in this area of generational social cost-benefit analysis are: the effects of automation on employment, on the obsolescence of acquired skills and on family stability; the impact of new scientific discoveries like thalidomide in generating a lifetime of personal dependency; the social, psychological and economic effects on those rejected as well as those accepted of rising standards of admission to educational systems, vocational and professional training, employment, promotion, occupational welfare, fringe benefits, middle-class housing areas, and even job corps programmes. Have we really any conception of the psychological effects on people of a continual process of social rejection and exclusion? Yet economic growth tends continuously to build ever higher these gateways to life and freedom of choice, and to widen the area over which credentialism rules;[3] the crowd outside finds it harder to clamber over, squeeze through, or look over the top.

In all these sectors relating to the divergence between social costs and private costs created partly by the disutilities of progress there is in continual motion an extensive and complex system of redistribution in life chances and command over resources. It is largely an uncompensated area; almost wholly uncompensated by the competitive market and only to a limited extent by law and social policy through the agency of public assistance and other social security instruments, retraining and work programmes, public education, housing and social welfare programmes. The reasons for the lack of compensation for damages and disservices are many and various; they lie in our inability to identify the victims; to name and hold responsible the causal agents, and to measure in material terms the social costs of change and economic progress. Other and related reasons have to be sought in the realm of values; in the deeply held belief, for instance, that men who are poor and sick deserve to be poor and sick, and that those who are excluded from society merit exclusion. They are the social pathologies of other people's progress.

These two assumptions about the future concerning income and wealth differentials and social costs and private costs are, I suggest, implicit in the model of economic progress I have instanced—a model we might call the 'optimistic automated model'. It is a model which tends to create the impression that economic growth is a problem in economics alone. We thereby find ourselves, as Gross has remarked, saddled with a new form of Gresham's Law: monetary information—or dollar number magic—of *lesser* significance tends to displace other information which may be of *greater* significance.[4]

Three central questions can now, I think, be formulated. First, will economic growth in a competitive market situation result in fair shares for all in proportionate terms with social policy performing a role in the economy similar to the one it plays now? In other words, is there in the dynamics of growth in our societies a 'natural', evolutionary, inherent tendency toward equality of distribution? As we become richer do we become more equal?

Secondly, is this tendency (supposing, for the moment, that it exists) toward fair shares for all in the product of future growth strong enough to allow a run-down in the proportionate role of social policy as a redistributive agent? In other words, will a doubling of the real income of the poor as well as the rich in x years (if it should take place) make possible a progressive decline in the role of social welfare—quite apart from the issue as to whether such a decline is or is not desirable?

Now I come to my third question, the most difficult of all to project into space. What can we say about the future consequences and costs of economic growth and of scientific, technological and social change? How will these consequences and costs of change be distributed and borne, and to what extent will they (or indeed can they) be compensated for in a profit-maximizing market? Can the market, for example, as an economic system resolve the problems of ethnic integration and accommodation? This is an important question now for Britain as well as for the United States.

What is indisputable is that in the last two decades the rate of change in highly industrialized societies has been rapid and pervasive, probably more rapid than in any similar period of time this century. There is, in general, no evidence that this rate of change is slowing down. It may even be expanding rapidly as more sophisticated techniques of production, distribution and supply are mastered and applied, and as medical science breaks new ground in the potential prevention of death and the prolongation of life. The addition of only five years to the existing biological life span for men as well as women, the poor as well as the rich, could present our societies with a set of immensely challenging problems.

With all that we now know, and recalling the enormous growth in scientific and technological research investment by Western society since the 1940s, it is reasonable to suppose that social and economic changes are likely to be as rapid—and probably more so —in the future as they have been in the recent past. Indeed, much of this research effort has not yet been generally applied in practice. Many years elapse before the full impact of research and innovation is experienced by the generality of individuals and families. It has also to be remembered, as Wilbert Moore has observed, that as the range of material technology and social strategies expands the net effects are additive or cumulative, despite the relatively rapid obsolescence of some procedures.[5]

This particular question concerning change is important for two reasons. First, the social costs of change rarely enter into the calculations and models of economists. They measure what they can more easily count. As yet, we cannot quantify in material terms social misery and ill-health, the effects of unemployment, slum life and Negro removal, the denial of education and civil rights, and the cumulative side effects from generation to generation of allowing cynicism and apathy to foster and grow. These are some of the costs which appear inescapably to accompany social and technical change. They are not embodied in any index of 'real' income *per capita*. We have, therefore, to remind ourselves continuously about their reality, partly because we happen to be living in a scientific age which tends to associate the measurable with the significant; to dismiss as intangible that which eludes measurement; and to reach conclusions on the basis of only those things which lend themselves to measurement.[6] Mathematical casework is not yet, I am glad to say, on the horizon.

Secondly, the facts of change are important because we need to ask questions about how these social costs—part of the *raison d'être* of social policy—are distributed, and may be distributed in the future, among the population by age, sex, family structure, ethnic group, income, and so forth. Is technological unemployment widely distributed or is it highly concentrated among certain groups? Who are the victims of depressed areas? Who bears the social costs of urban renewal or of 'gray-area' life? The answers to these and similar questions are critical for social policy, but, as yet, social scientists have been slow to develop techniques of analysis and indicators of positive and negative social growth. Different conclusions will be reached and different solutions required if the effects of change are widely experienced by rich and poor alike or if they are highly concentrated in certain social groups and areas.

At the heart of these speculations about the future distribution of social costs and the future of social policy lies the problem of stigma or 'spoiled identity', to use Goffman's phrase;[7] of felt and experienced discrimination and disapproval on grounds of moral behaviour, ethnic group, class, age, measured intelligence, mental fitness, or other criteria of selection-rejection. I believe that S. M. Miller was profoundly right when he wrote: 'The need in our society is for differentiation without stigma.'[8] There is, I think, no escaping the conclusion that if we are effectively to reach the poor we must differentiate and discriminate. We have to do so if we wish to channel proportionately more economic and social resources to aid the poor and the handicapped, and to compensate them as best we can for bearing part of the social costs of other people's progress.

The problem, then, is not whether to differentiate in access, treatment, giving and outcome but *how* to differentiate. What factors are or are not relevant? How in some respects can we treat equals unequally and in other respects unequals equally? We cannot now disengage ourselves from the challenge of distributing social rights without stigma; too many unfulfilled expectations have been created, and we can no longer fall back on the rationale that our economies are too poor to avoid hurting people.

This is, moreover, an issue which may well determine the future health of the professions—social work, medicine, education, nursing, public administration, and many others. They are, in many respects, the decision-makers of differentiation, the arbiters of welfare. To disengage themselves from the poor, as some social workers and physicians have tended to do in recent years,[9] is no answer for society. It could only mean, if such a trend continued, an ultimate decline in the ethical component in professional service.

But this is a controversial matter which cannot be pursued here. We must return to consider the questions and assumptions implicit in various economic models, an example of which is 'the optimistic automated model' I referred to earlier.

How valid are the assumptions, implicit and explicit, in such models? What evidence is there from the recent history of highly industrialized countries to confirm or refute these assumptions? Such questions can now be properly asked; for similar, though perhaps less sophisticated, models of economic progress played a powerful role in the shaping of policies fifteen to twenty years ago in both the United States and Britain.

I propose briefly to re-examine them; for the history of successful and unsuccessful essays in 'prediction' in the past may help us to construct more viable models for the future. At the very least, we may learn something from our failures that will help us to understand the nature of our societies and the process of change.

Around 1950 a number of propositions concerning economic growth and the role of social policy gained wide acceptance in Britain. It was said that:

1. Inequalities in the distribution of income and wealth were diminishing at a substantial rate.
2. Poverty would soon be virtually abolished (apart from a residual minority of incorrigibles and incompetents) under the impact of economic growth, full employment, and the redistributive effects of the social services (more vaguely described as 'the Welfare State').
3. Educational outcomes (or achievements) as well as opportunities were rapidly widening for all classes and income groups in the population.
4. Within a decade or so the housing problem would be largely solved, the slums abolished, and the objective of a 'decent home for every family' achieved.
5. As a consequence of these changes, and with the added effects of a free National Health Service ('socialized medicine'), income and social class differences in mortality and morbidity would soon dissolve.

It would be wrong to describe these as scientific predictions. They were not; but they did enter into the attempts of economists and policy-makers to estimate the future of the economy, and they are representative of a large body of genuine opinion at that time. Underlying them was the assumption of a declining role for social policy in the foreseeable future.

Similar opinions were current in the United States at about the same time, though less emphasis than in Britain was given to the issue of social stratification in education and other spheres since it was believed that the United States was a more mobile, egalitarian society. The first chairman of the Council of Economic Advisers under the Eisenhower Administration reflected these opinions about the efficiency of economic growth as a just allocator of resources when he said in 1951 (before his appointment to the Council):

'The transformation in the distribution of our national income . . . may already be counted as one of the great social revolutions in history.'[10]

Economic growth spelled progress—an evolutionary and inevitable American faith that social growth would accompany economic growth. Automatically, therefore, poverty would gracefully succumb to the diffusion of abundance. All this heralded, as Daniel Bell wrote ten years later, the end of 'ideological conflict'.[11]

Since the end of the 1940s our societies have indeed prospered. Economic growth has occurred on a scale and at a rate which few experts were prepared to suggest as targets fifteen years ago. What, then, has gone wrong?

Let us suppose, for one brief moment, that we are all back in the census year 1951, looking younger, just as intelligent, but wearing clothes which would now seem a little odd. Let us further suppose that we are convinced by our economists and policy-makers that the United States and Britain would be much wealthier societies in material terms within fifteen years. How many of us would then have dared to suggest that in 1966 one American child in four would be regarded as living in poverty and three elderly persons in ten would also be living in poverty;[12] that American society would be moving toward a more unequal distribution of income and wealth;[13] that many gray areas would have become ghettos;[14] that a nationwide civil rights challenge of explosive magnitude would have to be faced—a challenge for freedom, for the right to work, for a decent home, for medical care, and against stigma;[15] that, as a nation, the United States would be seriously short of physicians, scientists, teachers, social workers, nurses, welfare aides, and professional workers in almost all categories of personal service; and that it would be importing physicians, nurses, scientists, engineers, and other categories of human capital from many less affluent nations of the world?

In Britain, in 1951, there were few who would have thought that in the years ahead the proportion of children and old people considered to be living in poverty would increase;[16] that incomes would become more unequal;[17] that the distribution of personal wealth would be found to be more highly concentrated in the top 5 per cent of the population (and much more highly concentrated than in the United States);[18] that there would be no narrowing of differentials between working-class and middle-class children in the higher sectors of the educational system;[19] that the immigration of about 750,000 'coloured' people from the Commonwealth (or less than 2 per cent of the population) would result in illiberal policies and discrimination;[20] and that, like the United States, Britain would also be facing serious shortages of physicians, nurses, teachers, social workers, town planners, and many other categories of professional workers.

These trends have occurred in both our countries in a period of not only unprecedented economic advances but of progressive developments in certain sectors of social policy: significantly, in education and social security in the United States; significantly, in medical care, employment and national (public) assistance in Britain. Had social policies been less influential during these years; had there been less intervention by government (as some social analysts had advocated in the early 1950s), then, I believe, the trend toward inequality would have been more marked.

These are some of the lessons of history. They could, of course, be more fully described and documented; for there has been, particularly in the United States, a veritable explosion in recent years of research, demonstrations, projects, reports, and books on poverty and social deprivation. The poor are showing a remarkable tolerance about their re-emergence on the national stage as subjects for investigation, inquiry and doctoral theses.

One thing I am sure we are doing by all these searchings into poverty is to raise expectations—expectations of freedom from want, stigma, ignorance and social exclusion. If we are not to fail our fellow citizens again we might do worse than ponder on some of these 'lessons of the last fifteen years of welfare'. Perhaps I might make a start by offering a few generalizations about our past errors of omission and commission.

In the climate of political and social thought around the early 1950s there was a tendency to underestimate the significance for the future of social policy of a number of major forces and trends.

1. We underestimated the extent and rate of obsolescence of much of our social capital (houses, schools, hospitals, universities, welfare offices, public buildings, and so forth).
2. We underestimated the rate and effects of change, scientific, technological and economic, and thus we ignored or greatly minimized the impact of social costs on the poor, the unskilled and the underprivileged.
3. We underestimated the effects on people of stigma, discrimination, and the denial of civil rights (see, for example, Hughes's critique of sociology for failing to foresee the coming of the civil rights movement in the United States).[21]
4. We underestimated the cumulative forces and effects of selection

162

through the educational system, the labour market and the housing market; in other words, we failed to conceptualize the process of cumulative causation in these areas of deprivation.

5. We underestimated the extent of poverty and oversimplified its definition and causal origins.

But while we seriously underestimated the importance of some factors we greatly exaggerated the likely effect of others:

1. We overestimated the potentialities of economic growth by itself alone to solve the problems of poverty, economic, educational and social.

2. We exaggerated the trend toward equality during the Second World War in respect to income, employment and other factors—as we persistently have done for the last half century—and optimistically projected short-term trends into the future.

3. We exaggerated the effects of welfare programmes on incentives to work and moral values in general, and helped to create what we feared by nourishing systems of 'policing' and 'punishment'.

4. We overestimated the capacity of professional organizations, particularly in medicine and social work, to expand recruitment and training to meet present and future demands.

5. We overestimated the potentialities of the poor, without help, to understand and manipulate an increasingly complex *ad hoc* society, and we failed to understand the indignities of expecting the poor to identify themselves as poor people and to declare, in effect, 'I am an unequal person.'

6. We greatly exaggerated the capacity of the competitive private market to resolve social problems and to meet needs on the principle of differentiation without stigma.

7. Lastly, and perhaps most significant of all, we have sought too diligently to find the causes of poverty among the poor and not in ourselves. Poverty, we seem to have been saying, has its origins *either* in social pathology and a lack of self-determination *or* in agency delinquency and a failure in co-ordination *or* in the shortage of social workers and psychiatrists. Now, in the poverty programme, the United States appears to be discovering a new set of causal explanations—the lack of political power amongst the poor themselves. 'The fault, dear Brutus, is not in our stars, but in ourselves, that we are underlings.'

The historical study of the concept of social policy has, I believe, something to offer us. If there is any validity in these generalizations they suggest that our frame of reference in the past has been too narrow. Thought, research and action have been focused too heavily on the poor; poverty engineering has thus been abstracted from society. Social policy has been seen as an *ad hoc* appendage to economic growth, the provision of benefits, not the formulation of rights.

If we are in the future to include the poor in our societies we shall have to widen our frames of reference. We shall need to shift the emphasis from poverty to inequality, from *ad hoc* programmes to integrated social rights, from economic growth to social growth.

And what, in the end, do I mean by 'social growth'? When our societies are spending proportionately more on the educationally deprived than on the educationally normal; when the rehousing of the poor is proceeding at a greater rate than the rehousing of the middle classes; when proportionately more medical care is being devoted to the needs of the long-term chronically sick than to those of the average sick; when more social workers are moving into public programmes than into private child guidance clinics; when there are smaller differentials in incomes and assets between rich and poor, coloured and pink families.

These are a few among many of the quantifiable indicators of social growth that we could take pride in, the new status symbols of an 'affluent society'.

NOTES

1. Friedman, Milton, *Capitalism and Freedom*, University of Chicago Press, Chicago, 1962.
2. For example, Lees, D. S., *Health Through Choice*, Institute of Economic Affairs, London, 1961, and West, E. G., *Education and the State*, Institute of Economic Affairs, London, 1965.
3. For example, at present in the United States between 150,000,000 and 250,000,000 copies of several thousand different standardized ability tests—IQ, aptitude and achievement—are administered annually by schools, colleges, government agencies, business firms and the military services. See Goslin, David A., *The Search for Ability*, Russell Sage Foundation, New York, 1963, p. 13.
4. Gross, Bertram M., 'The Social State of the Union', *Trans-Action*, III, No. 1, 15, 1965.
5. Moore, Wilbert E., *Social Change*, Prentice-Hall, Englewood Cliffs, NJ, 1963, p. 2.
6. This is true even though many of the things which are measured and included in national accounts and tax reports contain a great amount of statistical error and guesswork. See 1966 reports on tax assessments in California, *The Economist*, March 5, 1966, p. 901; Morgenstern, O., *On the Accuracy of Economic Observation*, Princeton University Press, 1963, and Titmuss, R. M., *Income Distribution and Social Change*, Allen and Unwin, London, 1962.

7. Goffman, Erving, *Stigma; Notes on the Management of Spoiled Identity*, Prentice-Hall, Englewood Cliffs, NJ, 1963.
8. Miller, S. M., 'The Search for an Educational Revolution', in Hunnicut, C. W. (Ed.), *Urban Education and Cultural Deprivation*, Syracuse University Press, Syracuse, NY, 1965.
9. See, for example, Cloward, Richard A., 'Social Problems, Social Definitions and Social Opportunities', National Council on Crime and Delinquency, New York, 1963, mimeographed; Titmuss, R. M., 'The Ethics and Economics of Medical Care', *Medical Care*, I, No. 1, 1963, pp. 16–22.
10. Quoted in Miller, H. T., 'Is the Income Gap Closed? "No" ', New York *Times Magazine*, November 11, 1962, p. 50.
11. Bell, David, *The End of Ideology: on the Exhaustion of Political Ideas in the Fifties*, Collier Books, New York, 1961.
12. Orshansky, Mollie, 'Children of the Poor', *Social Security Bulletin*, XXVI, No. 7, 1963, pp. 3–13; Orshansky, 'Counting the Poor: Another Look at the Poverty Profile', *ibid.*, XXVIII, No. 1, 1965, pp. 1–29; Orshansky, 'Who's Who among the Poor: a Demographic View of Poverty', *ibid.*, XXVIII, No. 7, 1965, pp. 13–32.
13. Brady, D. S., *Age and the Income Distribution*, Research Report No. 8, Social Security Administration, US Department of Health, Education and Welfare, 1965. For other evidence on recent trends see Miller, S. M., and Rein, Martin, 'Poverty, Inequality and Policy', in Becker, H. S. (Ed.), *Social Problems*, John Wiley, New York, 1967.
14. See Hunter, David R., *The Slums: Challenge and Response*, Free Press of Glencoe, New York, 1964; Gans, Herbert J., *The Urban Villagers*, Free Press of Glencoe, New York, 1962; Taeuber, Karl E., 'Residential Segregation', *Scientific American*, CCXIII, 1965, p. 12, and Taeuber, Karl E., and Taeuber, Alma F., *Negroes in Cities: Residential Segregation and Neighbourhood Change*, Aldine, Chicago, 1965.
15. Office of Policy Planning and Research, US Department of Labor, *The Negro Family: the Case for National Action*, Washington, DC, 1965.
16. Abel-Smith, Brian, and Townsend, Peter, *The Poor and the Poorest*, Bell and Sons, London, 1965.
17. *Ibid.*; Nicholson, J. L., *Redistribution of Income in the United Kingdom*, Bowes and Bowes, London, 1965, and Titmuss, R. M., *Income Distribution and Social Change*, Allen and Unwin, London, 1962.
18. Revell, J. R. S., 'Changes in the Social Distribution of Property in Britain during the Twentieth Century', in Proceedings of the Third International Economic History Conference, 1965 (forthcoming).
19. Moser, C A , *Inequalities in Educational Opportunities*, London School of Economics, London, 1965.
20. White Paper, *Immigration from the Commonwealth*, HMSO, Cmnd 2739, London, 1965.
21. Hughes, Everett C., 'Race Relations and the Sociological Imagination', *American Sociological Review*, XXVIII, 1963, 879–90.

Chapter XIV

CHILD POVERTY AND CHILD ENDOWMENT*

CHILD ENDOWMENT REAPPRAISAL?

Public opinion has been slow to recognize the significance of three factors for the future development of social policies which concern the family and child endowment. The first is that Britain is experiencing a Western-type population explosion. The second is that it has absentmindedly evolved a remarkably generous pronatalist policy for a section of its population. The third is the accumulating evidence of hardship among substantial numbers of children of low wage-earners, fatherless families and other handicapped parental categories.

As to the first, the facts are fairly clear. Since 1955 the birth rate has risen sharply and continuously. Over one million more children have been born in England and Wales in the past nine years than were expected by the official population projections made in 1955. By 1964 the annual excess had reached 200,000. It would be an understatement to say that this trend has surprised population experts. In 1955, in tentatively looking to the future, they had to take account of the preceding ninety years which had seen a continuous fall in fertility in Britain. Equally surprising is the fact that the continuing upward trend in Britain is not in evidence in many other Western countries.

The latest official projections for England and Wales indicate a rise in the annual number of live births from 665,000 in 1955 and 875,000 in 1964 to 1,323,000 in 2000—a doubling in forty-five years.[1] Even if these trends continue only up to 1980 there will be 4,250,000 more children born in England and Wales during 1964–80 than were expected in 1955.

---

* These two articles, originally published in *The Times*, October 4 and 5, 1965, and since overtaken by events, are reprinted here for students of the recent history of social policy. In writing them the author wishes to acknowledge the help he received from Mr T. A. Lynes, now Secretary of the Child Poverty Action Group. Some references have been added; otherwise the text is unchanged.

While many factors have been at work during the past decade which might account for the increase in births, it seems that about two-thirds of the rise has been due to higher fertility, about 10 per cent to the increase in the number of married women, and just over one-fifth to earlier marriage. Recent analyses by the Registrar General indicate that the rise in fertility has produced a rise in the rates for second, third and fourth or higher birth order children and that it is likely to result in larger families.[2] The proportion of families in Britain with six or more children receiving family allowances rose by over 40 per cent between 1956 and 1964. All the evidence points in fact to a rise in the average ultimate family-size of women married at all ages under forty-five. What may also be significant is that fertility rates have increased most sharply in the more middle-class, non-manual regions of the country; and among women married over the age of twenty-five. In the taxable income range £5,000 and over in 1962–63 about 22 per cent of all children for whom tax allowances were claimed were in families of four or more.[3] Nearly half were in families of three or more. On the face of it these seem high proportions for the upper-income classes. They are probably surprising figures to those who, in the 1940s and early 1950s, were deploring the decline in family size among these classes.

While past experience in the admittedly hazardous field of population forecasting should make us cautious about these estimates for the future, at least it seems clear that Britain does not need to encourage, directly or indirectly, the procreation of larger families. In the past thirty-six years the population of Britain increased by eight million. The projected increase for the next thirty-six years is two-and-a-half times as large, with something approaching a doubling in the number of children under eighteen. For this to happen in one of the most densely-populated and congested countries of the world could present any Government with appalling problems of urban planning and renewal, land use, housing and traffic management, to say nothing of the difficulties of staffing the schools, the hospitals and many other services. The physical and psychological disciplines required to maintain any semblance of environmental and social order might well diminish the applicability of market principles in various sectors of the economy. There can, therefore, be few thoughtful observers prepared to support public policies to encourage larger families—particularly among those sections of the population who tend to set standards of family building habits.

At present Britain is devoting something like £770 million a year to child endowment, plus £30 million to maternity benefits. Has not the time arrived for a reappraisal? If so, the task falls more heavily on the shoulders of the Chancellor of the Exchequer than on those responsible for the current review of social security.

Of the total of £770 million, over £520 million is now being channelled through the fiscal system to families with children. The chief items here are tax allowances for children and public subsidies of the order of £17 million for covenants, settlements, and other arrangements which mainly benefit children and young people. Those who benefit most from these forms of child endowment are the minority in the upper income ranges. Cash family allowances now cost only about one-quarter of this sum (£146 million, less tax deductions). Supplements to sickness and unemployment benefit paid for children cost around £30 million, plus an unknown but smaller sum for national assistance.

In addition, there are two systems of financial aid for children continuing their education. For those aged fifteen-eighteen there are educational maintenance allowances costing £1,300,000 in 1964–65. For those aged eighteen and over, cash maintenance grants and scholarships for students in the higher education sector cost nearly £80 million in 1964–65. The standards of provision for those in the former group are in marked contrast to those made for the latter: in 1964–65 nearly 70 per cent of local education authorities only gave assistance (generally £50 to £70 a year) at fifteen when the gross parental income was below £400 a year. By contrast, the same authorities were simultaneously awarding much larger grants to some students who were three years older and where the gross parental income exceeded £6,000 a year. These grants increase in value as the size of the family increases and as more is spent by the parents on private education for other children and on mortgage interest. The no-limit rule for mortgage interest in the surtax class is a classic example of the application of the needs principle; the larger the family the greater the need for the ownership of house-room.

Public services in kind which may aid the larger family are more difficult to identify and estimate; they include, of course, school milk and meals, maternity and child welfare, and education. Of these, by far the most costly to taxpayers and ratepayers in relation to the numbers benefiting is university education. Making some allowance for capital expenditure, the cost of the average student in 1963 was probably around £1,000–£1,300 a year. If a wider definition of cost is adopted to include earnings or production foregone the so-called opportunity cost of the average university student to the economy might be around £2,000 a year. Students' fees (generally paid by local authorities) averaged only £69 a year in 1962–63.[4]

What does emerge from this broad survey is that those who benefit most from the more costly forms of child endowment are families with large numbers of children and incomes well above the average. The larger the family the higher the income must be to reap the maximum benefit from income and surtax allowances, covenants, settlements, mortgage interest and university grants. Looked at simply within the context of population growth, tax allowances and covenants in particular seem indefensible. They could have been designed to provide incentives to procreation among better-off families. They make no contribution towards solving the problems of poverty among large families who pay little or no income tax but make substantial contributions to the Exchequer by way of indirect taxation, rates and national insurance contributions.

PLAN FOR CHILDREN IN POVERTY

Recent studies of levels of living by family size and composition have shown that next to old age still the commonest cause of relative poverty in Britain today is the large family. We have been reminded of this fact in the past few years by the investigations conducted by Professor Townsend, Mrs Wedderburn, Mrs Wynn and others.[5] Their reports, and a recent analysis of the Ministry of Labour's household expenditure data by Professors Townsend and Abel-Smith,[6] suggest that something like 15 to 20 per cent of the nation's children are living in conditions of hardship or poverty. These findings have been accompanied by disquiet about nutritional standards. Dr Lambert, after an examination of the Government's national food surveys during 1950–60, concluded in a recent report '. . . the diet of families, with three or four children or with adolescents and children has shown no overall improvement and some notable falls in nutritional adequacy, absolutely and relatively, since 1950'.[7] Moreover, a succession of reports on housing conditions and costs, on the impact of rates, and on primary, secondary and higher education have all demonstrated that the child from the large family is far more likely to be socially and educationally underprivileged than the child from the small family.

Quantitatively, the underprivileged family of today is predominantly the family of three, four or five children. The primary cause of their hardships is to be found in low earnings. A secondary cause of child poverty is due to the absence of a father, or to the fact that the father or mother is disabled, seriously handicapped, or chronically ill.

169

Vicious Circle

The present income maintenance services, though a help to these families, are ineffective in enabling them to break out of the vicious circle of inherited poverty. For fatherless families and for families where the breadwinner is in semi-regular or even in regular employment, the family allowance and educational maintenance schemes have degenerated into little more than token payments. Taking price increases into account, the present rates of family allowances, for example, are actually worth today less than the 5s of 1946 (the value of which was only about half the sum recommended by Beveridge). In 1946, a man with four children earning an average wage received an additional 12 per cent of his weekly wage as family allowances. Today he gets less than 8 per cent. The gap in levels of living between the large and the small family has been steadily widening for the past twenty years.

It cannot be argued that we have been forced to punish these families because of a reluctance to develop pronatalist policies. During this period the cost of child endowment through the fiscal system has increased steeply (since 1955, for example, it has risen from £247 million to over £500 million). We now have to consider these issues of child endowment in the light of Britain's new population expansion.

One possible answer might be to reduce tax allowances by stages and to increase family allowances. But could the latter be raised to levels adequate for poorer families without the cost to the Exchequer becoming prohibitive? An alternative approach is to extend the benefit of the tax allowance to those below the tax-paying level, and to accompany this measure with a series of other changes in the structure of benefits and subsidies.

Adapting PAYE

Extending tax allowances to the poor could be achieved by adapting the PAYE machinery which is used to collect tax on the excess of the taxpayer's income over his total allowances. If the allowances exceed the income no tax is payable, but the excess allowances are 'wasted'. In such cases the machinery could be put into reverse and used to pay 'tax adjustments' calculated at the normal tax rates on the excess of allowances over income. As a simple example, take a man with a wife and three young children, earning £10 a week. Including family allowances, his annual income is £567. If he received a tax adjustment benefit his total income would be raised, at present rates, by £63 a year.

This example assumes that all the existing allowances would

170

remain unaltered. But other changes would be needed on grounds of cost as well as of population policy.

Among the changes that might be considered and some of which would save the Exchequer money are:

(1) Abolish the tax allowance for the first or only child in the family and (possibly) increase the allowances for the second and third children by 50 per cent.

(2) Extend family allowances to the first child (at present they start from the second). This would avoid any hardship that might result from abolishing the tax allowance for the first child.

(3) Abolish child allowances for surtax relief.

(4) Commence payment of allowances on the child's second birthday rather than at birth, aid for the mothers of younger children being limited to maternity benefits, benefits in kind and more extensive family planning facilities.

(5) Grade family allowances as well as tax allowances by age so that when the child reached sixteen the combined allowances would be a real discouragement to premature school-leaving.

(6) Revise educational maintenance allowances and bring them more into line with allowances for higher education.

Reversing Emphasis

The changes proposed under (1) to (4) would, broadly speaking, leave the one-child family rather worse off than at present (except at the lowest levels of income where the present tax allowance does not operate), while larger families at all levels of income would enjoy benefits of roughly the same order as those now given exclusively to some better-off sections of the population.

These figures do show the need to rationalize the whole system of allowances if it is desired to concentrate more help on the poorer families and to reverse the present emphasis on larger families among the better-off.

The tax adjustment scheme has other effects and potential uses. The amount of tax adjustment payable to any individual would depend not only on the size of his family but on the whole range of existing tax allowances and deductions. Thus, the allowances for life insurance and pension contributions, dependent relatives and blindness (to name only a few) would no longer be subject to an income qualification. All would be enjoyed equally by taxpayers and non-taxpayers. One probable—and wholly desirable—consequence would be to encourage a more critical approach to the whole subject of tax allowances. What would be the political reaction if the average wage-earner could obtain a large tax adjustment by executing a seven-year deed of covenant in favour of his widowed mother or his grandchildren?

Conflict of Aims

Once we have the machinery for providing allowances on an equitable basis to taxpayers and non-taxpayers alike, it would in principle be possible to give tax adjustments on mortgage interest payments to owner-occupiers below the tax-paying level, and also introduce a rent allowance to replace the existing subsidies to local authority housing and give some relief to the tenants of private landlords. Subsidies would then be given to families instead of to houses as they already are for middle-class owner-occupiers.

Twenty-three years ago the Chancellor of the Exchequer's White Paper on Family Allowances (Cmd 6354) drew attention to the need to consider the combined effects of cash allowances and tax relief for children. It is now time to examine afresh the role of state aid to families in all income classes in the context of population trends. The fundamental problem resides in a conflict of aims: to abolish child poverty and to remove direct incentives for large families. There can be no perfectly consistent answer. But that is no argument for not trying to find a less irrational and inequitable bundle of benefits and subsidies than we have at present.

NOTES

1. *Registrar General's Quarterly Return for England and Wales*, 4th Quarter, 1964, HMSO, London, 1965.
2. *Registrar General's Statistical Review of England and Wales for 1962*, Part III, HMSO, London, 1965.
3. *Report of the Commissioners of H.M. Inland Revenue for 1964*, Cmnd 2572, HMSO, London, 1965 For an analysis of socio-economic fertility differentials in England and Wales based on the census data for 1951 and 1961 see *Eugenics Review*, Vol 59, No. 1, March 1967. This analysis shows that the largest increases in family size have taken place in the professional, administrative and managerial classes. By contrast, the increase among unskilled and semi-skilled workers was substantially smaller; for all marriage durations combined, standardized for age at marriage, there was, in fact, a decline between 1951 and 1961.
4. *Higher Education*, Report of the Committee under the Chairmanship of Lord Robbins, Cmnd 2154, HMSO, London, 1963.
5. For references see Townsend, P., *Poverty, Socialism and Labour in Power*, Fabian Tract 371, 1967.
6. Abel-Smith, B., and Townsend, P., *The Poor and the Poorest*, Occasional Papers on Social Administration, Bell, London, 1965.
7. Lambert, R., *Nutrition in Britain 1950–60*, Occasional Papers on Social Administration, Bell, London, 1964.

Chapter XV

MODELS OF REDISTRIBUTION IN SOCIAL SECURITY AND PRIVATE INSURANCE*

For the purposes of this paper I am adopting the following definition of social security. I assume that social security systems relate to transactions by Government (or agencies approved by Government) which increase individual money incomes in certain specific circumstances of income loss or need for income protection; e.g. old age, widowhood, sickness, disability, unemployment, the dependent needs of children, and so forth. These increments to income may take the form of direct unconditional cash payments or of excusing cash payments by the individual to the Government or agency (as in the non-payment of social security contributions during unemployment or sickness—contribution 'credits'—and in the form of deductions from direct taxation). In this context, 'unconditional' means that the payments are not made for specific purposes, e.g. for the part or full payment of medical bills, drug bills, transport bills, etc., or for the reimbursement of charges for services rendered.

Broadly, therefore, this definition relates to unconditional money income transactions and not to services in kind. It follows the conventional definition of social security (whether described as such in Government programmes or as social insurance, national insurance, public assistance, social assistance, national assistance, etc.), but includes systems or methods of meeting comparable needs and contingencies through the operations of direct taxation.

By interfering with the pattern of claims set in the economy by the market and by Government, social security (as defined above) involves some redistribution in command-over-resources between individuals and groups in society. Whatever the method of finance and the role of contributions, benefits, credits, taxes and tax deductibles, the redistributive effects can be classified under two headings: (1) those effects brought about when the system meets *immediate demonstrated need* (e.g. public assistance); (2) those effects brought

* Discussion paper given at European Experts in Social Policy Seminar, Copenhagen, May 1965, organized by the Danish National Institute of Social Research. Some additional references have since been added.

about by transactions designed to meet *future presumptive need* (e.g. old age pensions).[1] The distinction is important in measuring the time-span of income distribution or redistribution; past, present and future.

In theory and practice then, every social security system—and there are several hundred different systems in the world—involves some redistributive effects; both vertical and horizontal. It has, however, been argued that if social security is seen as an integral part of the modern economy its essential function is the *distribution* rather than the *redistribution* of income.[2] Whichever approach is adopted, however, the character and extent of the systems' effects will depend on its objectives—modified, as they may be, by the role of taxation. Not all systems, of course, operationally attain their objectives; they may develop unintended or unforeseen redistributive effects as the result of various political, economic, administrative or technical factors. Few adequate studies have, however, been made of the effective impact of social security programmes on secular changes in the distribution of incomes between groups and classes in society.[3]

Disregarding at this point, however, the difference between theory (objectives) and practice (reality), I want now to consider some of the main 'models of redistribution' which underlie—or are thought to underlie—income maintenance systems. In a world of imperfect competition they are naturally not perceived (nor are they put forward here) as 'perfect models' of redistribution. They are approximate only and serve merely to indicate certain major differences in orientation and philosophy.

First, there is (what may be called) the *'individualized actuarial model'* (Model 1). This is the classical, abstract and idealized insurance model conceptually based on risk theory; individual, collective and general. It results in a contract whereby, for a stipulated consideration, called a premium, one party undertakes to indemnify or guarantee another against loss by a certain specified contingency or peril, called a risk, the contract being set forth in a document called a policy.

Incorporated in this private insurance model are a number of assumptions: (1) that it is a voluntary contract; (2) that the individual premium is related to the individual risk; (3) that the contract will be honoured; (4) that redistribution, insofar as it takes place, involves those to whom the contingency occurs and those to whom it does not. The process of redistribution is not, therefore, deliberate in the sense that the effects are predictable and intended.

This model of 'drawing-out-what-you-pay-in' (in the language of

174

the common man) has had some influence, idealogically and seman-
tically, on the shaping of social security systems in the past—particularly those parts relating to provision for old age. Along with
Model 2, it played a political role in the establishment of compulsory social insurance in Germany by Bismarck in the 1880s and in
the development of national insurance for unemployment and sickness in Britain in 1911.[4] Technically, it was also important in Britain
in creating the concepts of the 'fund' and of actuarially determined
insurance contributions. As the Government Actuary explained in
1957: in Britain we 'attempt to base the scheme to a certain degree
on an insurance principle in opposition to the repartition of cost
for each year between various contributing parties—that is to say,
to charge for the purpose of the insurance system what might fairly
be called an insurance contribution in opposition to a tax, so that
no one can say that what we make the individual pay for his social
insurance benefits is more than he would have to pay if he could
go to, and obtain those benefits from, some private insurance
organization'.[5]

The belief that national insurance did (and should) resemble the
private insurance model made it seem inappropriate that vertical
redistribution from rich to poor should be a deliberate function of
social security systems. The four assumptions we have mentioned as
underlying this model were thus little questioned in the past. They
were automatically taken to be part of the 'natural' functioning of
the private insurance market. Consequently, the closer that social
security approached this model the more effective and politically
acceptable would it be.

Yet, when we study the actual behaviour of the private insurance
market, it becomes clear that reality hardly ever takes the form of
an individualized contract. It is an abstract ideal. What is more
relevant is our second model, *'group insurance'*; this is the more
appropriate private model to consider for the purposes of this
paper. Incorporated in this model is the widespread belief by many
of those covered by group and collective schemes that they have
acquired (or have earned) an individual contract. Their contributions and those of their employer—conceived as wages or salaries
deferred or saved—'earn' their own benefits; no more, no less.
They do not, therefore, see themselves as involved in a system of
redistribution. Hence the equally widespread notion which sur-
rounds this model that benefits are 'tailored' to the individual's
requirements. He voluntarily chooses his tailored suit, and pays for
it himself with his own contributions and those earmarked by his
employer.[6]

Group insurance is the means by which individuals and corporate bodies obtain protection in the private market against one or more of a variety of risks: fire insurance, motor insurance, burglary insurance, life assurance, income reduction in old age, and so forth. If admitted to the group they obtain protection as members of a 'contractual sharing group'. The risks are said to be pooled or shared. According to the type of risk (fire, motor, etc.), the contributions or premia may or may not be set by the characteristics of the individual or the property to be covered. More generally today they are set by the broad class or category into which the individual or the property concerned is thought to fall—age, sex, occupation, construction and location of property, type of vehicle and its use, and so forth.

In considering this model of group insurance I am not concerned here, however, with the theories of risk-rating as applied to these forms of insurance except to make two points. The principle of 'pooling risks' is not seen by insurer and insured as *deliberately* redistributive. In practice, of course, the good risks may pay for the bad risks but, on the assumption that the bad risks have been correctly charged higher contributions, there is no deliberate intention of redistributing resources from the careful to the negligent property owner, from the good, non-drinking life to the impaired, alcoholic life, and so forth. A good deal turns, therefore, on the extent and degree of precision of risk-rating. If the rating of risks is absent, ineffectual or incorrectly calculated, then redistribution will take place as a direct consequence of the assumptions, guesses and methods adopted in price-fixing and the settlement of claims. Thus, an element of deliberate value judgment is interposed; 'deliberate' in the sense of *not* to risk-rate or to do so imperfectly; for example, when higher charges are imposed in the statistically unsupported belief that certain diseases are inherited; that Jews are poor property risks; that certain employees are accident prone; that working-class households are more negligent than middle-class households; that coloured people are poorer motor-car risks than pink people, and so on.

Developments in mathematical techniques during the past half-century in combination with technological advances in knowledge about risk causation have all tended to show that actuarial risk- and experience-rating in group insurance is today far from being an exact science. In other words, scientific advances have made us more aware of the inexactitudes and imperfections of risk-rating. Insofar, then, as use is consciously not made of these advances in knowledge, the model of group insurance is imperfect—and deliberately more imperfect than (say) fifty years ago—in achieving equity.

This, as Mr Reinhard Hohaus has stated (in what Professor E. Burns has described as 'a masterly analysis of the difference between private and social insurance'[7]), is the governing consideration. 'Because of its voluntary nature . . . private insurance must be built on principles which assure the greatest practicable degree of equity between the various classes insured. . . . Social insurance, on the other hand, is moulded to society's need for a minimum of protection against one or more of the limited number of recognized social hazards. . . . Hence, just as considerations of equity of benefits form a natural and vital part of operating private insurance, so should considerations of adequacy of benefits control the pattern of social insurance. . . . The foregoing need not necessarily imply that all considerations of equity should be discarded from a social insurance plan: rather the point is that, of the two principles, adequacy is the more essential and less dispensable.'[8]

For private group insurance to strive for the 'greatest practicable degree of equity' means the deliberate rejection of redistribution as a function of the pooling of risks and reducing to a minimum the extent of accidental or unintended redistribution. This is the theory embodied in the model of private group insurance. What today is the reality? How valid are the assumptions stated above in relation to the model?

First it must be acknowledged that in the insurance literature of the Western world in general, and Britain in particular, remarkably little is known about the bases of modern risk-rating.[9] It is a large and expanding area of ignorance in which myths abound and facts are scarce; an area virtually unexplored by economists. It is expanding because (and this much is known) the size of 'collectively shared pools' has become much greater and that collective, monopolistic price-fixing has increasingly been substituted for micro-risk rating.[10] In the absence of adequate statistical data we may tentatively submit the following hypotheses concerning the validity of the model. These are not entirely implausible: a certain amount of suggestive information has, for example, been published for many countries in the *Transactions of the International Congresses of Actuaries* during the past twenty years.

1. That the voluntary nature of the contract is tending to disappear from large areas of group insurance
The last twenty years have witnessed in Europe and N. America a great expansion in private insured pension schemes and occupa-

tional welfare benefits provided by employers. For the employee, these are generally compulsory whether or not they are contributory and represent wages or salaries deferred on the theory of human depreciation. The employee cannot contract out. He cannot decide to spend his total earnings in alternative ways. Moreover, even if participation is voluntary (which it rarely is) he has no choice in respect of (a) the cover afforded, (b) the insurer and, generally, there is a remarkable absence of any formal appeals machinery as there is in many social security systems. Compared with some of these systems, private group insurance offers less freedom of choice and few or no rights of appeal. The employee may not have a choice of 'best years' of earnings in pension schemes (this is particularly true of manual workers); he may lose some or all of his rights or expectations if he changes his job; his wife may not benefit if he dies before retirement, and so forth.[11]

A second example relates to fire and comprehensive risks insurance on private houses. The great increase in recent years in house purchase through mortgages obtained from building societies and other agencies has virtually eliminated choice of insurer. These agencies compel insurance with a stated company irrespective of the wishes and preferences of the home owner as to price, cover afforded and other considerations.

2. That over large areas of private insurance the individual premium or contribution is increasingly unrelated to the individual risk
This hypothesis is in part based on a study of the effects of the trend in modern society for the size of 'collectively shared private pools' to become larger and less subject to conventional market forces. To some extent this trend is a consequence of the growth in scale of the private insurance market through mergers, takeovers and amalgamations. Prices and policies have become more standardized over larger areas of group insurance;[12] less subject to risk- and experience-rating; possibly more subject to power-rating. Among other factors, what influences the price is less the nature of the individual risk and more the power of financial groups and intermediaries to sell large blocks of insurance business. American experience in the field of private health insurance suggests that '. . . group insurance has become, in large part, a "cost plus" operation . . . some insurance experts now allege that group insurance is no longer really "insurance" in the sense that the carrier assumes the risk but a highly sophisticated form of "insurance" service.' Moreover, price competition is said to be 'almost non-existent'.[13]

In short, considerations of individual equity are being increasingly

sacrificed for considerations of economy of scale in market operations. For instance, medical examinations are rapidly disappearing
as a condition of acceptance for privately insured group life assurance and fringe benefit schemes in Britain.[14] What is being substituted for the supposed exactitude of individual risk-rating by means
of medical examinations is exclusion on certain arbitrary, untested
criteria, e.g. absence from employment due to sickness or disability
on a specified date; exclusion on grounds of age; exclusion of certain groups because they are believed to be subject to a high rate of
turnover, e.g. unskilled workers, immigrants and women; exclusion
in the case of motor insurance on the basis of country of origin.[15]

They may or may not be 'bad risks'; immigrants may not be
rejected because of their colour but because they are unskilled,
short-term employees or because of their country of origin; the
point is that they are excluded (and thus led to believe they are 'bad
risks' and discriminated against) on grounds of administrative costs
and inadequate risk-rating due largely to the growth of large-scale
operations and other factors. Equity suffers in the conflict with
bigness and those who suffer most are those who fail to fit neatly
into pre-determined large-scale classes, categories and groups. Nor
is their exclusion from the private insurance market on arbitrary or
unsubstantiated risk-rating criteria the end of the matter. Increasingly today, with the spread of private group insurance, it may mean
for the individual the denial of work on grounds of age, disability
or other considerations or, at least, the denial of access to certain
preferred occupations and careers. American experience, after
twenty-five years of growth in the private pension field, has shown
the serious effects of private group schemes on older, displaced
workers, the disabled and Negroes. Displaced white-collar workers
over the age of forty-five, in particular, face considerable difficulties
in finding another job.[16]

*3. That for substantial numbers of employees covered by private
pension and welfare schemes the contract will not be honoured in full*
When workers change their jobs (for voluntary or enforced reasons)
or die in service some part of their accrued pension expectations are
lost. Some part of their 'saved' wages disappears. The number of
workers, particularly manual workers, affected in Britain is substantial and is growing.[17] In the USA, where the problem of the loss
of pension expectations has been more intensively studied, Bernstein
concluded that whereas 'about one-third to one-half of the civilians
who work in non-agricultural, non-Governmental jobs are under
private pension plans . . . only about one-sixth to one-quarter' will

actually receive any benefits at all. In short, private pension plans are unreliable, have serious discriminatory effects, provide virtually no cover for widows, lead to substantial losses in deferred wages and pension expectations, favour a minority of employees, often favour owners and managerial employees, and do not, in Bernstein's view, merit the continuation of a subsidy from taxpayers of approximately $3 billion annually.[18] Protection under private health insurance schemes and against other hazards is also lost for similar and other reasons in the USA.

Expectations are also eroded by inflation—a process that the model of private group insurance has not yet found an answer to so far as the mass of workers are concerned.[19] Inflation is, as Kenneth Boulding has said, 'a refined method of taking bread out of the mouths of the aged, the infirm, the widows and orphans' and other non-earners and feeding it to earners.[20]

4. That, contrary to the general belief, private group insurance does have redistributive effects and that these tend, on balance, to be regressive in character

Some of the arguments for this hypothesis have already been stated. These and others are briefly summarized below:

(*a*) The absence or inadequate basis of risk- and experience-rating. This means, for example, that the true social costs are not borne by the dangerous industries and causative agents. The 'bad risks' are not charged the true market price. The poor in non-dangerous trades may thus be subsidizing higher income groups employed in other trades. The poor, safe driver may be subsidizing the rich, bad driver.[21]

(*b*) The inexact and arbitrary nature of some categories of risk-rating. This allows, for example, more scope for the role of preju-dice in price-fixing, in the determination of excluded individuals, groups and classes, and in the settlement of claims. Those who are excluded from standardized schemes may thus be incorrectly charged higher prices for alternative cover or compelled to suffer penalties in other ways.

(*c*) The practice, in many compulsory pension schemes, of relating benefits to 'final' earnings, which are also maximum earnings for some groups (generally the higher paid classes) but not for other groups (generally the lower paid classes).[22]

(*d*) The fact that the costs are reduced or the profits of group schemes are increased by the higher rate of employment turnover experienced by lower-paid workers who (with their wives) lose part or all of their pension and other welfare expectations. Those who remain in these schemes or who are accorded full preservation and tax-free lump sums—mainly middle- and higher-paid workers —thus benefit from the greater rate of turnover among lower-paid workers.[23]

(e) The fact that a disproportionate share of the administrative costs of group schemes may be loaded on certain classes of insurance.[24] In some cases, these classes cater predominantly for lower-paid workers—as, for example, workmen's compensation insurance.

(f) The fact that in Britain and other countries the private insurance market has exacted substantial concessions from the fiscal system and that these concessions favour the higher income groups.[25] The 'impact effect' of these concessions is borne by the whole population.

(g) The fact that in an inflationary economy the 'impact effect' of employees' contributions for private group schemes is generally borne by the purchasers of the firms' products—in effect, the whole population of non-earners as well as earners—and may be regressive in character.[26]

(h) The fact that average mortality tables are applied indiscriminately to rich and poor alike over large areas of private group pension schemes. As it is now known that the higher income groups have a longer expectation of life on retirement than the lower, the result is on balance a substantial redistribution in favour of the former—particularly when account is taken of the effects of tax deductibles for contributions, premia, lump sums, loan charges and other factors.[27] In short, the poor pay more in the private pension market because they are poor and are statistically treated as non-poor, and because, in many cases, they are compulsorily contracted out of the state scheme by their employers without consultation and the exercise of choice.

It is arguable, of course, whether in the classical model of private group insurance there is (or should be) an obligation to publish information which would allow these various hypotheses to be tested. A case in the affirmative could be made out on the grounds of open competition and maximum freedom of choice for the consumer. This is the basis of the case argued by *The Economist*: 'Believe it or not, there are no risk statistics of any sort.'[28] However that may be, it must be emphasized again that the paucity of published data does not permit these hypotheses to be quantitatively put to the test in every case.[29]

Within this context I now consider the role of social security and I shall assume, for the purposes of discussion, that there is some validity in these hypotheses. We have, therefore, to define this role for Government on the assumption that the actual behaviour of private group insurance is as postulated above.

As Galbraith and others have said, a positive case has to be made out in the mixed economy to justify the intervention of Government in the field of social policy. In this instance, it has to be shown that the private market is incapable of meeting certain income maintenance needs and of performing certain functions considered desirable on social, economic and political grounds. On this basis, and in the light of the foregoing analysis, it is argued that the model of social security (Model 3) should have as one of its major objectives the function of progressively redistributing resources from rich to poor. In the past, this has not generally been a declared objective of social security systems. Rather, the emphasis has been on earners paying for non-earners and earning times paying for non-earning times through systems of 'social insurance', mutual aid and similar 'dividing-out' clubs for workers. In Britain, the Beveridge institution of flat-rate contributions from all represents a regressive form of taxation.[30] To a limited extent, this is countered by a progressive element insofar as lower-paid workers receive more from unemployment, disability and sickness benefits. But these benefits, it may be argued, are inadequate compensation for those who bear a disproportionate burden of the social costs of industrial and technological change.

I cannot, however, in this paper discuss all aspects of a 'model' for all social security risks. The main issue for discussion is the role of redistribution from rich to poor. On what grounds can this role be supported and what are the policy implications?

To answer these questions, we must first consider the conclusions to be drawn from the preceding analysis of the private market. I do so solely in relation to Britain. Accordingly, I suggest that the main conclusions are:

1. It is now widely accepted that in all sectors of the economy there is a national need to diminish both the absolute fact and the psychological sense of social and economic discrimination. This aim, it has been argued, should be applied to the problems of status discrimination between manual and non-manual workers; discrimination on grounds of age, sex and marital status; discrimination against those who have to change their jobs, learn new skills, move to other parts of the country, retire from work earlier or experience unemployment in the interests of economic growth; discrimination between pink and coloured people, and so on.

By its nature the private insurance market cannot fully meet this national need. On the contrary, as the analysis indicates, recent tendencies are in the other direction: towards hardening differentials and enlarging areas of felt discrimination.

2. In Britain, as in other countries, it is increasingly argued that one of the aims of social policy should be 'to concentrate help on those whose need is greatest' and to enable these groups in the population 'to share in rising national prosperity'. This is the basis of the American and Canadian 'Wars on Poverty'—campaigns that have been heavily influenced by the public recognition of (a) the human consequences of automation and cybernation, (b) the threat to society of increasing violence among the economically and socially deprived.

Again, in the field of social security, the private market has made and can make little contribution towards the attainment of these national objectives. Fundamentally, this derives in part from the basic difference between 'insurance' and social security. 'Insurance' is mainly concerned with enabling some individuals to provide against future contingencies; social security is mainly concerned with meeting present needs in the whole population.

3. Finally, it is also being argued that income maintenance systems (whether public or private) should offer *all* citizens, and especially the poor, the handicapped and minority groups irrespective of ethnic origin, (a) more freedom of choice, (b) more democratic participation in administration, (c) more opportunities for complaint and for the redress of wrongs.

It is less easy here to define the respective contributions of private group insurance and public social security. In Britain, it would seem that the former has had more to offer the higher income groups in respect of (a) and (c). 'Tailored' social security for the rich is possible, and 'money talks'. But for the mass of the population included in private schemes there is virtually no choice, no reality or sense of democratic participation, and few if any formal channels for the redress of wrongs. The recorded history of private workmen's compensation, health insurance and death and burial benefits has shown the limitations of the private market in these respects for the mass of the workers.[31]

What then in terms of equity, adequacy, redistribution and freedom of choice are the implications for the future development of social security?

For purposes of discussion I suggest that the following broad principles should form part of the 'model':

1. The principle of progressive redistribution in relation both to contributions and benefits
This means:

(*a*) the rejection of the concept of 'insurance';
(*b*) universal contributions and benefits;
(*c*) wage-related contributions from the whole population;
(*d*) an element of wage-related benefits up to stated maxima;
(*e*) an element of flat-rate benefits fixed at 'adequate' levels so that standards are raised for low income groups;
(*f*) the assimilation of social security and fiscal benefits for all income maintenance and dependency risks;
(*g*) the elimination of regressive tax allowances;
(*h*) a substantial proportion of the costs to be met from general taxes so that (i) some payment is made by unearned incomes, (ii) the financing of wage-related social security is progressive in its effects.

2. The principle of adequacy of benefits in relation to average standards of living
This means:

(*a*) fixing the combined flat-rate and wage-related benefits for the lower income groups as closely as practicable to their average earnings;
(*b*) minimum benefits to be based on assumed average need;
(*c*) in determining 'adequacy', the payment of children's allowances (financed from general taxation) on a sliding (progressively diminishing) scale during earning and non-earning;
(*d*) 'dynamizing' benefits, i.e. relating all benefits to some index of average incomes or earnings;
(*e*) reducing to a minimum residence and contribution requirements.

3. The principle of consumer choice and participation
This means:

(*a*) offering options and choices as to the form in which certain benefits are paid; for example, mortgage advances at retirement age, earlier payment of retirement pensions in special circumstances, etc.;
(*b*) the institution of consumer advisory groups and the development of local committees and tribunals to hear complaints, to redress wrongs and to criticize administrative agencies.

It has been said that in the past considerations of adequacy of benefit have controlled the pattern of social insurance. In the future, social security has to seek the best possible balance of equity, adequacy, redistribution from rich to poor and consumer participation. This conclusion follows, I believe, from an analysis of the actual functioning of the private market and from a wider appreciation of the goals of modern democratic society. In effect, social security has to be seen as an agent of structural change; not as a system reflecting and legitimating the *status quo*.

NOTES

1. For a full discussion of these concepts see Burns, E. M., *Social Security and Public Policy*, McGraw-Hill, New York, 1956.
2. Merriam, I. C., *Social Security Bulletin*, US Department of Health, Education and Welfare, Vol. 28, No. 4, April 1965.
3. For some references to the scanty literature see Gordon, M. S., *The Economics of Welfare Policies*, Columbia University Press, 1963, and Eckstein, O. (Ed.), *Studies in the Economics of Income Maintenance*, The Brookings Institution, Washington, 1967.
4. Gilbert, B. B., *The Evolution of National Insurance in Great Britain*, Michael Joseph, London, 1966.
5. Maddex, G. H., *Transactions XVth International Congress of Actuaries*, 1957, Vol. IV, p. 254.
6. See Seldon, A., *ibid.*, Chapter XII, and Lynes, T. A., *Pensions and Democracy*, Occasional Papers on Social Administration, 1968.
7. Burns, E. M., *ibid.*, 1956, p. 35.
8. Hohaus, R. A., *The Record*, American Institute of Actuaries, June 1938, pp. 82-4.
9. See references on p. 181.
10. On price fixing in relation to certain classes of insurance see articles in *The Times*, 'The Cost of Fire Insurance' (August 26, 1964) and 'Profit and Loss on Car Insurance' (April 12, 1960). According to Mr C. G. W. Whibley, deputy overseas manager of the Commercial Union Group, speaking at a Common Market conference, 'British insurance companies have not sought to undercut rates to secure business but have taken the view that their aim is to act as a stabilizing factor' (reported in *The Times*, July 26, 1962). See also 'Survey of Insurance 1967', *The Economist*, July 29, 1967, especially pp. v-vi.
11. See Chapter XII and Chapter XI ('The Irresponsible Society') in Titmuss, R. M., *Essays on 'The Welfare State'*, *ibid.* Other relevant sources are: Ministry of Labour, *Preservation of Pension Rights*, HMSO, London, 1966; Government Actuary, *Occupational Pension Schemes*, HMSO, London, 1966; Wedderburn, D., *White-Collar Redundancy*, Cambridge University Press, 1964; Rubner, A., *Fringe Benefits*, 1962, and Taylor, B., *Westminster Bank Review*, November 1962, p. 19. For an analysis of the employees' lack of freedom, participation in control and security rights under group pension schemes in the USA see Harbrecht, P. P., *Pension Funds and Economic Power*, 1959. In their analysis of the role of insurance companies in the British

economy, Professor Clayton's and Mr Osborn's findings substantially support Dr Harbrecht's conclusions (Clayton, G., and Osborn, W. T., *Insurance Company Investment*, Allen and Unwin, London, 1965, p. 242). In the field of group health insurance in the USA, it is said that 'the consumer is highly limited in his choice', Somers, H. M. and A. R., *Doctors, Patients and Health Insurance*, 1961, p. 408.

12. See 'Survey of Insurance 1967', *The Economist*, July 29, 1967, especially pp. v–vi.

13. Somers, H. M. and A. R., *ibid.*, 1961, pp. 286, 406 and 408. Some references to British experience in the pension field in relation to standardization, the non-competitive aspects of group insurance and risk-rating are to be found in Pilch, M., and Wood, V., *Pension Schemes*, 1960, pp. 68–74, 85–8 and 97, and *New Trends in Pensions*, 1964.

14. Hosking, G. A., *Pension Schemes and Retirement Benefits*, 1960, and *Trans. Faculty of Actuaries*, No. 220, 1965, p. 13.

15. For evidence of discrimination experienced by coloured citizens in regard to motor insurance see *Report of the Race Relations Board for 1966–67*, HMSO, London, 1967, p. 20, and Political and Economic Planning, *Racial Discrimination*, 1967.

16. Bernstein, M. C., *The Future of Private Pensions*, Glencoe Free Press, New York, 1964; Harbrecht, P. P., *ibid.*, and National Bureau of Economic Research, *Survey of Pension Funds*, reported in *The Times*, September 29, 1966. The denial of motor insurance cover can mean the denial of a job in many occupations today (see Political and Economic Planning, *ibid.*). On the serious effects of private pension schemes in Britain restricting the engagement of older workers and disabled people see *National Advisory Committee on the Employment of Older Men and Women, First and Second Reports*, Cmd 8963 and 9628, HMSO, London, 1953 and 1955, and *Report on the Rehabilitation, Training and Resettlement of Disabled Persons*, Cmd 9883, HMSO, London, 1956. No later official studies have been made.

17. See earlier references in this chapter and, in particular, the Government Actuary's Report, *Occupational Pension Schemes*, 1966. This shows that of 535,000 exits from employment in the private sector in Britain in 1963 (505,000 voluntary exits and 30,000 dismissals) 27 per cent received no private pension benefit, 62 per cent received only a return of personal contributions (with or without interest) and only 6 per cent had their pension rights fully preserved (Table 45).

18. Bernstein, M. C., *ibid.*, pp. 299–300, and paper read at the annual meeting of the American Risk and Insurance Association, August 29, 1966.

19. See, for example, Ratcliff, A. R., and Round, A. E. G., *Transactions of the 17th International Congress of Actuaries*, 1964, Vol. III, Part 1, pp. 367–93.

20. Boulding, K. E., *Principles of Economic Policy*, 1959, p. 250.

21. Report by McKinsey & Co. to British Insurance Association on Motor Insurance summarized in *The Times*, May 10, 1965. One conclusion reached by the report was that safe drivers were subsidizing bad drivers.

22. See, in particular, Pilch, M., and Wood, V., *ibid.*

23. See Chapter XVI.

24. This is conjectural but some historical evidence is suggestive—see *Social Insurance and Allied Services* (the Beveridge Report), Appendix D, 1942.

25. Lynes, T. A., 'Life Assurance through Pension Schemes' (App. D), in Titmuss, R. M., *Income Distribution and Social Change*, 1962.

26. See Gordon, M. S., *ibid.*, 1963, p. 69.

27. See report by Institute of Actuaries on experience of assured male lives

1959–63 in *Trans. Faculty of Actuaries*, No. 220, 1965. The mortality at ages sixty-five to eighty-five of pensioners under 'works schemes' (manual workers) exceeded that of pensioners under 'non-work schemes' (non-manual workers) by 19 per cent in 1961–63 calculated on an amounts basis.

28. *The Economist*, 'Survey of Insurance 1967', July 29, 1967, p. v.

29. *The Economist* referred in 1965 to the 'secrecy and obscurity with which their own' (British insurers) 'McKinsey report had been clothed' (Insurance Supplement, July 24, 1965, p. vii). A year later it said that the failure to publish this report when it was first submitted 'must rank as one of the most disastrous collective decisions the British insurance industry has ever taken' (*The Economist*, May 14, 1966, p. 728). Over the whole field of British insurance activities *The Economist*'s comment in 1967 was that the industry's 'statistics remain primitive' (July 1, 1967).

30. In the USA, effective social security contribution rates were regressive in 1954 over the income distribution as a whole and fairly uniform for tax brackets under $5,000 (Musgrave, R. A., *Federal Tax Policy for Economic Growth and Stability*, 1955). See also Harvey, E. C., 'Social Security Taxes —Regressive or Progressive?', *National Tax Journal*, Vol. XVIII, No. 4, 1965, p. 408, and Deran, E., *National Tax Journal*, Vol. XIX, No. 3, 1966, pp. 284–5.

31. See, for example, 'The Problem of Industrial Insurance', Appendix D, *Social Insurance and Allied Services* (the Beveridge Report), 1942, p. 249.

Chapter XVI

THE ROLE OF REDISTRIBUTION IN SOCIAL POLICY*

In the literature of the West, concepts and models of social policy are as diverse as contemporary concepts of poverty. Historically, the two have indeed had much in common. They certainly share diversity. There are today those at one end of the political spectrum who see social policy as a transitory minimum activity of minimum government for a minimum number of poor people; as a form of social control for minority groups in a 'natural' society; as a way of resolving the conflict between the religious ethic of compassion and undiluted individualism. In this view social policy is not good business. Statistical estimates of the national income per capita look healthier if the infant mortality rate rises. At the other end of the political spectrum there are writers like Macbeath who has comprehensively stated that 'Social policies are concerned with the right ordering of the network of relationships between men and women who live together in societies, or with the principles which should govern the activities of individuals and groups so far as they affect the lives and interests of other people.'[1]

Somewhere between these extreme visionary notions lives a conventional, textbook, definition of social policy.[2] The social services or social welfare, the labels we have for long attached to describe certain areas of public intervention such as income maintenance and public health, are seen as the main ingredients of social policy. They are obvious, direct and measurable acts of government, undertaken for a variety of political reasons, to provide for a range of needs, material and social, and predominantly dependent needs, which the market does not or cannot satisfy for certain designated sections of the population. Typically, these direct services are functionally organized in separate and specialized ministries, departments or divisions of government, central and local. They are seen as the 'social policy departments'. What they do is thought to be

* Lecture delivered to the staff of the Social Security Administration, Department of Health, Education and Welfare, Washington, USA, in December 1964, and published in *Social Security Bulletin*, Washington, June 1965.

explicitly redistributive; they politically interfere with the pattern of claims set by the market. They assign claims from one set of people who are said to produce or earn the national product to another set of people who may merit compassion and charity but not economic rewards for productive service. In short, they are seen as uncovenanted benefits for the poorer sections of the community. And because these separate functional units of social service are accountable to the public their activities are, in large measure, quantifiable. We can thus measure the size of the presumed burden (as it is conventionally called) on the economy.

This, I propose to argue, is a very limited and inadequate model of the working of social policy in the second half of the twentieth century. In its distance from the realities of today it is about as helpful (or unhelpful) as some recent models of economic man maximizing his acquisitive drives. Later, I attempt to support and illustrate this statement by examining some of the lessons of experience of nearly twenty years of so-called 'Welfare Statism' in Britain. First, however, I want to briefly consider one or two of the factors which have contributed to this limited concept of social policy—particularly in relation to its role as a redistributive agent.

Perhaps the most important causative factor in Britain has to do with the heritage of the poor law (or public assistance). Less than sixty years ago social policy was, in the eyes of the middle and upper classes, poor law policy. This model of 'welfare use' was part of a political philosophy which saw society as an adjunct of the market.[3] As Karl Polanyi puts it, 'instead of economy being embedded in social relations, social relations are embedded in the economic system'.[4] The essential, though financially reluctant, role of the poor law was to support industrialism and the attempt in the nineteenth century to establish a completely competitive, self-regulating market economy founded on the motive of individual gain. It thus had to create a great many rules of expected behaviour; about work and non-work, property, savings, family relationships, cohabitation, men-in-the-house, and so forth.[5] Poverty, as Disraeli once said, was declared a crime by industrialism. Laws about poverty became associated with laws about crime.

This system, which legally survived in Britain until 1948, inevitably involved personal discrimination. The stigmata of the poor law test, moral judgments by people about other people and their behaviour, were a condition of redistribution. The requirements of poor law and public assistance administration were, we can now see, remarkably attuned to the characteristics of bureaucracy drawn by Weber and others.[6] It was theoretically a neat and orderly world of eligible and

189

ineligible citizens; of approved and disapproved patterns of dependency; of those who could manage change and those who could not. From its operation for over a century Britain inherited in 1948 a whole set of administrative attitudes, values and rites; essentially middle-class in structure; and moralistic in application. The new social service bottles of 1948 had poured into them much of the old wine of discrimination and prejudice. It has taken nearly two decades of sustained programmes of new recruitment, training, retraining and intraining, and the appointment of social workers to the public services, to eradicate part of this legacy of administrative behaviour.[7]

The history of the poor law and public assistance is thus still important to an understanding of social policy concepts today. If one disregards the social costs of industrialism, of allowing a large part of the disservices of technological progress to lie where they fall, then the system (of public assistance) was clearly redistributive. It directly benefited the explicit poor. Those in the greatest need did receive some benefit. But with the limited instruments of policy and administrative techniques to hand in the past, the system could only function by operating punitive tests of discrimination; by strengthening conceptions of approved and disapproved dependencies; and by a damaging assault on the recipients of welfare in terms of their sense of self-respect and self-determination. Within the established pattern of commonly held values, the system could only be redistributive by being discriminatory and socially divisive.

All this is now well documented in the archives of social inquiry and is somewhat ancient history. Equally well-known is the story of society's response to the challenge of poverty during the past thirty years or so: the discovery that this system of public aid was administratively grossly inefficient; the discovery that it could not by its very nature absorb the new dimensions of social and psychological knowledge and that, therefore, it could not function effectively both as a redistributive agent and as an agent to prevent social breakdown; and the discovery that the system was fundamentally inconsistent with the need to grant to all citizens, irrespective of race, religion or colour, full and equal social rights.[8]

Gradually in Britain, as we tried to learn these lessons, we began to discard the use of discriminatory and overtly redistributive services for second-class citizens. The social services on minimum standards for all citizens crept apologetically into existence. In common with other countries we invented contributory national insurance or social security and provided benefits as of right. The actuary was called in to replace the functions of the public assistance relieving officer. Free secondary education for all children, irrespective of the means of their parents, was enacted in 1944 as part of a comprehensive educational system. Public housing authorities were called upon in 1945 to build houses for people and not just for working-class people. A limited and second-class health insurance scheme for working men was transformed, in 1948, into a comprehensive and free-on-demand health service for the whole population.[9]

All these and many other changes in the direct and publicly accountable instruments of social policy led to the notion that, in the year 1948, the 'Welfare State' had been established in Britain. While there was general political consensus on this matter there was, on the other hand, much confusion and debate about cause and effect.[10] There were many, for instance, who thought that these policy changes were brought about for deliberately redistributive reasons and that the effects would be significantly egalitarian. This, perhaps, was understandable. Direct welfare in the past had in fact been redistributive (considered apart from the effects of the fiscal system). Therefore it was natural to assume that more welfare in the future would mean more redistribution in favour of the poor. There were others however (among whom I count myself) who believed that the fundamental and dominating historical processes which led to these major changes in social policy were connected with the demand for one society; for non-discriminatory services for all without distinction of class, income or race; for services and relations which would deepen and enlarge self-respect; for services which would manifestly encourage social integration. From some perspectives these major changes in policy could be regarded as ideological pleas to the middle- and upper-income classes to share in the benefits (as well as the costs) of public welfare.

Built into the public model of social policy in Britain since 1948 there are two major roles or objectives: the redistributive objective and the non-discriminatory objective. To move towards the latter it was believed that a prerequisite was the legal enactment of universal (or comprehensive) systems of national insurance, education, medical care, housing and other direct services.

What have we learnt in the past fifteen years about the actual functioning of these services? What has universalism in social welfare achieved? Clearly, I cannot give you a full account of all aspects of this development during a period when, for thirteen of these years, the Government in power was not, in the early stages at least, entirely committed to the concept of the 'Welfare State'. I shall therefore concentrate my conclusions, brief and inadequate

191

though they are, on the theme of redistribution.

Up to this point I have dealt only with what I sometimes call the 'Iceberg Phenomena of Social Welfare'. That is, the direct public provision of services in kind (e.g. education and medical care) and the direct payment of benefits in cash (e.g. retirement pensions and family allowances).

I now turn to consider two other major categories of social policy which have been developing and extending their roles in Britain and other countries over much the same period of time as the category we call 'the social services'. Elsewhere, I have described the former as 'Fiscal Welfare' and 'Occupational Welfare'.[11] These are the indirect or submerged parts of the 'Iceberg of Social Policy'. In both categories a remarkable expansion has taken place in Britain during the past twenty years.

All three categories of social policy have a great deal in common in terms of redistribution. They are all concerned with changing the individual and family pattern of current and future claims on resources set by the market, set by the possession of accumulated past rights, and set by the allocations made by Government to provide for national defence and other non-market sectors. Social welfare changes the pattern of claims by, for instance, directly providing in kind education or mental hospital care either free or at less than the market cost. Fiscal welfare changes the pattern of claims by taking less in tax (and thus increasing net disposable income) when a taxpayer's child is born, when its education is prolonged, when men have ex-wives to maintain, when taxpayers reach a specified age, and so on. An individual's pattern of claims on resources is today greatly varied through fiscal welfare policy by his or her change in circumstances, family responsibilities and opportunities available (and taken) for prolonged education, home ownership and so on. In Britain, the United States and other countries the tax system has recently been regarded as an alternative in certain areas to the social security system; as a policy instrument to be used to provide higher incomes for the aged, for large families, for the blind and other handicapped groups, and for meeting part of the costs of education which today may last for up to twenty years or more.[12]

Occupational welfare, provided by virtue of employment status, achievement and record, may take the form of social security provisions in cash or in kind. Such provisions are legally approved by Government and, as in the case of fiscal welfare, they may be seen as alternatives to extensions in social welfare. Their cost falls in large measure on the whole population. It is thus, like social welfare and fiscal welfare, a major redistributive mechanism.

In Britain, occupational welfare may include: pensions for employees; survivors benefits; child allowances; death benefits; health and welfare services; severance pay and compensation for loss of office (analogous these days to compensation for loss of property rights); personal expenses for travel, entertainment and dress; meal vouchers; cars and season tickets; residential accommodation; holiday expenses; children's school fees at private schools; sickness benefits; medical expenses; education and training grants and benefits ranging from 'obvious forms of realizable goods to the most intangible forms of amenity'[13] expressed in a form that is neither money nor convertible into money.

A substantial part of these occupational welfare benefits can be interpreted—again like fiscal welfare—as social policy recognition of dependencies; the long dependencies of old age, childhood and widowhood, and such short-term dependencies as sickness and the loss of job rights.

The populations to which these three categories of welfare relate differ, but a substantial section of people may be eligible for benefits in respect of all three. In Britain, most of the social welfare services (except national assistance and university education) are universalist and citizen-based; they are open to all without a test of means. Thus, access to them does not depend upon achieved or inherited status. Fiscal welfare relates to a smaller population; only to those who pay direct taxes and not those who pay property taxes and social security contributions. Occupational welfare relates to the employed population and, at present, predominantly favours white-collar and middle-class occupations. Benefits are thus related to achievement.

All three categories of welfare are, as we have seen, redistributive; they change the pattern of claims on current and future resources. They function redistributively as separate, self-contained systems and they do so also in relation to the whole economy. Here is one example. Many private pension schemes, which include manual and non-manual workers, tend to redistribute claims on resources from lower-paid to higher-paid employees. This happens because the lower-paid workers change jobs more frequently; in doing so they do not have credited to them the full amount of pension contributions or premiums. It is estimated in Britain that the cost of full preservation of pension rights for all employees in the private sector (an objective in the present Government's proposals for the reform of social security) could add 15 to 25 per cent to the actuarial costs of private schemes.[14] Moreover, as at present organized, the cost to

N   193

the Treasury (the whole community) of private pension schemes substantially exceeds the Treasury contribution to social security pensions for the whole population. The pensions of the rich are more heavily subsidized by the community than the pensions of the poor.[15]

This in part happens because occupational welfare and fiscal welfare benefits are fundamentally based on the principles of achievement, status and need. If there is need, then the higher the income the higher is the welfare benefit. By contrast, social welfare benefits generally take account only of needs—the need for medical care, for education and so on irrespective of income or status.

I have now described in very general terms three categories of social policy redistribution—with particular reference to their operation in Britain. At present, they are publicly viewed as virtually distinct systems. What goes on within and as a result of one system is ignored by the others. They are appraised, criticized or applauded as abstracted, independent entities. Historically, they have developed different concepts of poverty or subsistence; different criteria for determining approved dependencies; different standards of moral values in determining eligibility for welfare. Some examples will illustrate this point.

The social policy definition of subsistence as developed in the fiscal system for determining exemption from taxation, income needs in old age, and so on, differs markedly from the definition used in public assistance.[16] In some areas of policy the fiscal definition of poverty is employed—as, for instance, in determining grants to university students.[17] In other and similar areas of policy the public assistance definition is employed—as, for instance, in determining aid for poor parents of 16-year-old children at school.[18] It is odd, when you come to think of it, that dependency at age 16 is assessed at a lower standard of assistance than dependency at 18 or even 23 (in the case of medical students and graduates).

We have in fact two standards of poverty for determining aid from the community; both highly subjective and unscientific; both employed to assist dependent states; a working-class standard and a middle-class standard. The former has been investigated, studied, measured and argued about for long by sociologists, social workers and economists, and made the subject of many books and doctoral theses. By contrast, the latter has been virtually ignored.

One further example of double standards operating in different categories of welfare may be selected from a large field—this one to illustrate the role of moral values in social policy.

In the category of social welfare, cash aid from public funds for

194

unsupported mothers and their children may be stopped if it is believed that cohabitation is taking place. This is an event—or a relationship—that can rarely be legally proved. It is hardly a scientific fact. We have in Britain a cohabitation regulation;[19] you have a man-in-the-house regulation.[20] They amount to the same thing; they cannot be spelt out in precise operational terms. Their application in practice depends in large measure, therefore, on hearsay and moral judgment.

The same problem of to give or not to give aid arises in the category of fiscal welfare. As an example I quote from a memorandum by Lord Justice Hodson to a Royal Commission on Marriage and Divorce: 'A super-tax payer may, and quite frequently nowadays does, have a number of wives living at the same time since after divorce his ex-wives are not treated as one with him for tax purposes he can manage quite nicely since he is permitted' (a social policy decision) 'to deduct all his wives' maintenance allowances from his gross income for tax purposes leaving his net income comparatively slightly affected.'[21]

In both instances redistribution takes place; the community renders aid in these situations of need and dependency. But while the decision to help the public assistance mother may involve judgments about moral behaviour, in the case of the taxpayer the decision is automatic and impersonal. The logic of the double standard is not apparent. If one is socially acceptable and approved behaviour then why not the other?

Now I must begin to draw these reflections together. What have been the lessons of experience in Britain about the actual functioning of these three categories of welfare during the past fifteen years? Obviously, I cannot give you more than a fragment of an answer, and even this involves over-simplifying to a dangerous degree. To analyse and measure the redistributive effects of this process of the social division of welfare would be an immensely complex task— even if the essential statistical data were available which, in many areas, they are not. All I can offer are a few generalized conclusions.

The major positive achievement which has resulted from the creation of direct, universalist social services in kind has been the erosion of formal discriminatory barriers. One publicly approved standard of service, irrespective of income, class or race, replaced the double standard which invariably meant second-class services for second-class citizens. This has been most clearly seen in the National Health Service. Despite strict controls over expenditure on the Service by Conservative Governments for many years it has maintained the principle of equality of access by all citizens to all branches of medical care. Viewed solely in terms of the welfare objective of non-discriminatory, non-judgmental service this is the signal achievement of the National Health Service. In part this is due to the fact that the middle-classes, invited to enter the Service in 1948, did so and have since largely stayed with the Service. They have not contracted out of socialized medical care as they have done in other fields like secondary education and retirement pensions. Their continuing participation, and their more articulate demands for improvements, have been an important factor in a general rise in standards of service—particularly in hospital care.[22]

But, as some students of social policy in Britain and the United States are beginning to learn, equality of access is not the same thing as equality of outcome. We have to ask statistical and sociological questions about the utilization of the high-cost quality sectors of social welfare and the low-cost sectors of social welfare. We have to ask similar questions about the ways in which professional people (doctors, teachers, social workers and many others) discharge their roles in diagnosing need and in selecting or rejecting patients, clients and students for this or that service. In the modern world, the professions are increasingly becoming the arbiters of our welfare fate; they are the key-holders to equality of outcome; they help to determine the pattern of redistribution in social policy.

These generalizations apply particularly when services in kind are organized on a universalist, free-on-demand basis. When this is so we substitute, in effect, the professional decision-maker for the crude decisions of the economic market-place. And we also make much more explicit—an important gain in itself—the fact that the poor have great difficulties in manipulating the wider society, in managing change, in choosing between alternatives, in finding their way around a complex world of welfare.

We have learnt from fifteen years' experience of the Health Service that the higher income groups know how to make better use of the Service; they tend to receive more specialist attention; occupy more of the beds in better equipped and staffed hospitals; receive more elective surgery; have better maternity care, and are more likely to get psychiatric help and psychotherapy than low income groups—particularly the unskilled.[23]

These are all factors which are essential to an understanding of the redistributive role played by one of the major direct welfare services in kind. They are not arguments against a comprehensive free-on-demand service. But they do serve to underline one conclusion. Universalism in social welfare, though a needed prerequisite towards reducing and removing formal barriers of social and economic discrimination, does not by itself solve the problem of how to reach the more-difficult-to-reach with better medical care, especially preventive medical care.

Much the same kind of general conclusion can be drawn from Britain's experience in the field of education. Despite reforms and expansion during the past fifteen years it is a fact that the proportion of male undergraduates who are the sons of manual workers is today about 1 per cent lower than it was between 1928 and 1947. Although we have doubled the number of university students the proportion coming from working-class homes has remained fairly constant at just over a quarter.[24]

The major beneficiaries of the high-cost sectors of the educational system in 'The Welfare State' have been the higher income groups. They have been helped to so benefit by the continued existence of a prosperous private sector in secondary education (partly subsidized by the state in a variety of ways including tax deductibles), and by developments since 1948 in provisions for child dependency in the category of fiscal welfare.[25] Take, for example, the case of two fathers each with two children, one earning $60,000 a year, the other $1,500 a year. In combining the effect of direct social welfare expenditures for children and indirect fiscal welfare expenditures for children the result is that the rich father now gets thirteen times more from the State than the poor father in recognition of the dependent needs of childhood.

Housing is another field of social policy which merits analysis from the point of view of redistribution. Here we have to take account of the complex interlocking effects of local rate payments, public housing subsidies, interest rates, tax deductibles for mortgage interest and other factors. When we have done so we find that the subsidy paid by the State to many middle-class families buying their own homes is greater than that received by poor tenants of public housing (local government) schemes.[26]

These are no more than illustrations of the need to study the redistributive effects of social policy in a wider frame of reference. Hitherto, our techniques of social diagnosis and our conceptual frameworks have been too narrow. We have compartmentalized social welfare as we have compartmentalized the poor. The analytic model of social policy that has been fashioned on only the phenomena that are clearly visible, direct and immediately measurable is an inadequate one. It fails to tell us about the realities of redistribution which are being generated by the processes of technological and social change and by the combined effects of social welfare, fiscal welfare and occupational welfare.

How far and to what extent should redistribution take place through welfare channels on the principle of achieved status, inherited status or need? This is the kind of question which, fundamentally, is being asked in Britain today. And it is being directed, in particular, at two major areas of social policy—social security and housing. Both these instruments of change and redistribution have been neglected for a decade or more. We have gone in search of new gods or no gods at all. It is time we returned to consider their roles afresh and with new vision. Perhaps we might then entitle our journey 'Ways of Extending the Welfare State to the Poor'.

NOTES

1. Macbeath, A., *Can Social Policies be Rationally Tested?*, Oxford University Press, London, 1957.
2. For some discussion of the problems of definition see Wilensky, H. L., and Lebeaux, C. N., *Industrial Society and Social Welfare*, Russell Sage Foundation, New York, 1958; *Social Welfare Statistics of the Northern Countries* Report No. 9, Stockholm, 1964; Myrdal, Gunnar, *Beyond the Welfare State*, Yale University Press, 1960, and Titmuss, R. M., *Essays on the 'Welfare State'*, Allen and Unwin Ltd, London, 1958.
3. See, for example, Dicey, A. V., *Law and Opinion in England During the Nineteenth Century*, London, 1905.
4. Polanyi, Karl, *Origins of Our Time*, Beacon Paperbacks, No. 45, London, 1945, p. 63.
5. *Reports of the Royal Commission on the Poor Laws*, HMSO, London, 1909.
6. Gerth, H. H., and Mills, C. W., *From Max Weber: Essays in Sociology*, Oxford University Press, New York, 1946.
7. See, for example, *Annual Reports of the National Assistance Board*, 1950–63, HMSO, London, and *Seventh and Eighth Reports on the Work of the Children's Department*, Home Office, HMSO, London, 1955 and 1961.
8. Illustrated in the recommendations of the Beveridge Report, *Social Insurance and Allied Services*, Cmd 6404, HMSO, London, 1942.
9. Hall, M. P., *The Social Services of Modern England*, Routledge, London, 1952.
10. Titmuss, R. M., *Income Distribution and Social Change*, Chapter 9, Allen and Unwin Ltd, London, 1962.
11. Titmuss, R. M., *Essays on the 'Welfare State'*, Allen and Unwin Ltd, London, second edition, 1963.
12. *Reports of the Royal Commission on the Taxation of Profits and Income*, 1952–55, HMSO, London, 1955.
13. *Final Report of the Royal Commission on Taxation*, Cmd 9474, HMSO, London, 1955, p. 68. See also Rubner, A., *Fringe Benefits*, Putnam, London, 1962.
14. See references in Titmuss, R. M., *Income Distribution and Social Change*, Chapter 7, and *British Tax Review*, January–February 1964.
15. Titmuss, R. M., *The Irresponsible Society*, Fabian Tract 323, London, 1959.

16. *Reports of the Royal Commission on the Taxation of Profits and Income*, 1952–55, HMSO, London, 1955.
17. Ministry of Education, *Grants to Students*, Cmd 1051, HMSO, London, 1960.
18. *Report of the Working Party on Educational Maintenance Allowances*, HMSO, London, 1957.
19. National Insurance Act, 1946, section 17 (2), and *Digest of Commissioner's Decisions*, HMSO, London, 1946–64.
20. See *Report of the Public Welfare Crisis Committee*, Metropolitan Washington Chapter of the National Association of Social Workers, Washington, 1963.
21. Hodson, J., *Royal Commission on Marriage and Divorce*, MDP/1952/337, HMSO, London, 1952.
22. Lindsey, A., *Socialized Medicine in England and Wales*, University of North Carolina Press, 1962.
23. Titmuss, R. M., *Essays on the 'Welfare State'*, Appendix on the National Health Service, second edition, Allen and Unwin Ltd, London, 1963.
24. *Robbins Report on Higher Education*, Appendix 2, Volumes A and B, HMSO, London, 1964.
25. *The Economist*, London, October 26, 1963.
26. Nevitt, D., *Essays on Housing*, Occasional Papers on Social Administration (No. 9), Codicote Press, London, 1964.

Chapter XVII

PENSIONS AND PUBLIC SERVANTS: A STUDY OF THE ORIGINS OF THE BRITISH SYSTEM*

For most of mankind, the approach of old age has always meant a growing sense of insecurity. The processes of ageing, physical and psychological, bring with them the actualities of dependence on others for many daily needs and an awareness of the indignities that can accompany the loss of status and independence. This is all part of what the Western world now calls 'the problems of old age'. But only in scale and intensity is it a new problem. The Psalmist implored 'Cast me not off in the time of old age,' and the ancient Greeks, those lovers of movement and form, looked upon old age with much distaste. To Hippocrates, who divided man's life into seven climacterics, old age began at 56.

Different societies throughout history have sought to incorporate in their cultures ways and means of resolving this problem and, in many instances, of making the realities of dependent old age less painful for the individual and for society. The old were attributed to be repositories of all wisdom. They were often the law-makers and controllers of authority. They demanded respect, required economic support, and accumulated prerogatives through the exercise of property rights. The unalienable effects of these final dispositions were not only powerful in themselves but helped to safeguard the authority of the next generation of aged. And by having many children, men and women hoped to insure themselves against want in their declining years.

These social and cultural systems were made possible in the past by the fact that few people survived into old age. Those who did were respected and honoured for an achievement which is commonplace today. For the vast majority of people, however, life was short and often brutal. They died before they had time to learn the social roles of old age. This is true of many primitive societies in Africa and the

* Foreword to book by Dr Marios Raphael, published by the Social Sciences Centre, Athens, Greece, in collaboration with the École Pratique des Hautes Études—Sorbonne—VIe section, *Sciences Économiques et Sociales* Mouton & Co., Paris, 1964.

East today. Anthropological studies have shown that in more primitive and rudimentary forms of association fewer old people are found and these, quite generally, with old age attributed to them at a much earlier chronological date than in advanced societies.

The revolution of individualism which accompanied the economic, technological and social changes in the Western world had far-reaching consequences for the status and functions of the old. The growth of urban societies, the separation of home and workplace, the decay of old crafts and the need to learn new and specialized skills all contributed to a more widespread sense of insecurity in old age. Yet, from some points of view, as Professor Notestein has remarked, the 'problem of ageing' today is no problem at all.[1] It is the only pessimistic way of looking at a great triumph of civilization. The population of the Western world has grown older because it has learnt to be efficient in the renewal of its life. Today, one thousand births yield about twice as large a fund of life as they produced in the seventeenth century. As a collective philosophical view this may be taken as one definition of progress. But societies which foster changes to save human life cannot escape responsibility for the quality of life thus extended.

The development in modern times of the concept of formal retirement from gainful employment strengthened the need for the acceptance by employers and the public at large of some measure of responsibility for the welfare of those denied the right to earn life. Retirement as we know it today is a comparatively new feature of human history. Demanded in the interests of economic efficiency and labour productivity, men and women have been 'cast off', insecured against want, more dependent on others in an increasingly complex world, and with a longer expectation of life than their ancestors before the industrial revolution.

One response to this challenge of poverty in old age has taken the form of pensions and superannuation schemes provided by employers. Another and more recent development in the West has been the establishment of State organized social security schemes. Both these systems, now to be found in many countries in a great variety of complex structures, are generally thought to be the product of the past century.

The value of Dr Raphael's study of the public records in England is, however, to show that the origins of these schemes lie much further back in history. We are thus led to understand some of the social and administrative problems of the seventeenth century; from, in fact, a date in 1684 when the first public pension was granted by the Government of the day to Martin Horsham, a landwaiter in the

201

Port of London, who was 'soe much indisposed by a great melancholye that he is at present unfit for business'. Unfitness was the criterion; not chronological age.

From then on Dr Raphael's study increases in complexity and fascination. We see the slow evolution and shaping of principles. Between 1684 and 1712 there were three main phases of development. The first was, in essence, the sale of an office by the holder to a personally nominated successor. Such transfers of office were allowed in the national administration of the Customs and other branches of the civil service on grounds of infirmity, sickness and old age. The new office-holders then became responsible for making payments—either lump sums or regular payments—to provide some income in old age for the previous holders.

In the second phase, the payment of pensions ceased to be personal. The initiative was taken by the public authorities. They proposed that a pension should be granted and appointed the successor whose salary was then charged with the cost of the pension. The principle operating during this phase was that individual pensions were charged against individual positions.

The third phase introduced the concept of the 'average'; saw the invention of the superannuation fund, and established the principle of collective responsibility. These developments were enshrined in a Treasury warrant 250 years ago—to be precise, on May 3, 1712.

It is a record of men in search of some acceptable principles of equity by which the costs of pensions for the aged and infirm should be distributed. The search moved outwards—from the individual to the group; and it started first among the poorer employees. By 1712 it was established that the cost of pensions should be borne collectively by new entrants by way of regular contributions to a publicly organized fund. Collectively, the young became responsible on average terms for the income-maintenance of their aged predecessors in office.

Throughout the eighteenth century, as Dr Raphael shows, new issues were identified and new problems emerge with the growth of public administration. These are described in two of his central chapters—Chapters III and IV. In terms of the definition of pension principles, they culminate in one of the great landmarks in British social policy—a Treasury Minute of August 1803. This was a State paper as momentous in its day—and, indeed, for the twentieth century—as the Beveridge Report of 1942. Significantly, both took shape and were influenced by the experience of two of the greatest wars in which the British people have been engaged.

The principles of 1803 were embodied in an Act of 1810. Contributions were abolished and the first foundations were laid for a comprehensive, non-contributory and generous public superannuation scheme for civil servants. This legislation and subsequent Acts of 1822, 1824, 1857 and 1859, wrestled with most of the intricate problems of pension planning which policy-makers in Western countries are confronted with in the 1960s: the equitable distribution of costs; the proportionate relationship of benefits to earnings; the problem of inflation, length of service and peak earnings in later life; the application of discretionary means tests as opposed to pensions 'as of right'; the definition of retirement and the age of retirement, and many other issues.

There is, indeed, much of contemporary interest in this study. Those who hold the view, for instance, that the past century has witnessed great improvements in conditions of health among the middle-aged and elderly will learn with some surprise that the age of retirement in the British civil service was lowered from 65 to 60 in 1859. It has broadly remained the same ever since. It came about as a result of an almost accidental parliamentary bargain but the underlying forces were, first, the need for a more efficient administration and the abolition of widespread corruption and nepotism in the service and, second, the emergence of the civil service as an independent and powerful professional pressure group or trade union.

Today, the British civil service is probably unique in the Western world in having the most generous non-contributory pension scheme, with tax-free lump sums and other benefits. Its non-contributory nature is largely the result of the price that was paid by the Government over one hundred years ago for the abolition of various forms of corruption and patronage and a monstrous welter of sinecures, fees and mediaeval survivals in the civil service.

All students of social policy will be indebted to Dr Raphael for the painstaking way in which he has unravelled, from the original sources, the genesis of the public superannuation system in Britain. His history covers a tumultuous period of nearly two hundred years of industrial, technological and social change. By 1859, Britain had been transformed into an industrial society. The social costs of change were borne in part by the aged; by the middle of the nineteenth century their conditions were a challenge to the public conscience. This was the context in which the superannuation Act of 1859 was passed. The civil servants were the first large organized group of workers to obtain security in their old age. The foundations of the system, firmly settled by the Act of 1859, remain today; the governing principles, applied more generously with the passage of time, still rule authoritatively. In 1963, the system was still a model and a goal for the vast majority of Britain's workers.

Appropriately, Dr Raphael ends his account with the Act of 1859. In doing so, he demonstrates the value of bringing the lessons of the past to bear on the problems of the present. As his academic adviser several years ago and his friend today, I end this Foreword by thanking him for his study.

NOTE

1. Notestein, F. W., 'Some Demographic Aspects of Aging', *Proceedings of the American Philosophical Society*, Vol. 98, No. 1, 1954.

PART IV

DILEMMAS IN MEDICAL CARE

THE ROLE OF THE FAMILY DOCTOR TODAY IN THE CONTEXT OF BRITAIN'S SOCIAL SERVICES*

Family doctors must not think that they are alone and unique in facing a 'crisis' in their professional roles. All service professions in Britain today are confronted with the problem of quality of service and of reconciling often conflicting interests. Let me put it like this as a teacher of London University. Should I spend ten minutes or an hour with this or that student? Should I acquiesce in a proposal that more of the teaching of undergraduates should be done by post-graduate students and less by the academics? The less time that we spend on teaching the more we shall have to pursue our own interests, to cultivate the garden, or ride a variety of hobby-horses. We are not paid by item of service or by piece-rates. We are not paid by examination results. We are not paid more if we see our students in the evenings or at the weekends. We are worse off if we spend money on books than if we borrow them from the library or give up reading because, like Ibsen, we find reading 'irrelevant'.

This system, like the family-doctor service and the National Health Service, is peculiarly British. It allows some academics to overwork grossly (and perhaps pushes them into the doctor's surgery). It allows others to lead a life of comparative calm and elegance. Frankly, I do not know what the answers are: except to strengthen the processes of professional self-examination and find ways of rewarding, mostly in non-material values, those who serve well their students, their clients, and their patients. I mention this matter simply to underline the fact that all professions (and not medicine alone) are involved in this problem of raising the standard of professional service.

Now I want to make explicit some of my personal and subjective views about the family doctor and the health services. Broadly, two

* The substance of this paper was given at the annual scientific meeting of the British Medical Association in Manchester on July 23, 1964, and in the Lecture of the Year to the City Division of the BMA on October 27 1964. It was published in *The Lancet*, 1, i, 1965.

value judgments underlie this paper. First, I regard the National Health Service Act as one of the most unsordid and civilized actions in the history of health and welfare policy. It put family doctors on a footing with university teachers, and patients on a footing with university students. Both professional groups—of doctors and teachers—are expected to give generously of what they know without a price being put on time or knowledge. The presumption in the relationship is thus more social than economic. Moreover, both are expected to give more than they can conceivably give because knowledge advances, men are not computers, and there are only 24 hours in the day. In this sense, professional service is never stationary, it knows no limits, and there is no resting-place or terminus, especially for the 'general man' in medical care and education. We may sigh for the apparent certitude of the specialist, the scientist, and the technician; but for all of our days we shall have to go on living with uncertainty, and with our clients' or students' dislike of uncertainty. Teachers in modern society can now say to doctors that the fear of not passing an examination is almost as pervasive as the fear of growing old. Examinations are increasingly the gateway to success in life. Doctors are thus no longer alone in wielding personal and professional authority in the determination of other people's life chances.

My second value judgment—or article of faith—is a belief in the importance to society of the generalist—the 'non-special mind' (in Bagehot's phrase). We live in an age of uncritical worship of technocracy—partly because its benefits can be measured by the monsters it produces and we think we love. We cannot measure the rewards of general practice or the rewards of teaching in the language of productivity or the economic market-place. As I see it, the role of the family doctor is in part to protect the patient from the excesses of specialized technocracy; to defend him against narrow-mindedness; and to help him humanely to find his way among the complex maze of scientific medicine without resort to self-diagnosis or charlatanism. In a quite different context, the role of the liberal educator or generalist is similar. Both inhabit more insecurely a world of uncertainty; it is safer (and easier) to specialize than to generalize. Both perform roles which unlike those of the technologist are difficult to evaluate in economic criteria; they happen to be about personal freedom which, as we all know, is without price.

So much for values. In now turning to the topic of my paper I find I cannot speculate about the role of the family doctor without considering some of the factors—including developments in the social services—which are likely to affect his future place in the medical and social care field.

The question of the family doctor's role in the hospital is bound up with the future of specialization. From Godber's analysis of the distribution of hospital work, it is clear that there has been since 1949 a great increase in specialization and in the division of hospital medical labour.[1] This has beneficially affected outpatient departments as well as inpatients—note, for example, the remarkable increase in traumatic and orthopaedic surgery attendances in recent years making this now the largest of any specialized outpatient service.

All that we know of advances in the basic sciences, of the results of medical research, and of the application of new techniques and tools—such as electronic recording systems and the operating microscope—suggests that this trend towards specialization and technological expertise will continue. The pace may well accelerate in the next decade or so, particularly as more of the younger specialists find opportunities and satisfactions in research and scientific inquiry.

Already this trend in the work of the hospital has led a number of thoughtful medical leaders in the United States like John Romano to ask the question: what is the future of the clinician.[2] Is he to be healer or scientist? Can he be both? 'The emphasis on bench research in laboratories in most medical schools has become so great,' according to Kerr White, writing recently on general practice in the United States, 'that teaching medical students and caring for patients are subsidiary activities carried out by those who, for one reason or another, are not doing the former.'[3]

To these questions we may add one more which stems from another observable trend in Britain and the United States, and again a trend which we may reasonably project into the future. All patients under (let us say) the age of 70 are likely to stay in hospital for progressively shorter but possibly more frequent periods. Hospital experience is thus likely to be briefer, more episodic, and discontinuous, and more intensive. The opportunities, therefore, for the hospital doctor to be a healer in the broader dimensions of social, psychological, and familial care are likely to decrease unless there is a strong movement for hospitals to develop into community institutions with psychiatric departments and other functional responsibilities for what we are now pleased to call 'community care'. The implications seem inescapable. If there is to be a major place for the family doctor in most of the hospitals of the future it is less likely to be a general role, and more likely to be a technical and specialized role.

But what of the care of the patient in his own home and his own environment? Assuming that the family doctor system survives in Britain, what are the major foreseeable factors which seem likely to affect his responsibilities and his relations with his patients? Let me enumerate briefly some of the more important ones before I turn to discuss (as I must) the Gillie Report.[4]

Owing to the shortsightedness and self-interest of the medical profession during the 1950s in alliance with the Treasury, we are going to be seriously short of doctors for many years. Even before the Willink Committee (which was dominated by the profession) recommended in 1957 a cut in the intake of medical students, many medical schools had reduced their numbers.[5] Although steps have recently been taken to increase the number of students these measures are, according to Hill, grossly inadequate.[6] The situation will be much worse if the 3,600 foreign-born doctors (on whom many hospitals at present rely heavily) return to their own countries. But even if we do get the crash programme for medical education advocated by Professor Hill and others to provide 12,000 additional doctors by 1981 (an increase of 25 per cent on present numbers) we shall clearly face serious shortages in the next ten years.

The conclusions seem inescapable. Far more use will have to be made of auxiliaries and ancillaries in all fields of medical care. The family doctor, in particular, will have to organize his time more effectively. In most areas of the country he will not be able to continue to function in splendid isolation as an independent contractor. This means more genuine group practice with a preventive outlook (as distinct from legal and financial partnerships); it means transforming the general hospital into an adjunct of general practice, extending outwards into the community (and much more generously than hitherto) a battery of technical and specialist facilities; and for the family doctor it means asking what is involved, socially, psychologically, and therapeutically, in being a member (let alone leader) of a community health team. This again is a problem of communication and of understanding the roles and functions of a variety of health and social workers in the community.

In short, I suggest that a growing shortage of doctors combined with other factors (which I shall come to in a minute) will require that applied medicine should become more of a group or team affair. Radical changes in the organization of medical care may thus be called for at the community level. We may, for instance, have to ask—if the family doctor becomes more of a community doctor— whether there is still a place for a medical officer of health. Perhaps his place could be assumed by a well-trained social administrator, sensitive to the needs of family doctoring.

Now I must turn to other factors which are likely to affect the future of the family doctor. Population trends mean more patients. Current population projections suggest that over the next twenty years the population of England and Wales will rise by over 7 million to around 54 million. What will also affect the family doctor service are changes in the age and social structure of the population. Owing to Britain's new population explosion the proportion of children in the population will rise substantially and there will also be a rise in the other main dependent age-group—those over retirement age. Perhaps most important of all for the family doctor is the fact that, if the Registrar General's estimates are borne out, we are likely to have in the next ten years just over 1 million more people aged over 65. Nearly a third of this additional population is expected to be aged 75 and over; 7 per cent of this increase (nearly all of them women) will be aged 85 and over. Indeed, by 1972 we are likely to have over 1 million people who have passed their 80th birthday—most of them women, many alone, slightly eccentric and unconforming, with memories of husbands or of husbands and children who might have been.

These are some of the more objective quantitative factors which must affect the work of the family doctor. As yet, there is little evidence to suggest that the institution (hospitals for the physically and mentally sick and infirm and other residential provisions) is likely to make in the future a substantially larger contribution to meeting the medical and social needs of the elderly. For a variety of reasons, the reverse seems more likely to happen. Thus, as the Gillie Report says, these needs will represent one of the central problems of general practice.

What of the more subjective and intangible factors of social change that are under way? First, it seems reasonable to expect continuing advances in medical science: more effective (as well as ineffective) drugs; more knowledge and better tools for the diagnosis and treatment of physical and mental illness; more specialization and division of labour in general medicine and surgery; and more emphasis on scientific research in the science-centred seats of medical power. It does not, of course, necessarily follow that these trends will make the hospital a more isolated institution of medical practice. But there will be pressures which can only be countered by the building of more bridges between the community and the hospital. In any event, the concept of the 'safe physical medicine doctor' as the permanent end-product of medical education will increasingly become just an interesting historical idea. Without a sure philosophy of family doctoring and the growth of community-minded hospitals, the family doctor of the future seems likely to feel more like a marginal man, more irresolute about his role in medical care and his place in the profession of medicine.

And what of the patient? He or she will increasingly be looking for four major elements in medical care: (1) scientific expertise; (2) personal interest and psychological understanding; (3) continuity of care, and (4) some right to choose whether to be treated at home (if it is medically possible) or in hospital. The family doctor in the future must expect, in company with workers in other service professions, a more demanding and critical public who, nevertheless, will not be sure which of these elements should have priority. Higher standards of education in the nation as a whole and a more sophisticated adult population are likely to herald the gradual disappearance of an uncomplaining, subservient, class-saturated acceptance of low standards of professional service.

Many sociological studies have shown that the less educated, working-class patient is more easily 'disciplined' and 'managed'. In this situation the doctor did not feel threatened and could persuade himself that a 'well managed' practice was also a 'well doctored' practice. This factor of patient-doctor subservience has contributed to the high status and prestige which the medical profession now commands (as it did not in the past) in the eyes of the British public, and partly explains the failure of the medical consultation-rate to rise significantly during the 1950s.

For too long, university teachers outside Oxbridge, family doctors outside Harley Street, workers in other professions, and bureaucrats in Whitehall and Town Hall have lacked the challenge and incentive of a critical clientele. In this setting of unequal relationships, low standards have flourished. In the long run, an educated public opinion is, as J. H. F. Brotherston has said, the most powerful ally of the medical profession.

This does not mean making the consumer and the lawyer king through the operation of the price mechanism—as American medicine is now in danger of doing. Signs of consumer dissatisfaction in that country are today to be found in various forms of medico-scientific charlatanism, resort to the corner drugstore, demands for osteopaths, chiropractors, and naturopaths, and the steeply rising costs of malpractice insurance. In California, the young doctor has now to pay around $820 a year for such insurance, and one doctor in four has been the target of a malpractice suit or claim. In Britain, the comparable figure is about $6. Malpractice suits are thought to be a symptom of a breakdown in doctor-patient relationships. They are also a consequence of making the consumer king: self-diagnosis, self-medication, self-selection and purchase of the specialist in the medical market-place.

Another consequence is that, following the Food and Drugs Amendment Act of 1962, more and more hospitals, clinics, and doctors are abandoning the clinical trial of new drugs for fear of malpractice claims. Hence the search in other countries by some sectors of the American pharmaceutical industry for uncritical and less sophisticated publics to cooperate in the testing of new drugs and the advancement of scientific knowledge.

What should the response be in Britain to the challenge of rising expectations for better standards of medical care, social work practice, university and school teaching, and, in general, higher qualitative standards in all professional services? I do not think the answer lies in paying academics by student results, by tipping doctors for special indulgences and overtime, or by turning social workers into private entrepreneurs with legitimated practice expenses and so forth. One of the most important alternatives to such a renaissance of professional market-places must lie in a sustained process of group and individual professional self-examination. The corollary of the impact of scientific curiosity is applied professional curiosity. In the field of medical care, the spectrum of re-examination has therefore to run all the way from the first MB to the role of research in general practice, postgraduate education, the reformulation of concepts of ethical behaviour, and community and hospital relations.

Hitherto, the medical profession in Britain and the United States has been *the* model for other professions seeking status, prestige, and privilege. For many reasons it is likely to continue to be in Britain one of the most influential reference groups in the shaping of professional behaviour patterns. The more that the family doctor gets mixed up in community care, the more chance he will have of setting standards of behaviour for other professional workers.

On this somewhat controversial note I come to the Gillie Report (*Field of Work of the Family Doctor, 1963*). While it had much to recommend that was admirable concerning the need for research and self-examination it did not itself quite live up to its own precepts. Consider, for example, two of the main theses advanced in the report. First, the family doctor was cast in the role of co-ordinator, mobilizer, director, stage manager, and leader of community care in psychological as well as physical terms. No factual evidence was adduced in the report to indicate that the trend has been in this direction, that more family doctors are establishing relations with social workers and other members of the local health and welfare team without the intervention of the medical officer of health, that fewer family doctors are delegating mental health responsibilities to mental welfare officers, and that, in general, proportionately more family doctors are gradually assuming a role of leadership in community care. Some general comments were made about the attachment of health visitors to individual practices and to family doctors undertaking more maternity and child welfare duties but no facts were provided.

On relations with consultants the report did supply one piece of evidence. While the number of domiciliary consultations had risen by 1962 to nearly 300,000 a year it was 'estimated that consultation with both doctors present at the patient's home takes place today at less than half of the visits, and this proportion is probably still falling'. Considering all that is said about the 'professional loneliness' of the family doctor (to quote again from the Gillie Report) and his need for a place in the hospital scheme of things, this fact is surprising. Yet the committee made no attempt to set out the reasons or set on foot an inquiry. Had they done so the results might have shown that the family doctor is not wholly responsible for this disquieting trend in professional relations and patient care.

A second main theme in the report was concerned with (what it calls) 'the barely tolerable pressure on the family doctor, the length of his working day and his 24-hour-a-day responsibility'. It also drew attention to the undoubted fact that the family doctor had been at the receiving end, so to speak, of the biological consequences of explosive advances in medical and scientific knowledge during the past twenty years. 'The results', said the report, 'in survival of the less physically fit and the aged have added to the scope, but also to the load of the family doctor's work. This increased load is the central problem in general practice today.'

There is unfortunately no factual material available for recent years relating to demands on the family doctor by the elderly or by people of all ages. Between 1905 and 1956 the number of studies of medical consultations with family doctors (providing figures on a yearly basis) totalled at least thirty-one. Of these inquiries into the work of the family doctor, just over half made some claim to be representative of the population as a whole. So far as I can ascertain, the British Medical Association has published national figures for eleven years, the last one relating to 1939. The results of the one comprehensive inquiry conducted since the National Health Service was introduced, and sponsored by the Association, have not yet been published, although they relate to the work of the family doctor in the early 1950s. The latest information we thus have is for 1955–56 and resulted from the fruitful collaboration on morbidity statistics

214

between the College of General Practitioners and the General Register Office.

It is often said today that general practice in Britain has been subject in recent years to a plethora of research and inquiry. While this may be true of certain special aspects, the impression that is left after an analysis of all these thirty-one studies between 1905 and 1956 is that more is known about the basic facts of the family doctor's day before, rather than since, the health service was introduced. Introspection, psychiatric and professional, there may have been, but not about the fundamentals of demand and supply.

This examination of all the medical consultation-rate studies that have been made, local and national, gives no indication that there has been since 1948 any notable increase in the rate—either for elderly people or for the population as a whole. On the contrary, there are hints of a fall. For example, according to the reports, *Morbidity Statistics from General Practice*, the medical-consultation rate for elderly men was 5.9 and for elderly women it was 6.4 in 1955-56 (the latest year for which we have any representative figures). Though there are difficulties in comparison, these were lower than the rates for 1948–49 reported by the Survey of Sickness and published by the Registrar General. All such figures are, of course, averages and to some extent representative of general practice in England and Wales.

These and other figures, and, in particular, the absence of any evidence that medical-consultation rates have risen, are especially puzzling because of the advent of a free family doctor service for all old people. Three other facts could have led to some rise in consultation-rates since 1948: the proportion of over-75s in the population of old people has substantially increased, death-rates among the elderly were higher during the 1950s than the Registrar General had estimated, and evidence from research carried out by the Social Medicine Research Unit of the Medical Research Council shows that disability among men aged 61–63 steadily increased during the 1950s.[7]

It is all the more remarkable, therefore, that, apart from the unpublished study by the British Medical Association about fourteen years ago, no objective and comprehensive inquiry has been made into the basic facts of the family doctor's work either by the profession itself, the medical faculties of the universities, or the Ministry of Health. We thus know little about recent trends, what have been the medical care consequences of changes in age and social structure, why there are extraordinarily wide differences from practice to practice, and whether it is true that the Scots have substantially higher consultation-rates than the English.

Three recent trends which have a bearing on the work of the family doctor do, however, make more difficult the problem of recording, estimating, and comparing changes in demand and response over time. First, general practitioners have been using more often the diagnostic and technical facilities of the hospital; secondly, hospitals—and particularly mental hospitals—have been discharging patients more quickly; thirdly, emergency-call or commercial deputising services have spread rapidly in London and certain other areas (in London it is said that about 50 per cent of all general practitioners now make use of these services), and it is not known whether these items of service are included in doctors' records.

In the absence of the basic facts about patterns and trends in medical care—about who uses the Health Service and with what results—it is hazardous to speculate about the future. This problem of professional self-assessment in terms of both quantity and quality of service is not, I should emphasize again, peculiar to the medical profession. It is now of growing concern to the legal profession, for example, and also to university teachers. How effective is the law in meeting the needs of the general public? Is the present system of entrance, education, call, and control of the Bar consistent with the principle that justice must not only be done, but must be seen to be done? Are university teachers as overburdened with teaching duties (and as short of time for reading) as their own trade union has claimed? Why are there such great differences in student failure-rates in similar faculties in different universities? Are these high failure-rates in one of the most generously staffed university systems in the world due to faults in the students themselves or to the neglect of undergraduate teaching and other causes? Is there not a real danger today, with the growth of specialization, the advancement of research, the prestige value of graduate supervision, and the general *ambience* of academic entrepreneurship, that the more generalized teaching of undergraduates will come to be regarded as a low-status occupation?

The dilemmas of the general man in medicine, as in other professions, are serious ones—more serious perhaps in the long run than the problem of the two cultures. They are a critical part of the wider problem of quality of service and of the growing need for professional self-examination.

The time is opportune for change and self-appraisal. Informed public opinion has been increasingly recognizing in recent years the need for greatly improved community services. This trend in opinion thus favours maintaining and strengthening the family doctor system. It is for the profession to decide whether the system should be maintained, and whether it is prepared to make all the necessary changes in organization, functions, and relationships that will be involved.

NOTES

1. Godber, G. E., *Brit. Med. J.*, 1961, ii, p. 843.
2. Romano, J., *J. Med. Educ.*, 1963, 38, p. 584.
3. White, L. Kerr, *ibid.*, 1964, 39, p. 333.
4. 'Field of Work of the Family Doctor', *Report of the Sub-committee of the Standing Medical Advisory Committee*, HMSO, 1963.
5. Abel-Smith, B., and Gales, K., 'British Doctors at Home and Abroad', *Occasional Papers on Social Administration*, Welwyn, Herts., 1964.
6. Hill, K. R., *Lancet*, 1964, ii, 517.
7. Morris, J. N., *Uses of Epidemiology*, Second Edition, Livingstone, 1964.

Chapter XIX

SOCIOLOGICAL AND ETHNIC ASPECTS OF THERAPEUTICS*

I

As a student of medical care looking at therapeutics, I move in a world inhabited more by speculative thought and empirical social studies than by experimental science, quantitative measurement, and controlled trials in the laboratory and the hospital. This means that I shall have to take a broader definition of the word 'drugs' than a scientist might and a wider interpretation of what we mean by 'our society'. I shall also have to draw attention to the fact that man does not (and cannot) live by drugs alone.

Although this essay is largely concerned with some of the effects of developments in drug therapy on the doctor-patient relationship, I want, first of all, to say a few words on the question of consumer costs. As we are all aware, technical developments in drug therapy during the past thirty years have been on a massive and breathtaking scale. In most Western countries some 80 to 90 per cent of the prescriptions are written today for drugs not on the market ten to fifteen years ago.[1] In the United States some three to four hundred new drugs are now marketed every year.[2] The annual sales of prescription drugs manufactured in the United States rose from $200,000,000 in 1939 to over 2.5 billion dollars in 1961. In addition, over one billion dollars was spent for self-medication.[3] In Britain, the national drug bill practically doubled between 1949 and 1956 and led to a series of official inquiries into the costs and problems of prescribing.[4] Under the National Health Service, there are today approximately some 10,000 possible 'remedies' which may be prescribed.

Over the last decade national expenditures on drugs per head of the population have been rising rapidly in most countries, and particularly in the low-income or underdeveloped countries of the

* Paper given at a conference on Drugs in our Society, Johns Hopkins University, Baltimore, USA, November 1963, and published in *Drugs in our Society* (Ed. Talalay, P.), Johns Hopkins Press, 1964.

world. There are, of course, difficulties of definition and measurement and broadly comparable statistics are only available for a small number of countries.

These statistics show, however, remarkable differences in national expenditures.[5] Britain, Holland and Denmark appear to be the three low-cost countries, while expenditures in France, Western Germany, the United States and Italy are 50 per cent to 200 per cent higher. Differences of this order are puzzling and cannot be explained without much more research. They are even larger and more difficult to explain when we include a number of low-income countries in Latin America and Africa for which some statistics are available. Considered in terms of the proportion of the national income devoted to drugs, some of these countries are spending more than the richer countries of the West. The cost per person of drugs as a percentage of income per head is three times higher in Venezuela than in Britain. To take another example, Mauritius is today spending a higher proportion of its national income on the products of the pharmaceutical industry than Britain.[6]

The impact of the therapeutic revolution has radically changed in these countries the allocation of scarce resources and the order of social and economic priorities. Relatively more may be spent on drugs and curative medicine; relatively less on food and preventive health measures. There has been an economic as well as an ecological disturbance.

II

As many other participants in our discussions, and especially Professor Owsei Temkin, have already said, man's addiction to potions and 'medical' remedies is as old as history. Two hundred years ago Voltaire defined medical treatment as the art of pouring drugs of which one knew nothing into a patient of whom one knew less. It was not until medical therapeutics began to deserve the name of a science in the 1940s that this cynical generalization lost some of its validity. Even so, most Western-trained physicians practising today in all countries of the world completed their training before the flowering of this scientific revolution in therapeutics. It has even been said that 'any doctor who has been out of medical school for five years and has not learnt any more is practising outdated medicine'.[1]

One problem then for most doctors is how to handle ignorance and uncertainty. Confronted with the patient, they have to deal with this situation in much the same time (on average) as they and their predecessors had before the scientific revolution. There is little evidence for most Western countries that family doctors now spend significantly more time on each patient consultation. Doctors, like members of other 'service' professions, have, of course, always had to perform their role in a large area of uncertainty: about the patient as a person; about the nature of his disease or presumed abnormality; about the effects of therapy. What is different—or what has changed—so far as the doctor is concerned, is his greater relative *awareness* of ignorance in the field of drug therapy. The better he is as a diagnostician (and he certainly has more effective aids today than thirty years ago) the more likely it will be that his awareness of ignorance will be correspondingly increased. More specific diagnosis means more specific therapeutic choices; 'blanket' or 'blunderbuss' treatments will not suffice and will consciously be recognized as inadequate or potentially harmful.

Many more factors operate today than in the past to remind the doctor constantly of his therapeutic inadequacies: the growing emphasis on postgraduate medical education; pressure from patients in a science-worshipping world; specialization in skills and functions; the proliferation of medical journals which, on an international count, now number over 7,000; and perhaps most important of all for the family physician, the avalanche of advertising and advice in a variety of forms from the pharmaceutical industry. The makers of drugs are not only telling the doctor what to prescribe and why, but they are also continually telling him indirectly that he does not know. According to one British medical writer, who is not an admirer of the National Health Service, the growing complexity of scientific therapeutics has meant that 'the medical profession has to a great extent lost control. That commerce should attempt to take over the task of academic instruction, using its immense resources in the palatable presentation of scientific facts, is a matter of deep significance. For if doctors are in fact reduced to receiving instruction from trade, what becomes of their claim to be considered a learned profession?'[7]

Whatever the professional implications, it seems clear that the general message being delivered daily to the doctor is, first, to remind him of how much he does not know and, second, to impress on him that being up-to-date about the latest developments in therapeutics is the mark of a 'good' doctor. New drugs, like new concepts, often have a remarkably short life. The pharmaceutical industry, like many an academic in the natural and social sciences, is now teaching on the uncertain frontiers of advancing knowledge.

The dilemma for the family physician, unlike the university

teacher in other disciplines who can take refuge in some specialized tower, is that it is much harder for him to confess or admit his self-awareness of ignorance. 'Leave medicine to medical men', now almost a universal slogan, is one symptom of the attempt to escape from the dilemma. It is being accentuated today by a number of external and internal forces in achievement-oriented Western societies. The claims of the profession itself to higher status and greater rewards make confession more difficult. A similar effect operates when systems of paying for medical care appear to require that the patient be given something in return for his payment. 'Whatever men expect they soon come to think they have a right to.'[8] In this contractual relationship, it is harder for the doctor to withhold the benefits of science. He has been invested by the patient with the role of a 'giver' of concrete objects. These idealized expectations carry with them the assumption that the doctor knows what the objects contain and what their effects are. To the patient, science has come to mean something tangible, something that 'works', something that means action. He—and society at large—communicate compulsively this conception of the doctor's role performance.

The patient's urge to act, to do something about his illness or about the illness of a loved one, to conform to the activity values of society, meets, reinforces and is reinforced by the doctor's urge to fulfil the high expectations invested in him by society and the profession itself. To expect that anything is possible can lead to trying everything possible. The public behaviour of the pharmaceutical industry, both in relation to the doctor and to the generality of patients, plays the role of a third force in stimulating action. The whole drug revolution has greatly accentuated the time factor in the interplay of these forces. The drug houses, operating under patent laws, know that monopolistic situations may be today very short-lived; consequently, they are in a hurry to change prescribing behaviour quickly. Doctors, anxious to make up for long years of training and to accumulate patients quickly, are in a hurry to be 'at their best' today; tomorrow will be too late. Where are we to look for the countervailing forces which will remind us of the more leisurely 'wisdom of the body'?

III

Before the scientific explosion, the patient's expectations were of a less *specific* kind. The placebo bottle of medicine certainly had its place (and potentially a much less toxic place) and often formed part of the contract. But it did not dominate the contract or relationship as scientific drugs do today. The bottle of medicine from the doctor, domestic remedies of various kinds and self-medication with cure-all patent medicines all contributed to and often exchanged for one another in the pragmatic 'folk medicine' of the nineteenth century. In most classes in Western society, consumption of these remedies was on a massive and empirical scale. But the patient of those days, in his relationships with the doctor, looked to a larger extent than the patient today for assurance, experience, personality—authoritarian medical wisdom.

Discipline and social control in situations of serious illness found their expression through the personality of the doctor. He deployed his personality as an instrument of therapy. He did not consciously have to remember to be what he was. Self-awareness of inadequate personality on his part in those days has its counterpart today in self-awareness of ignorance of scientific therapeutics. Patients can more easily make choices about the former than they can about the latter. In the competition for patients, failure in the past was more a matter of personality, social connections, or external factors such as the financial resources of the community.

Today, it is thought by the doctor to lie to a greater extent in fulfilling (or failing to fulfil) the patient's conception of his role as a purveyor of scientific therapeutics. In one sense then, he has surrendered to the expectations of patients and to the prevailing value system. The more that a society as a whole values success in life and fears death, the higher may be its demand for medical care in some form or other. The more that the individual personality is sensitive and self-conscious about the roles he thinks he is expected to play in society, the more demanding may be his perception of what constitutes 'efficient function' or wholeness for himself and others. What man himself regards as sickness and as his role as a sick or well person are the critical factors, for, as Charles Lamb observed, 'sickness enlarges the dimensions of a man's self to himself . . . supreme selfishness is inculcated upon him as his only duty'.

Surrender to consumer behaviour in presumed competitive conditions which are powerfully influenced by exacting standards of 'efficient function' may thus be one consequence of the scientific revolution in therapeutics. It carries with it too the implication, noted by a number of observers, of surrender to the makers of drugs.[7] Yet, in another sense, it is the patient who has surrendered by worshipping uncritically at the shrine of science. As Professor Freidson of New York concluded in his perceptive analysis of relationships, '. . . the amount of control that the patient can exercise over his fate in the consulting room is being reduced.'[9] He is the victim of the assumptions that he and society have made about the doctor and of his inability today to assess scientific competence in medical therapeutics. 'Everything,' said Professor Péquignot, 'has passed beyond his (the patient's) understanding, and he feels like a pawn in the game. This is because medicine, in becoming a science, has been transformed (like thermodynamics or nuclear physics) into something which can only be understood from within, and after long studies.'[10]

IV

This speculative 'model' (if it may be so described) of the doctor-patient-drug relationship requires to be qualified and substantiated at many points. It is largely derived from the work of sociological theorists and medical philosophers; no attempt has been made to document it fully from the growing literature on medical sociology.[11] Nor was it thought necessary to present anything in the nature of a cost-benefit analysis in economic and technical terms of the physical and psychological effects of drug therapy. These are to some extent dealt with in other papers; and Dr Dickinson Richards and others have paid tribute, on the credit side, to the immense benefits that have accrued to man as a result of these scientific advances in medicine.

What is lacking in the research field are concrete and controlled studies which would give precision to these speculative observations suggesting that the doctor-patient relationship has been profoundly affected by the impact of scientific therapeutics. They are particularly needed to deepen our understanding of the role played in this relationship by three major variables:

(1) *Time and Continuity of Care.* The problems of knowledge, choice and use of drugs are probably different in degree if not in kind in the case of relatively unfamiliar patients with short-term, episodic illness as compared with relatively familiar patients with long-term illness or disability.[12] Does continuity of care by the family physician act in the patient's interests as a form of social control, as a protection against the feeling of being regarded as an 'object', as a precondition for allowing psychological insights to come into play, and as a stimulus to the doctor not to surrender to ignorance and the latest, perhaps inadequately tested, therapeutic innovation?

(2) *Class and Inequality of Communication.* Questions of time and continuity in relationships clearly cannot be disassociated from the social, ethnic and educational characteristics of the doctor and

the patient. The evidence of such empirical studies as have been attempted suggests that these 'social distance and deference' variables may be quite critical. Their importance has been shown in mental health studies, in the treatment of tuberculosis, in the impact of a new therapy on diabetes, in partially explaining geographical differences in prescribing behaviour by family physicians in Britain, in experimental social survey research in the United States, in studies of teacher-pupil relationships in American and English schools and, most sharply of all, in studies of the impact of Western medicine on primitive cultures. This body of knowledge, accumulating unevenly in various sectors of the behavioural sciences, does show that there are group differences—whether we ascribe them to class, culture, education or language—in respect of the perception and self-diagnosis of need; in respect of the action taken to satisfy need; and in respect of the effectiveness of use of such need-services as are available.[13] Little empirical work has so far been done, however, on the interplay of these dependent variables in relation to drug therapy.

(3) *Systems of Organizing Medical Care.* Different ways in which medical care is organized, financed and administered are known to influence the quality and quantity of doctor-patient relationships independently and in association with other variables. Such systems cannot be neutral. Every type of system, private and public, embodies a set of rights and obligations for both doctor and patient. These become part of the doctors' and patients' expectations of each others' role and role performance and, simultaneously, their self-images of expected behaviour. In these situations of doctor-patient expectations, which may coincide or conflict, the modern drug is today playing an increasingly significant part. How significant and with what consequences will depend, *inter alia*, on the values and goals of different medical care systems.

v

Lastly, we come to the question of medical ethics and the impact on traditional codes of behaviour of the scientific revolution in therapeutics. If medical care were not controlled (or assumed to be controlled) by some special ethical prescriptions, much of this discussion would be irrelevant. It would have to be conducted in the language of the marketplace. But in all Western societies it is declared that the supreme object of medicine is service and not personal profit.[14] The essence of professional behaviour and the patients' confidence in a profession is thus *predictable service to people*. Predictable, in this context, can be translated as 'truthful'. Practitioners have a fiduciary trust to maintain certain standards predictable to patients. This is the basis of the rule restricting competition, the rule which forbids a physician from treating another physician's patient without his authority. It is, however, the special nature of the relationship which creates the dilemmas for the physician in the field of drug therapy. How can he be helped to raise standards of ethical behaviour, faced as he is with the challenge of uncertainty, ignorance, and error in the choice, use and effects of drugs? What are the implications for the doctor's training and education, for the education of patients, for the making of medical-care policy, for the evaluation of new drugs and for the production of drugs?

These are international problems, for the therapeutic revolution has taken place in many parts of the world before the development of professional codes of behaviour. These codes were slow to evolve in the West. The shape and direction they took depended as much on the will of society in general as it did on the policies of the profession itself. Above all, they depended on the growth of the idea of disinterested service. As many witnesses have testified in the last ten years, the advent of science has subjected these codes to serious and widespread stresses.[15]

But in many countries of Africa, Latin America and the Far East the drug revolution is spreading at an ever-quickening pace and, virtually, in an ethical vacuum. The soil is richly receptive. Traditional cosmologies and attitudes to health and disease readily absorb modern therapeutics. The popularity of the administration of intramuscular injections, for example, with its ritual of aseptic precautions and the apparently magical quality of the act of acupuncture, has been reported by observers in practically every underdeveloped society. It is, moreover, profitable; it enables the doctor to avoid time-consuming human relationships; it does not require the patient to change his habits and ways of life, and it thus allows the doctor to contract out of the aspirations of the newly independent nations. Societies which desperately need preventive health practices are being told by Western scientific medicine that they can purchase health passively. Drugs become substitutes for cultural change. Standardized therapeutic procedures substitute for medical humanity. And the pharmaceutical industry and other agencies simultaneously provide 'an amazing variety of ancient and ineffective drugs from overseas'.[16]

These are not the only consequences. Drug addiction is growing in Africa. The emergence and rapid spread of drug-resistant organisms in India and many parts of Africa is worsening the problem of control over tuberculosis and other diseases. Pharmacies are owned by doctors (and sometimes financed by the industry), and these sell potentially toxic compounds over the counter on credit terms and on an irregular basis to all comers. One authority, writing in 1960, concluded that one of the dangers threatening medicine in Africa was the private doctor. He was not observing any medical code and was 'playing on the credulity of the naive and superstitious'.[17]

Two very general propositions emerge from this brief survey. The first is that these scientific advances in drug therapy now need, for their efficacy, stricter professional codes of behaviour—more explicit and comprehensive value-systems of expected norms of medical behaviour derived from professional reference groups.

The second is that the greater the social and cultural differences between the doctor practising Western medicine and his patient, the greater is the need for high standards of professional ethics. The fewer the differences in language, perception, behaviour and modes of life, the easier understanding and treatment becomes, thus reducing the potential power of the doctor over the patient. Their relationship must remain fundamentally unequal, despite, one might add, the Drug Amendments of 1962 and the establishment of the voluntary Dunlop Committee in Britain; we have to strive, however, for less inequality. These generalizations apply with added force to countries undergoing rapid social change, detribalization and urbanization, with all their concomitant effects in diminishing the sway of fatalism and creating new expectations of health and well-being.

NOTES

1. Romano, J., *Tomorrow's Challenge to the Medical Sciences*, London, 1957.
2. Rozenthal, A. A., in Sanders, M. K. (Ed.), *The Crisis in American Medicine*, New York, 1961, p. 100.
3. us, Congress, Senate, Sub-committee on Antitrust and Monopoly, *Hearings: Drug Industry Antitrust Act*, 87th Cong., 1st Sess., 1961, p. 2580, testimony of Secretary Ribicoff. See also Somers, H. M. and A. R., *Doctors, Patients and Health Insurance*, Washington, 1961.
4. United Kingdom, Ministry of Health, *Final Report of the Committee on Cost of Prescribing*, London, 1959, p. 1.
5. Dunlop, D., quoted in *Brit. Med. J.*, 1962, 2 : 1366, and International Labour Office, *The Cost of Medical Care*, Geneva, 1959.
6. Titmuss, R. M., and Abel-Smith, B., *Social Policies and Population Growth in Mauritius*, London, 1961.
7. Roberts, F., *The Cost of Health*, London, 1952, p. 80.
8. Lewis, C. S., *The Screwtape Letters*, London, 1959, p. 152.

9. Freidson, E., *Patients' Views of Medical Practice*, New York, 1961, p. 227.
10. Péquignot, H., *Impact of Science on Society*, V, No. 4, December 1954, p. 235.
11. See 'The Sociology of Medicine: A Trend Report and Bibliography', *Current Sociology*, 1963, X/XI, No. 3.
12. On the use and misuse of drugs for different conditions see Peterson, O. L., and others, 'An Analytical Study of North Carolina General Practice', *J. Med. Educ.*, December 1956, 31 : 12.
13. Comprehensive bibliographies are provided in: Morris, J. N., *Uses of Epidemiology*, Second Edition, Edinburgh, 1964; Freidson, *Patients' Views*; Paul, B. D. (Ed.), *Health, Culture and Community*, New York, 1955; Gartley, J. E. (Ed.), *Patients, Physicians and Illness*, Glencoe, Ill., 1958; Susser, M. W., and Watson, W., *Sociology in Medicine*, Oxford, 1962; Martin, J. P., *Social Aspects of Prescribing*, London, 1957.
14. For example: 'The prime object of the medical profession is to render service to humanity; reward or financial gain is a subordinate consideration' (Principles of Medical Ethics of the American Medical Association, 1953).
15. See, for example, Landis, B. Y. (Ed.), 'Ethical Standards and Professional Conduct', *Annals of the American Academy of Political and Social Science*, 1955, 297, and 'Medicine and the Drug Industry in Germany', *Lancet*, 1956, 2 : 1304.
16. Prentice, C. R. M., 'The Land of the Million Elephants', *Lancet*, 1963, 2 : 290.
17. Gear, H. S., 'Medicine in the New Africa', *Lancet*, 1960, 2 : 1020. For other references to the use and misuse of drugs in underdeveloped countries see Titmuss, R. M., 'Medical Ethics and Social Change in Developing Societies', *Lancet*, 1962, 2 : 209; Lambo, T. A., 'Further Neuropsychiatric Observations in Nigeria', *Brit. Med. J.*, 1960, 2 : 1696; Klokke, A. H., 'Medical Care in the Tropics', *Lancet*, 1961, 1 : 1336; Macdonald, N., 'New Drugs Needed for Tuberculosis', *Lancet*, 1962, 2 : 92, and Keppel Club (London School of Hygiene) papers on Drugs and Medical Care, April 1962 (unpublished).

Chapter XX

TRENDS IN SOCIAL POLICY: HEALTH*

My task is to explore the relations between thought and action in the field of health legislation since the appearance in 1905 of Dicey's *Law and Opinion in England in the Nineteenth Century*.

In one of these lectures last term, Professor Robson was a little unnerved by the thought of Dicey's ghost lurking in the audience. I am not afraid of ghosts but I am of doctors. Let me hasten to explain, therefore, that in this lecture I am not concerned with the theory and practice of medicine in clinical terms nor, except in the broadest way, with the changing pattern of health and disease. What I have chosen to examine, expressed at its simplest, is the organiza-tion of medical care within the social and scientific context of the last fifty years. What forces have shaped those institutions and systems, public and private, individual and collective, through which doctor and patient are brought together? There have, of course, been many: health is a relative concept, deeply embedded, as a doctor has said, 'in the domains of politics, philosophy, etiquette, religion, cosmology and kinship.'[1] All I have attempted in this paper is to single out a few of the principal strands of influence on thought and action in the twentieth century.

Political and legal developments, affecting the role of medicine in society, have already been largely sketched in for me by previous lecturers in this series.[2] The significance, in political terms, of the National Health Insurance Act of 1911 and the National Health Service Act of 1946 has been emphasized more than once. These Acts summarize the two great periods of legislative activity in the provision of personal health services in England. During both periods the figure of a Welshman galvanized BMA House into action. The decisions of these two men, the counsellors they chose, and the bargains they struck have profoundly affected the structure of our health institutions and the place of the doctor in modern England.

Accordingly, this paper concentrates attention on the events of

* Public lecture at the London School of Economics and Political Science, March 1958, and published in *Law and Opinion in England in the Twentieth Century* (Ed. Ginsberg, M.), Stevens, London, 1959.

1911 and 1946. First, I shall discuss some of the difficulties of disentangling the current of social forces and opinion from the influence of war on policies for health. Secondly, I describe the conditions of general practice before the Act of 1911—the general practitioner's Act. Thirdly, I attempt to trace the impact of science on medicine as one of the forces which contributed to the Act of 1946—the specialist's Act. Binding these topics together, I employ a common political thread. In a sentence, it is the unreality of the antithesis between 'collectivism' and 'individualism' in the problem of the clash between equality and freedom.

This was one of the problems which dominated the debates about health and social policy at the beginning of the century. In framing the Act of 1911, Lloyd George, as he impishly remarked, renounced vice, in the person of Beatrice Webb with her scheme for a public salaried medical service, and virtuously embraced insurance.[3] She turned out to be the lady from the Pru.; courted and introduced by a rising young solicitor in the insurance world, later to become Chancellor of the Exchequer, Sir Kingsley Wood. Though of respectable actuarial parentage she had an uncommonly high record of lapses. These, however, she successfully concealed and got herself 'approved' as a friendly body, cheerfully able to dispense on the doorsteps of the poor both health and burial benefits. Thus fortified, Lloyd George was able to provide working-class bread-winners with medical benefits and free choice of doctor. In 1946, Mr Aneurin Bevan climbed on to Lloyd George's shoulders and gave to the middle-classes and to women and children what the working-man had received in 1911. Not only did Mr Bevan renounce vice, on this occasion represented by the Coalition Government's plan for a salaried medical service controlled by local government, but he also renounced Miss Prudential, leaving her to be cultivated by Lord Beveridge and a new generation of pension consultants and retirement counsellors.

The question that is often asked by students from abroad of comparative social policies is why has State intervention in the field of medical care in England advanced further than in any other country in the Western world. Part of the answer is, I think, that the 1946 legislation would have assumed a very different and less comprehensive form but for the fact of 1911, and but for the fact that it happened when it did—paradoxically, so close in time and in thought to the philosophy of individualism. We are thus led to examine the social and economic problems of medical care during the first decade of the century.

In the introduction to the second edition of his book, written in

1914, Dicey sagaciously remarked: 'A collectivist never holds a stronger position than when he advocates the enforcement of the best ascertained laws of health.'[4] He was apparently led to this view by a political interpretation of Chadwick's and Simon's work for a sanitary England and by Lloyd George's 'collectivist' Health Act of 1911. But to assess these developments solely in political terms does not, by itself, shed much light on the many causal factors at work. Dicey, however, explained both the law and the ideas that shaped it in the language of politics.[5] For the State to act in the interests of 'the best ascertained laws of health' meant, to him, a grave threat to liberty, for such action signified 'government for the good of the people by experts, or officials who know, or think they know, what is good for the people better than either any non-official person or than the mass of the people themselves'.[6] This was collectivism or socialism (Dicey used both terms as synonyms though he preferred the former because it was a convenient antithesis to individualism). In any event, the motive behind the law and the effect of the law itself signified to Dicey more redistributive taxation in favour of the poor. He assumed that all State intervention in the field of health had this consequence.

Both theses, that more enforcement of the laws of health means more collectivism and less personal liberty, and that such measures benefit only the poor, may be examined in the light of other ideas and forces which Dicey neglected.

He conceived of opinion as 'law-making opinion' that 'body of beliefs, convictions, sentiments, accepted principles, or firmly rooted prejudices' which, taken together, makes up the 'tone of England' at a particular time.[7] I must stray from this conception. Though Dicey, at the time he wrote, may justly be absolved from neglecting Freud, no one who attempts to trace the course of ideas and action in the field of health over the past half-century can fail to note the impress of a growing body of psychological and psycho-analytical knowledge. New knowledge has put health and disease in a new cultural perspective. Personal illness has acquired a social definition. Psychiatry and society may now confirm the patient's subjective definition of illness. The patient, as Péquignot has recently said, has once again to be listened to.[8]

Advances in knowledge in other scientific fields have also had a profound influence on law and opinion about health; about what Sherrington, the biologist, called 'the urge-to-live'.[9] I think of the influence on medical opinion, if not on lay opinion, even when Dicey was writing, of Darwin and Galton, Virchow and Pasteur, Koch and Ehrlich, Gowland Hopkins and others.[10] By the beginning of the twentieth century the new scientific era in medicine was well under way. The discovery of the germ theory of disease, of radium, X-rays and blood groups and other bacteriological triumphs of the laboratory, was beginning to affect medical practice; advances in biochemistry were influencing drug therapy; the successful use of nitrous oxide, ether and chloroform meant that the battle for the relief of pain had started; nevertheless, Dicey found no place in his survey of opinion for the influence of these and other developments in the natural sciences. By 1905 they were important for at least three reasons: diagnosis now began to matter more as the empirical role of expectant treatment, of folk therapeutics, waned in face of the advances of rational medicine; specialization in knowledge and skill was developing rapidly, thus affecting the organization of medical service, the structure of the profession, accepted norms of ethical behaviour, and the doctor-patient relationship; lastly, the costs of medical care to the individual were beginning to rise,[11] the first warning of the coming technological revolution.

These movements, scientific, professional and economic, were shifting the emphasis, in matters of health and disease, from the situation to the person; from the environment to the individual; from the public health officer to the general practitioner. Scientific intervention from without and changes in medical training within were altering the pattern of practice. Together, they produced the professional concept of the general practitioner. He had not existed before as a separate, distinctive branch of the medical profession with a set of recognizable roles and functions. He had to be created to enable the new medicine at the end of the century to be practised.[12] But this was not enough. What was also needed were systems and institutions which would allow and, indeed, encourage the doctor to practise as he wanted to practise. In what he wanted to do and be he was, of course, influenced by the changing expectations placed on him by the 'new' medicine of the times. Basically, it was a problem of social organization. The natural sciences were responsible for making it a social problem.

Simultaneously, developments in the comparative method of studying society, statistical and sociological, were helping England to identify its problems of health and disease more precisely and more historically (there now being available a more adequate body of knowledge for estimating trends over time). The concept of progress, of improvement or the lack of it, came to be applied in more sophisticated ways to the national health. Population groups, their social, occupational and class characteristics, increasingly became the material for epidemiological studies of disease and death. What had been in the forefront in medical thought and action half a century earlier was 'the health of towns'. By the beginning of the twentieth century, the emerging problem of ascertaining the 'best laws of health' was the health of the individual in his social setting, especially the health of mothers and children. Society was beginning to count and reassess the health costs of industrial progress in terms of the life chances of its next generation of workers, mothers and soldiers.

Significantly, the century was ushered in with a Midwives Act, and the health, nutrition and medical care of mothers and babies, schoolchildren and military recruits became a respectable, even a popular, subject of parliamentary debate. No longer could it be said, with Bagehot, that 'the character of the poor is an unfit topic for continuous art'. War as a measure of national, even imperial, stamina, exploded the doctrine of 'natural justice', confounded the works on political economy which, as Bagehot remarked, always began with the supposition of two men cast on an uninhabited island, and stimulated a burst of medical inquiries and legislative activity concerning the ills of the working-classes.

The prolonged social inquest that followed the South African War showed that little comfort could be drawn from the study of historical trends in mortality rates as indicators of levels of health. Three-quarters of a century of industrial and sanitary progress, of accumulating wealth and the acquisition of an Empire, had had no obvious effect, for example, on the infant death rate.[13] It was as high at the beginning of the twentieth century as it had been in the 1840s; higher than it was to be, fifty years later, in most of the 'under-developed' areas of the world. Considered in this biological context, England, at the turn of the century, was falling behind the rest of Western society in its care of the young. In 1902, the Inspector-General of Army Recruiting spoke gloomily of 'the gradual deterioration of the physique of the working-classes from whom the bulk of the recruits must always be drawn'.[14] Whatever its moral implications, here was a clear warning. Society was giving insufficient thought to investment in the next generation. Material thrift was not enough.

What emerged from all this debate about our military fortunes and our standards of communal fitness was a new accent on pre-vention; a redefinition of the idea in personal terms—the prevention of premature death, sickness and ill-health; the 'seeds of decay' among the young. But to accept this redefinition of prevention and advocate its endorsement meant, however, a challenge to prevailing social values in at least two respects. It meant enlarging the area of social responsibility—attaching more responsibility to someone, some group, some authority—and it also meant practical action.

As knowledge increased of the causal factors in disease, and as advances in the natural sciences began to penetrate the practice of medicine, it became clearer that action meant social action and responsibility collective responsibility. The logic of knowledge, and an increasing public awareness of the potentialities of action based on advances in knowledge, revealed the limits within which the individual could determine his own health. The expert (disliked by Dicey) knew better. Supported by science, by the need for forethought and prediction, by the demand for national well-being, by the idea of progress, the potential power of technical medicine increased. The story of medicine in society over the ensuing fifty years is, in general, a story of the accelerating force of these ideas and trends—a process dramatically hastened by two world wars and the scientific discovery of malnutrition during the 1930s.

During the first decade of the century, however, the organized structure of applied medicine was in no condition to absorb and practise either the 'scientific triumphs of the laboratory' or the idea of prevention. The advance of these conflicting yet complementary forces, the scientific and the social, was hindered by a variety of barriers; economic, professional and institutional. Changes were needed, for instance, in the economic structure within which most doctors practised if the benefits of these advances in knowledge were to be reaped in terms of an improvement in the quality of medical care. The general practitioner was the key figure in this problem of change. Then, as now, hospital provision, public and voluntary, catered for only a tiny proportion of the total expressed demand for medical attention.[15] The provision of medical care for the mass of the people centred round the general practitioner; his training, his conditions of work and his relationships with his patients and fellow doctors. The intervention of the State in the field of medical care in 1911, and to a greater degree in 1948, cannot be fully understood unless account is taken of the situation of general practice prior to the rise of 'socialized' medicine. The opinion of the doctor, particularly the rank-and-file doctor, was a powerful force in shaping the future course of the law in relation to health.

Before the Act of 1911, the working lives and material standards of the majority of general practitioners were profoundly affected by their relationships with not only the administrators of the poor law but with a network of long-established social institutions.[16] These took many forms, for their primary functions were not to provide medical care. Most of them were voluntary and philanthropic associations; friendly society clubs, trade union clubs, slate clubs, works clubs, tontines, breaking societies, charitable dispensaries and so forth. Then there were the medical aid societies run on private enterprise lines by insurance companies. The dominant system of medical care, organized through this complex of institutions and groups, was known as 'contract medical practice.'[17] The doctor was the 'club' or group doctor; for a stated sum of money per week or per year (generally a capitation fee) he contracted to provide professional service (and in many cases medicine) for the members of the group.

The mass of the wage-earning population, small shopkeepers and a substantial proportion of the middle-classes received their medical care through this system of contract practice. Generally there was no maximum wage or salary limit, though the doctors strongly opposed the inclusion of middle-class members, partly because they made greater demands on their services than the working-classes.[18] Consequently, they criticized, though without much success, the system of fixing contributions, in each individual club, on a flat-rate basis.[19] In the opinion of the doctors a few years later, one of the signal gains made by the profession from the 1911 legislation was the exclusion of the middle-classes not only from the benefits of State insurance but also from contract practice. With the withdrawal of the working-classes, club and contract practice virtually collapsed after 1911. It could no longer be sustained without the contributions of the workers.

Before this happened, however, we should note that contract practice, expressly developed for wage and salary earners, generally excluded the wives and other dependants, the old, the disabled and other 'bad' risks. It was a system of medical care for men at work, regularly at work. Then, as now, the actuarial bad risks were not courted by any insurance system, voluntary or commercial, of prepaid medical care. All these excluded classes thus had to seek their medical care elsewhere, mainly from out-patient departments, 'sixpenny doctors' and the poor law. In so far as they were treated, they generally saw a different doctor. Thus, for the mass of the population 'family doctoring' did not exist. Perhaps 10 per cent to 20 per cent of families had a private, 'fee-for-service' doctor for the whole family.[20] The term 'family doctor' was not then in use. It does not figure, for instance, in the 96 page report by the British Medical Association in 1905 on *Contract Practice*.[21] Its gradual acceptance later in the century, as a principle of more effective medical care, grew out of the concept of prevention.

This period of transition from the folk medicine of the nineteenth

century to rational medicine in the twentieth century was character-
ized by a widespread revolt among the doctors against the developing
system of contract practice. Culminating in the legislation of 1911,
this period can be seen as one in which the doctors were engaged in a
Hobbesian struggle for independence from the power and authority
exercised over their lives, their work and their professional values by
voluntary associations and private enterprise.[22] The 'Battle of the
Clubs', as it was called, was, fundamentally, a struggle for professional and private freedom. Scientific developments in medicine,
the emergence of a stronger hierarchical structure based on more
specialization in knowledge and skill, and new ideas about health
and disease, called for radical changes in the ways in which doctor
and patient were brought together. One change that was needed was
an enlargement of professional freedom.

Though, as a professional group, they are by no means alone in
this respect, doctors have, at various times since at least the beginning
of the century, shown a marked dislike for organization; for administrators; for bureaucrats—especially local bureaucrats and bourgeois
councillors. They showed this dislike, for instance, during the
negotiations with the Government before the introduction of the
Health Service. It was then made clear that in no circumstances
whatever would the profession entertain the idea of local government
having any responsibility for the hospital and general medical
services.[23] The present structure of the Health Service owes more to
the opinion of doctors than to political and public opinion.

Medical hostility to lay organization was fomented and sharpened
before the Act of 1911. We may briefly consider some of the forces
which helped to strengthen this powerful heritage.

First, there was the issue of professional independence and clinical
freedom. Under these contract systems of medical care, doctors had
no security of tenure. They could be dismissed at any time. They were
forced to compete and tender for these appointments. There was no
free choice in the doctor-patient relationship. As they were always
liable to be reported to an 'impertinent' lay committee for inattention
they felt unable to resist demands from patients for medicine.[24] They
had no right of appeal under the 'administrative law' of these
voluntary associations.[25] As full-time salaried doctors they were
often 'unmercifully sweated' by insurance companies[26] at rates of
pay which worked out at 3d a consultation[27]; they were under
pressure to sign certificates and life assurance forms against their
medical judgment, and they were expected to canvass for new
patients. In short, the power over their professional lives exercised by
these voluntary associations and private concerns was felt by the

majority of general practitioners as an intolerable infringement on their liberty to practise medicine. The system of medical care under the poor law had similar degrading effects on the large number of doctors who undertook these part-time appointments.[28]

Secondly, the doctors complained of the demoralizing influence on their work and their patients of many patent and proprietary medicines; the 'Secret Remedies' (as they were called) courageously attacked for a decade or more by the British Medical Association. Out of a total estimated expenditure of £12 million on all drugs, dressings and appliances in 1907 over one-quarter (£3¼ million) was spent on these 'secret remedies' which claimed to cure every conceivable disease.[29] For most newspapers the advertising of these drugs (on which £2 million annually was spent) constituted a major source of income. Newspaper proprietors (later to oppose the National Health Insurance Bill with unexampled violence) played no small part in the formation of opinion on matters of health and disease.

An incredulous public, dazzled by the new scientific jargon, misled by doctors who cut their ethical corners, confused by Chambers of Commerce who defended these 'secret remedies' in the name of freedom of contract, exploited by the entire press of the country, became, as one critic said, 'permanent medicine swallowers'. The average doctor, caught in the moral void of club and contract practice, found himself in the role of purveying and stimulating the use of these preparations. His sense of powerlessness under contract practice was accentuated by this traffic in drugs in which every man, according to Dicey, was (or should be) a better judge of his own 'secret remedy'.[30] As a scientific revolution in medicine developed, the 'bottle of medicine habit' became more deeply embedded in the culture of health and disease.[31]

Thirdly, the doctors complained bitterly about their standard of living. Beatrice and Sidney Webb concluded their survey in 1910: ' ... the medical profession in the United Kingdom stands at this moment in a position of grave danger. A very large proportion of its members earn incomes which can only be described as scandalously inadequate, whilst many of those who now enter its ranks after a long and expensive education fail altogether to secure a footing.'[32] The cost of five to seven years' training, fees and maintenance was approximately £1,000[33] (equal to about £4,000 in 1957 prices); the average income of general practitioners was estimated by the *British Medical Journal* in 1907 at £200 to £250 per annum[34] (about half as much again as a certificated male school teacher[35]); bad debts incurred by doctors varied according to the district from 10 per cent to 50 per cent[36]; and many doctors went bankrupt.[37] It is doubtful whether many general practitioners were the products of 'public' schools; certainly not as high a proportion as now enter the teaching hospitals.[38]

Low standards of living, combined with the competitive practices of voluntary associations, philanthropic institutions and commercial insurance companies, led to widespread abuses. The medical journals of the period resound with the cries of doctor against doctor about the bribery and corruption, the employment of unqualified assistants, the fee-splitting, the canvassing, the under-selling and commission-taking that was apparently widespread. As a body, general practitioners campaigned against the voluntary hospitals for giving the middle-classes cheap out-patient treatment; against the rising generation of specialist surgeons and consultants for reducing the standard of living of general practitioners; and against the clubs for allowing the middle-classes to obtain medical care at the same capitation fee as the working-classes.[39] In its values and goals, the profession was divided against itself; a reflection, in some senses, of the increasing division of labour within medicine. In this situation, more power fell into the hands of the organization men of the times; the administrators, lay committees and bureaucrats of the voluntary associations and insurance companies. 'The cause of these evils', concluded the BMA Report, 'is the advantage which non-medical organizations are able to take of the competition between individual medical practitioners.'[40]

In February 1910 (before Lloyd George had introduced his Health Insurance Bill), the *British Medical Journal* wrote: 'We are thus reduced to a dilemma from which most people see no escape except by some form . . . of State assistance.'[41] It went on, in this and succeeding editorials, to offer to collaborate with the Government in a State scheme provided that no lay committee or 'sham philan-thropy' came between the profession and the Government.

The rest of this story of how the foundations of the National Health Service were laid is better known.[42] In the battle over the 1911 legislation the doctors forced Lloyd George to give them satisfaction on most of their important claims: control of medical benefit not by friendly societies and clubs but by special 'insurance committees' on which doctors would be represented; freedom of choice; the right of every doctor to take part in the service; security of tenure, the exclusion of the middle-classes, and higher capitation fees. Compared with what had obtained before, the material rewards for most general practitioners were approximately doubled.[43] Years later, the Association's official historian had no doubt that the position of the profession had been 'vastly improved'.[44] In terms of professional service, the law of 1911 provided more opportunity for the better expression of the ethical code of medical practice; corruption and competition could diminish; and for a large section of doctors and patients alike freedom of choice became a more genuine possibility.

This is my interpretation of the health law of 1911 and the ideas and movements that helped to shape it.[45] To Dicey, it 'vehemently expressed the growth of collectivism'[46] for the benefit of the working-classes—'the pampered classes', as *The Times* described them in 1911.[47] The fundamental issue in 1911 was not, I suggest, between individualism and collectivism, between contract and status; but between different forms of collectivism, different degrees of freedom; open or concealed power. To whom should the doctor be accountable in society? How was scientific progress to be incorporated into the practice of medicine? What, in the light of advancing physical and psychological knowledge, were 'the best ascertained laws of health'?

I must now move on from 1911. In retrospect, it represents one of the great dividing periods in the development of systems of medical care. It happened when it did because of the conjunction of many historical forces. The power of private contract practice was perhaps the most important single factor. Its origins are clearly traceable to the social conditions created by industrialization. It grew to power in the vacuum left by individualism. By the turn of the century there had developed (what may be called) a coalition of interests between the needs of the doctor to incorporate new knowledge in his practice and to pursue his calling in accordance with the ethics sanctioned by his group, and the needs of the working-man to conserve his health and wage-earning power from all the hazards of industrial and technological change. Both were conscious of the power exercised over their lives by these different external forces. Thus, the Act of 1911 had more to do with professional liberty than with class warfare; more with freedom of contract than with equalitarian redistribution.

By 1946 the fundamental issues were in some senses the same, in other senses different. The emphasis shifted to the social rights of all citizens to better health. By then, science had become a much more potent force in the problems facing modern society of choosing between alternative systems of medical care. Not only was medicine more powerful but more had been learnt about the inequalities of health and medical care between different social classes and occupations. Studies of infant mortality by social class had shown, for example, that despite the great absolute decline among all classes, the relative gap between the highest and the lowest rates was, if anything, somewhat greater in 1950 than in 1911.[48] Elsewhere, evidence was growing that the rich were benefiting more and earlier than the poor from advances in scientific knowledge. The most striking instance here is the long period that elapsed, after the early 1920s, before the working-classes drew anything like a proportionate benefit from the discovery of insulin for the treatment of the young insulin-sensitive diabetic.[49]

As more recognition was accorded to the social factors in health and disease it became clearer that the quality and distribution of medical care was one of the central issues for social policy. The advent of scientific medicine made it clearer still.

In other papers I have discussed the impact of the natural sciences on the theory and practice of medicine in relation to the introduction of the National Health Service and the structure of the medical profession.[50] All I can do here is to pick out one or two strands of thought.

During the period between these two health laws of 1911 and 1946 science was invading medicine at an accelerating pace. After the discovery of prontosil in 1935 the process became more marked and challenging. Once the medical significance of new knowledge in the biological and natural sciences has been grasped, the flood-gates between theory and practice in medical care burst wide open. Developments in recent years now read like a story of geometrical progression: they include the elaboration of penicillin, streptomycin, oleandomycin and other antibiotics, the application of nuclear physics, improvements in anaesthesia and thoracic surgery, the treatment of coronary thrombosis with anti-coagulants, knowledge of blood compatibility and the discovery of cortisone and polio vaccines.

When we reflect on these dazzling achievements in the natural sciences during the twentieth century, the advances made in our understanding of the psychology of man since Freud published in 1900 *The Interpretation of Dreams* may seem prosaic by comparison. Seen, however, in a broader and larger perspective the work of Freud and his successors has been of revolutionary importance to medicine. It has changed our attitudes to the mentally ill (as the recent *Report of the Royal Commission on the Law Relating to Mental Illness* bears ample witness[51]), it has at least helped towards the alleviation of mental suffering, it has greatly enlarged the possibilities of preventive therapy, and it has given us new ways of looking at the growth of personality and the origins of illness. For all these reasons it has added a new potential of awareness to clinical skill; as John Rickman wrote: 'it has given a new dimension to the medical interview'.[52] To public opinion as well as medical opinion, the concept of health and disease is radically different from that held in the days when Dicey could write of the law relating to health simply in terms of the germ theory of infection.

What, today, constitutes health? What do we expect from the doctor for ourselves and our fellows? What do we now think is expected of us in our various roles? These are some of the questions which lie at the heart of the movement for better health and better medical care. What man himself regards as sickness and his role as a sick person has been profoundly affected by the advent of rational medicine and developments in psychological knowledge. Together, they have led to the growth of the idea in Western society that pain is avoidable by rational, non-mystical means. As standards of education and living rise greater significance is attached to sensations of pain as signals of danger to the individual and his sense of self-preservation. An American study of 'cultural components in responses to pain' has shown that the educational background of the patient plays an important role in his attitude to the symptomatic meaning of pain sensation. 'The more educated patients are more health-conscious and more aware of pain as a possible symptom of a dangerous disease.'[53]

The support that middle-class opinion in England has given to the National Health Service and the nature of the demands that these classes have made upon it become explicable in the context of ideas and expectations of this kind.[54] What has been learnt in recent years from a variety of medical and sociological studies suggests that the middle-classes are more conscious of the need for health as an essential element in achieving 'success in life'; more aware of the technical and psychological potentialities in medicine; readier to see, as Professor Clark-Kennedy has said, that the power of medicine over individual lives 'has increased, is increasing and is likely to increase still further',[55] and, above all, quicker to recognize that the costs to the individual of medical care have been pushed to unprecedented heights by a technological revolution.[56]

For the Labour Government, in 1946, to have simply extended the old Health Insurance Scheme to include wives and dependants and hospital benefits would have meant excluding the middle-classes. From a working-class standpoint this could well have been interpreted as a perpetuation of the pre-war system of two standards of medical care—'panel' and private. In practice, however, the likelihood is that the position of the classes would have been reversed. The 'protected' working-classes would have been, relatively speaking, the largest beneficiaries of scientific medicine. The middle-classes, fully exposed in a private market to the initial inflationary phase of technical change, would have suffered. Technical progress would have behaved towards them as the gods behaved towards Tantalus.

This, however, was not one of the decisive arguments in 1945. But many of the consultants (represented by the Royal Colleges) did see the writing on the professional wall. They foresaw the coming bankruptcy of the voluntary hospitals; the threat (to the profession) of greater local government control; the harmful financial effects on doctors as well as patients of the rise in the private costs of health; and the dominant role to be played in the future by the hospital—and especially the teaching hospital—as it increasingly became the focus of medical science and technology, the laboratory for 'the Golden Age of surgery',[57] and the main source of prestige and power. With shrewdness and foresight, the Royal Colleges led the medical profession into the National Health Service and helped to shape a law which made available the benefits of scientific medicine to all classes in the community.

But this, I believe, would not have come about but for the Second World War and the Labour Government. The first supplied the decisive motive-power, the second the will. One of the lessons of the war, as a citizens' war, was the popular demand for the abolition of the poor law; of ineligible citizens; of personally merited disease; of inequality before 'the best ascertained laws of health'. The National Health Service Act of 1946 was, in part, an expression of this war-time mood for justice and equality of opportunity. But in a longer perspective of time and social change it was a renewal of the argument for the freedom of patients and doctors. Once again, though in circumstances dramatically altered by technical progress, the choice was between different forms of collectivism and a different distribution of power between the doctor and the administrator, and between the representatives of the people and the profession.

There are some who still see the Act as a collectivist device for the sole benefit of the working-classes. As the offspring of 1911, it is depicted as the apex of 'Welfare State' benevolence. But this is too simple, as it was too simple a view of 1911. Of course the working classes have benefited. But the middle-classes have benefited even more, and the medical profession most of all.[58] The economic and financial effects of State intervention in the sphere of health and disease since 1946 are complex and, I have no doubt, have worked out differently from the often accepted views of what 'Welfare Statism' is thought to mean in practice.

Though the demand for social justice has been one of the major forces shaping law and opinion in the field of health since the beginning of the century, other forces have played an equal—and sometimes more important—role. One, as I have shown, is the advancement of scientific knowledge. Another is represented by the movement from fatalism to awareness in popular attitudes towards health and disease. Yet another is the recurrent business of liberal thought to release the individual (whether, in this context, doctor or patient) from unalterable dependence on any particular social group. In short, the underlying aim of health legislation has been to prevent social injustice by countering power with power. The law of 1946 was directed towards the diffusion of power; the diffusion of the power of medicine, and the diffusion of the benefits of science. These were its aims; what has happened in reality is inevitably another story.

NOTES

1. Paul, B. D., *Health, Culture and Community*, New York, 1955, p. 459.
2. A number of medical writers have also surveyed the social factors in the development of health services since the nineteenth century. Among these I would single out Mackintosh, Professor J. M., *Trends of Opinion about the Public Health 1901–51*, 1953. This book covers much of the important territory of public health, housing and local government services which I have not examined in this lecture.
3. See Bunbury, H., and Titmuss, R. M., *Lloyd George's Ambulance Wagon* ('The Memoirs of W. J. Braithwaite'), 1957.
4. Dicey, A. V., *Law and Opinion in England in the Nineteenth Century* (1926 Edition), p. 74.
5. Dicey's abstract interpretation of political opinion is analysed by Mr Oliver MacDonagh in 'The Nineteenth-Century Revolution in Government: A Reappraisal', *The Historical Journal*, 1958, 1, 1, p. 52.
6. Dicey, *op. cit.*, p. 73.
7. *Op. cit.*, p. 19.
8. Péquignot, H., *Impact of Science on Society*, 1954, Vol. V, No. 4, p. 256.
9. Sherrington, C., *Man on His Nature*, 1955 Edition, p. 180.
10. Perhaps more surprising is Dicey's neglect of the influence on law-making opinion of Marx, Alfred Marshall and Durkheim.
11. In any discussion of trends in the costs of medical care it is necessary to distinguish between (a) the total national cost (public and private) of medical care measured in terms of the use of real resources, and (b) the money costs borne by individuals. The former can be usefully related to the gross national product and the latter to disposable income. It is not certain that during the past fifty years national costs have risen as a proportion of the gross national product. No clear answer can be given until more research has been done into trends of national outlay on medical care services, though there has probably been a shift from private to public payment. What is indisputable is that partly owing to the advent of scientific medicine the potential expenditure by an individual on medical care for one illness has

expanded much more than disposable income per head. This applies to practically all levels of income, particularly when account is taken of the incidence of all forms of taxation.

12. See editorial review in the *Lancet* on Dr Charles Newman's book, *The Evolution of Medical Education in the Nineteenth Century*, 1957, *Lancet*, 1957, ii, 411.

13. See Logan, W. P. D., *Population Studies*, Vol. IV, No. 2, 1950, p. 132, and Stolnitz, G. J., *Population Studies*, Vol. IX, No. 1, 1955, p. 24, and *Trends and Differentials in Mortality*, Millbank Memorial Fund Report (1955), p. 26.

14. Annual Report for 1902, quoted in *Report of the Inter-Departmental Committee on Physical Deterioration*, 1904, Cd 2176.

15. Voluntary hospitals in the United Kingdom provided only about 25,000 beds in 1910. The number of beds in poor law and public health authority institutions of all kinds (mental, poor law, tuberculosis and isolation) was probably about four to five times greater. Webb, S. and B., *The State and the Doctor* (1910), and McCurrich, H. J., *The Treatment of the Sick Poor of this Country* (1929).

16. In 1912 the British Medical Association estimated that there were 27,567 practising physicians in England, Wales and Scotland (including consultants and whole-time medical officers) of whom 22,567 were general practitioners engaged in attending (though not exclusively) on that section of the population earning less than £160 a year (including dependants, approximately 36,000,000). *Brit. Med. J.*, 1912, Supp. ii, 29.

17. For a detailed description of this system, see *Report on Contract Practice*, *Brit. Med. J.*, Special Supplement, July 1905.

18. For evidence on this point, see *Report on Contract Practice*, pp. 7, 8 and 14.

19. These varied, according to the club and the district, from 2s to 10s per member per year including all drugs supplied. There is a considerable body of evidence in the literature of the period which suggests that the inclusion of drugs in the fee had two effects: first, because of the low level of fees, the system encouraged the provision of cheap and ineffective medicines; secondly, a more liberal supply of drugs became one of the competitive baits to tempt people to transfer from this system of prepaid medical care, voluntary and commercial, to private practice. The influence of these drug consumption incentives was one of the factors which led Lloyd George to separate the National Health Insurance capitation fee from the cost of drugs (see Statement by the Chancellor of the Exchequer to the Advisory Committee, October 23, 1912, *National Insurance Accounts and Papers, 1912–13*, pp. 5–12).

20. When account is taken of the numbers dealt with by the poor law medical service, by dispensaries, by out-patient departments and by 'sixpenny shop doctors' it seems unlikely that the proportion was as high as 20 per cent. Approximately 12 per cent of the adult population of the United Kingdom were income tax payers with incomes over £160 a year (Money, Chiozza, *Riches and Poverty*, 1912).

21. This report was published in the *Brit. Med. J.*, Special Supplement, July 1905.

22. According to Horner ' "club doctoring" grew to monstrous size in the early years of this century, and had become little other than a means for exploiting the less prosperous members of the medical profession' (Horner, N. G., *The Growth of the General Practitioner of Medicine in England* (privately printed, 1922)).

23. For references, see Titmuss, R. M., *Essays on the 'Welfare State'*, Allen and Unwin, London, 1958. Eckstein is inclined to attribute this distrust of local government to class differences. Doctors, he says, are less afraid of central control because civil servants of the administrative class have a more similar social background to doctors than have *petit bourgeois* lay councillors. Eckstein, H., *Political Quarterly*, 1955, XXVI, No. 4.

24. British Medical Association, *Report on Contract Practice, Brit. Med. J.*, Supp., July 22, 1905, especially pp. 20–2. The report is liberally illustrated with comments from general practitioners about the effects of contract practice on their status. The following is fairly typical. 'Members are frequently impudent because you are the "club doctor". Consultations are never extra and they dismiss you with scant ceremony, and are always talking behind your back, and you receive more injury than advantage in this way, as they influence private patients against you, and you lose caste' (p. 42).

25. By contrast the profession now enjoys a privileged position under the administrative law of the National Health Service (see *Report of the Committee on Administrative Tribunals*, Cmnd 218, and *Minutes of Evidence*, Days 6–7, 19, 20, 21 and 24, 1957).

26. Little, E. M., *History of the British Medical Association 1832–1932* (1932), p. 201.

27. The equivalent purchasing power in terms of prices in May 1957 would have been about 1s in 1905 (Chancellor of the Exchequer, *Hansard*, July 11, 1957, adjusted for 1905–11 by indices linked by Layton, W. T., and Crowther, G., *An Introduction to the Study of Prices*).

28. See *Minority Report of the Royal Commission on the Poor Laws* (1909); Webb, S. and B., *The State and the Doctor* (1910), and British Medical Association, Report of the Poor Law Reform Committee, *Brit. Med. J.*, Supp. (1910), i, 41.

29. The estimate of £12 million is taken from *Consumers' Expenditure in the United Kingdom, 1900–19* (Prest, A. R., and Adams, A. A., 1954, p. 157). The source of other data on drugs and advertising is the *Report from the Select Committee on Patent Medicines*, H. of C. paper 414, 1914. This Report estimated that only about 1 per cent to 2 per cent of the retail price of these 'secret remedies' represented the cost of ingredients.

30. Dicey, A. V., in discussing the Drugs Act of 1899 in relation to the growth of collectivism (*op. cit.*, pp. 263–4).

31. For the evidence on which these paragraphs are based, see British Medical Association, *Secret Remedies: What They Cost and What They Contain*, 1909, and *More Secret Remedies*, 1912; *Report of the Select Committee on Patent Medicines*, 1914; Cox, A., *Among the Doctors*, 1950, p. 210; Webb, S. and B., *The State and the Doctor*, 1910; Brend, W. A., *Health and the State*, 1917; Heald, A. F., *Brit. Med. J.*, 1900, i, 119, and Shryock, R. H., *The Development of Modern Medicine*, 1948.

32. Webb, S. and B., *The State and the Doctor*, 1910, p. 253. See also Conybeare, J., 'The Crisis of 1911–13', *Lancet*, 1957, ii, 1032.

33. *Brit. Med. J.*, editorials, 1900, ii, 470, and 1912, ii, 536. (Fees in teaching hospitals ranged in 1912 from £100–£150 a year.)

34. After deducting the cost of medicines and appliances supplied, the salary of assistants, and allowing for bad debts and commission taken by collectors (varying from 10–25 per cent of fees) (*Brit. Med. J.*, September 7 and 14, 1907, and Supp., July 22, 1905, p. 13). It is probable that this estimate only

applied to the poorer sections of the profession—perhaps one-half to three-quarters of all general practitioners. Other estimates in 1910–11 gave figures on a roughly comparable basis of £600–£700. None of these estimates made allowance for such practice expenses as travel, surgery accommodation, equipment and other items. (See *Plender Report*, Cd 6305, 1912; Redmond, G. S., *Brit. Med. J.*, 1910, ii, 240; Moore, B., *Brit. Med. J.*, 1910, ii, 47; British Medical Association, *Report on Contract Practice*, 1905; *Brit. Med. J.*, leaders, 1900, i, 1036, and ii, 471, and advertisements of medical vacancies for the years 1900–10 in the *Brit. Med. J.* and the *Lancet*. The equivalent purchasing power of £200–£250 in terms of prices in May 1957 would have been about £800–£1,000 in 1905 (for basis of calculation, see footnote 27).)

35. Tropp, A., *The School Teachers*, 1957, App. B, p. 273. The low incomes of many general practitioners in the decade before 1911 may be compared with the incomes and earnings of other middle-class occupations. For example, actuaries and principal clerks in the civil service were paid £550—20—£700; chief inspectors and principal medical officers £1,000; medical officers £500 to £800; assistant actuaries £350—15—£500 (Cd 6540, 1912). Rates of wages for skilled workers (e.g. boilermakers and smiths, iron-moulders, fitters and compositors) ranged from 38s to 50s per week in 1906 (Cd 4844, 1909). Members of Parliament were paid £400 a year in 1911.

36. *Brit. Med. J.*, 1910, ii, 1558, and Moore, B., *Brit. Med. J.*, 1910, ii, 47.

37. See figures collected by Sir James Paget at the end of the nineteenth century (*Lancet*, 1900, ii, 1176). The extreme poverty of many practitioners was also shown by the large amount of charitable aid dispensed by medical societies among doctors, their families and widows (see Hardy, H. Nelson, *The State of the Medical Profession in Great Britain and Ireland in 1900*, 1903, p. 25).

38. According to the 1955–56 study, *Applications for Admission to Universities*, ex-public school boys were more heavily represented in medical schools than in any other faculty for which figures were given. In London the proportion was about one-third, in Oxford and Cambridge nearly three-fifths and, for all medical schools studied, one-quarter (Kelsall, R. K., *Report on an Inquiry*, 1957).

39. The *Report on Contract Practice* in 1905 had much to say on the extent to which the middle-classes joined these clubs and made greater demands on the doctor than the working-classes. An analysis of some 40,000 club members showed that those members paying an annual subscription of 5s and over received over 50 per cent more attendances than those paying between 2s and 3s a year (pp. 7, 8 and 14).

40. British Medical Association, *Report on Contract Practice*, *Brit. Med. J.*, Supp., July 22, 1905, p. 28.

41. *Brit. Med. J.*, editorial, 1910, i, 521 and 713.

42. Bunbury, H., and Titmuss, R. M., *Lloyd George's Ambulance Wagon* ('The Memoirs of W. J. Braithwaite'), London, 1957.

43. Compare the difference, for example, between Lloyd George's first and final offer in the dispute over the capitation fee (*Brit. Med. J.*, 1912, ii, 87).

44. Little, E. M., *History of the British Medical Association 1832–1932*, 1932, p. 328.

45. Others have interpreted differently the medical history of the first decade of the century. Thus, Sir Heneage Ogilvie, writing about the state of the profession at the beginning of the century, said: 'In Britain medicine was a cultured and scientific calling, one which offered a secure livelihood, interesting and humane employment, an honoured position in society, and the

choice between many careers with a common background . . . every practitioner had a consultant's gold-headed cane in his surgery' (*Lancet*, 1952, ii, 820).

46. Dicey, A. V., *op. cit.*, pp. 33 and 53.
47. *The Times*, June 10, 1911.
48. Morris, J. N., and Heady, J. A., 'Social and Biological Factors in Infant Mortality', *Lancet*, 1955, i, 554.
49. Demonstrated in Professor J. N. Morris's book, *Uses of Epidemiology*, 1957, p. 27.
50. Titmuss, R. M., *Essays on the 'Welfare State'*, Allen and Unwin, London 1958.
51. Cmnd 169, 1957. Similarly, the concept of mental defect (or social incompetence) has also been changed and enlarged (Penrose, L. S., *The Biology of Mental Defect*, London, 1949).
52. Rickman, J., *Brit. Med. J.*, 1950, i, 37.
53. Zborowski, M., *Journal of Social Issues*, 1952, Vol. VIII, No. 4, p. 27.
54. For some evidence of social class demands on the Health Service, see Abel-Smith, B., and Titmuss, R. M., *The Cost of the National Health Service*, 1956, and Titmuss, R. M., *Essays on the 'Welfare State'*, 1958.
55. Clark-Kennedy, A. E., *Human Disease*, 1957, p. 7.
56. Costs to the individual as defined in footnote 11.
57. Writing in the *Lancet* in 1957, Sir Cecil Wakeley said: 'We are now living in the Golden Age of surgery . . .' (*Lancet*, 1957, ii, 906).
58. Dr A. Cox, former Secretary of the British Medical Association, concluded in 1950: 'Since 1914 the change in the position of the general practitioner has been phenomenal' (*Brit. Med. J.*, 1950, i, 78). See also Titmuss, R. M., *Essays on the 'Welfare State'*, Allen and Unwin, London, 1958, Chapters 8, 9 and 10.

Chapter XXI

ETHICS AND ECONOMICS OF MEDICAL CARE*

(I)

The notion that medical care requires to be deliberately organized through the medium of a third party is not a new one in the history of medicine. In the days of Hippocrates, salaried physicians were appointed by the community to treat the sick without a fee. The Romans employed many of their physicians and surgeons on the same basis. Nor was it unknown among third parties for the method to be used of paying doctors on a capitation basis. The introduction by the British of a free-on-demand health service in 1948 was not, therefore, in its essential principles a novel event.

Yet it is now being regarded by a growing number of economists, supported in London by the Institute of Economic Affairs and in the United States by the American Medical Association, as a unique aberration. This is attributed to what one economist, Dr D. S. Lees, describes as 'a strange neglect of general economic principles'. In his pamphlet, *Health Through Choice*,[1] as widely known in North America[2] as in Britain, he attempts to repair this omission. Applying classical economic theory to the Health Service and its development since 1948 he postulates an alternative to organized medical care—namely, the invisible hand of the private market. The fundamental choice, he argues, lies between individual consumer sovereignty and collective arrangements. The function of consumers is to choose, bargain and buy—not to organize supply. No third party is presumed to intervene or is required to intervene in the private transactions between two people—patient and doctor.

One of the assumptions implicit in Dr Lees' thesis is that economic principles were not neglected in the past in the relations between doctor and patient in Britain. This suggests, therefore, the existence at some time of a state of affairs in which the consumer was sovereign and no third parties intervened in the financial dialogue between buyer and seller. How much historical truth there is in this proposition depends, of course, on the period selected for comparative purposes.

* Originally published in *Medical Care*, January–March 1963, Vol. 1, No. 1.

Something akin to the model of a free market may have prevailed in the centuries of folk-medicine just as it still does today among primitive peoples in Africa and Asia. We know from the studies of social anthropologists that one of the essential characteristics of folk or non-rational medicine is that of shared knowledge between patient and doctor. It therefore fulfils one of the requisites of a free market: the buyer should not be placed in a subordinate position to the seller.

Dialogue and transaction take place—or can presumably take place—on the basis of some equality of knowledge. But if—as was often the case—the purveyor of medical care also had priestly functions the analogy with the market broke down—as it may do today when the doctor assumes an apostolic role. The consumer thus relinquishes his claim to sovereignty. Submission to higher authority demands behaviour which is inappropriate and ineffective in the market place.

Such comparisons with the distant past or with primitive cultures are not, therefore, particularly helpful in the testing of economic theory. Perhaps the most appropriate period to select for the examination of Dr Lees' assumption is that immediately preceding 1911 and the advent of organized National Health Insurance. Even here, however, the model of consumer sovereignty does not fit at all easily for the mass of patients and general practitioners.

Apart from the employment of many practitioners under the poor law during the early years of the century there were also large numbers engaged in club and contract practice.[3] Free choice of doctor did not obtain in these conditions, and the doctors were paid by third parties either on a salaried basis or by piece-rates. Professionally, their work was often strictly controlled by the administrators and lay committees of voluntary associations, insurance companies and poor law authorities. It is probable that there were proportionately more salaried general practitioners during this period of presumed free market conditions in medical care than there are today under the health service. 'The cause of these evils,' said the British Medical Association in 1905, 'is the advantage which non-medical organizations are able to take of the competition between individual medical practitioners.'[4] This helps to explain what Professor Eckstein has noted, that the Association was then far more hostile to private than to public control.[5] Hence its objection in these circumstances to payment by piece-rates. Some fifty years later much the same conclusion was reached by the President of the American Hospital Association. He remarked in 1959 that public control over voluntary hospitals was to be preferred to private control.[6]

Only among a section of the profession do we find from the historical studies that have been made anything resembling free market conditions prevailing during the Edwardian period.[7] Competition for patients, an essential attribute of a free market, was inevitably accompanied as theory would imply by widespread fee-splitting, commission-taking, canvassing, the dispensation of 'secret remedies', and the employment of unqualified assistants. Monopolistic conditions did not then obtain for there was much competition from the medically unqualified and various other purveyors of 'secret remedies'. Outside the poor law and club and contract practice, the price of medical care was not administered or regulated in the sense understood by modern students of imperfect competition.

It would seem, therefore, that Dr Lees' assumption of free market conditions operating without the intervention of third parties has only limited validity in respect of the period before organized health insurance in 1911. Insofar as the thesis does hold, however, we should note the implications of consumer sovereignty for professional standards of medical behaviour and medical ethics. But these are matters which Dr Lees does not discuss. Nor are they referred to in another recent economic analysis by Professor and Mrs Jewkes 'The Genesis of the British National Health Service'. 'It is reasonable to suppose,' they argue, 'that even without a National Health Service, Britain would have enjoyed after 1948 medical services more ample and better distributed than those which existed before the war.'[8] No doubt their reason for omitting any consideration of professional ethics is to be found in the statement by another economist, Dr F. G. Dickinson, Head of the American Medical Association's Bureau of Medical Economic Research in 1956.

'The doctor is essentially a small businessman,' he wrote, 'he is selling his services so is as much in business as anyone else who sells a commodity.'[9]

It would thus follow that if a private medical market place, envisaged by these Conservative and Liberal economists, is to operate effectively in Britain it should be peopled by the kind of doctors described by Professor D. Lowell Kelly of the University of Michigan in 1957. Reporting on the personality characteristics of medical students, he said that they revealed 'remarkably little interest in the welfare of human beings ... the *typical* (author's italics) young physician ... is generally not inclined to participate in community activities unless these contribute to his income ... he is still essentially an entrepreneur'.[10]

The logic of the case presented by Dr Lees and Professor Jewkes would thus appear to demand quite different considerations in the selection and training of medical students in Britain than those which are accepted today. They would need to be taught to give preferential treatment to consumers who will pay most for what they have to sell; consumers who are presumed, as a result of the free play of the market, to be more worthwhile in genetic or productive terms. This proposition is akin to the thesis advanced by Dr Ffrangcon Roberts in his *The Cost of Health*[11]—a 'brilliantly argued' book according to Dr Lees.

In embracing the market system, doctors would thus relinquish their role (as Durkheim put it) as 'centres of moral life'.[12] Logically again, it would thus follow that society could no longer depend upon doctors to give truthful information about their patients, or even information as reliable as one normally expects from the average shopkeeper.

(II)

What makes even more speculative these attempts to apply classical economic theory to systems of medical care is the advent of science. In terms of diagnosis and therapy, the scientific revolution gathered momentum after the discovery of 'prontosil' in 1935. The tremendous impact on medical practice and professional ethics of scientific and technological developments during the past two decades has been described by many writers and requires no detailed comment here. Its effects on the doctor-patient relationship may, however, be summarized under four related heads: (i) a great increase in specialization and in the division of medical labour; (ii) the proliferation at an accelerating pace of more and more technical and para-medical instruments of diagnosis and therapy; (iii) an apparent rise in the price of medical care continually exceeding the rise in the price of other consumer goods and services; (iv) in consequence of these and other trends, an immense enlargement—in relative terms—in the average patient's ignorance about medical matters. The more it becomes a science like thermodynamics and nuclear physics, the more will medicine place the patient in a position of inequality not unlike that he occupied before the Renaissance. As Professor Péquignot has observed, it is now impossible to explain medicine to a sick man, for it is as difficult to describe Hodgkin's disease or acute leukaemia in everyday language as it is to find everyday words for a curve of the fifth-degree or the notion of entropy.[13]

Yet Dr Lees argues, in drawing an analogy between the role of the doctor and the functioning of washing machines, that, in both cases, the consumer has to call in the expert. In concluding, therefore, that medical care is no different from such commodities, he fails to make three distinctions: first, between services and objects; secondly, between events that are a threat to life and those that are not; thirdly, between costs that can be estimated in advance and predicted over time and costs that cannot be so estimated and predicted. To disregard these distinctions means, in technical terms, therefore, that ordinal analysis applied to consumer demand equates mink coats with Caesarean operations in childbirth. At given rates, they are assumed to exchange for one another.

It may be objected, of course, that there are many other parallels for calling in (or relying on) the expert. Engine drivers and garage mechanics who do not do their jobs properly are a threat to life. But trains and cars are different from human minds and bodies. This is a value judgment, but it is one which few would dispute. We can decide to stop running a car but most of us cannot decide to stop breathing. Nor do cars have babies or have to care for other cars. Nor do we, as ignorant laymen, always know that we want medical care until we have 'consumed' it.

All these imponderable and quantitatively immeasurable factors have to be taken into account in any attempt to equate medical care with mink coats or car repairs.

We can also examine these matters not only by making comparisons in historical terms but by looking at contemporary experiences in other countries. The obvious one to select for this purpose is the United States; the citadel of 'free enterprise medicine'. Professor and Mrs Jewkes would no doubt endorse this selection for not only do they suggest that the United States has a better record in medical care since 1948 than Britain but their book, published in Oxford, bears the imprint of a dollar price. We propose, therefore, in analysing more closely some of these economic views about the health service, to draw on American experience over the past fifteen years.

This exercise is not perhaps as pointless and academic as it may seem. The notions of consumer sovereignty, individual freedom of choice, variety versus conformity, and centralized control versus the free market, have been increasingly applied in recent years to other social services like education, housing, and social security as well as medical care. The case for the market has been ably presented by economists and other writers on behalf of the Conservative and Liberal Parties and needs no documenting here.[14] It is sufficient to outline the general thesis.

251

These services, collectively organized by the State, are seen as a temporary economic phenomenon peculiar to a specific historical phase in the development of large-scale industrial societies. They were needed as social supports when the masses were poor; in times of war; and when the future of capitalism was uncertain. These conditions, it is argued, no longer obtain. Thus the 'Welfare State', after another celebrated example, should wither away, and more and more people should have resort to a self-regulating market—to quote Dr Lees 'the superior means of registering preferences'. It is more sensitive than government; it automatically corrects for mistakes in supply; it enables individuals to adjust their consumption and saving more easily; it provides more variety and thus increases consumer satisfactions; it is less bureaucratic and, administratively, more efficient. Private responsibility should thus replace public paternalism. These are the main arguments and appealing phrases for removing the present State impediments to a free market in education, housing, social security and medical care. Is this thesis supported by the behaviour of the medical care market in the United States?

(III)

We must begin with the American consumer. From his point of view one of the more obvious and striking facts of life is the continuing rise in the cost of medical care. Since 1948 it has risen much more than in Britain. The rise began in the early 1940s and has steadily accelerated. Between 1947 and the end of the 1950s the cost of medical care services rose more than twice as fast as all items in the Bureau of Labour Statistics Consumer Price Index. By June 1960 it was rising three times as fast. By far the steepest rise has been registered by the price of hospital rooms and group hospital insurance premiums. These are now rising at the rate of over 7 per cent per year, or twice as fast as the national income. All the evidence points to continuing price inflation, particularly because of the growing shortage of doctors and nurses, the advent of more profit-making hospitals as a source of capital gains, the trend from domiciliary to hospital care, and other factors. A recent projection of patient day costs in voluntary hospitals expects a further rise of between 39 and 45 per cent over the next five years.[15]

The price indexes do not show changes in the quantity or quality of medical care purchased. Over the last fifteen years total expenditures on health and medical care have steadily risen and now stand at something over 5 per cent of the gross national product. Included in this total, personal consumption on private medical care rose from 2.9 per cent of GNP in 1947 to 3.7 per cent in 1958. These figures show that effective demand has been increasing, but it is hard to say what proportions of the additional expenditures are due to: (i) the increasing population—particularly among older people; (ii) price inflation; (iii) higher administrative and selling costs; (iv) more items of service per head; (v) better quality services; (vi) duplicated and under-utilized services and other factors.

The problem of disentangling the respective contributions of all these factors is one of great complexity. It is much too simple to suggest—as Dr Lees and Professor and Mrs Jewkes do—that if the Americans are spending a higher proportion of their gross national product on medical care it necessarily confirms the private market as superior in supplying a better service in quality as well as quantity. The reverse might be true if many Americans are today being forced to pay more for the same measured service. As one example, we may note that in 1959 some $750 million were spent on drug promotion or nearly one-quarter of personal consumption spending on drug preparations and sundries. This proportion was considerably higher than ten years earlier.

No-one who devotes any serious attention to the vast literature on medical care in the United States in recent years can fail to observe the many signs and symptoms of frustration and consumer dissatisfaction. According to a report to Congress in 1959, 'the supply of available medical care, in terms of medical personnel and medical facilities, is declining in relation to population growth and rising health consciousness. Shortages of supply exist already and will grow more serious in the future. . . . '[16]

The number of hospital beds per 1,000 population dropped from 9.7 in 1948 to 9.2 in 1962.[17] In England and Wales over the same period the number of staffed beds rose from 10.2 to 10.3. Moreover, the American figures include a recent spectacular growth in the number of proprietory and profit-making hospitals in various areas—most of them small and inadequately staffed and equipped—despite the technical rationale for large units.[18] Investment in these hospitals is said to be 'particularly attractive for investors seeking capital gains'.[19]

One developer, writing in the *Wall Street Journal*, envisages a coast-to-coast chain of such hospitals, viewing them as a 'bread and butter item—just like food stores'.[20] Some of these hospitals are connected with pharmacies, and in 1961 it was reported that at least 450 doctors were whole or part owners of pharmacies in the State of California alone.[21]

In 1962 the US Public Health Service reported that the country faced a shortage of more than one million 'acceptable' hospital beds.[22] There is serious over-building of hospitals and gross duplication of expensive equipment in some areas, growing shortages in others, and a general trend towards greater maldistribution in important sectors of medical care. One part of the price of non-planning—a 26 per cent average non-occupancy rate in short-term general hospital beds in 1957—cost American consumers $3.5 billion in idle investment and $625 million in operating costs.[23]

At the same time, the shortage of less expensive long-term facilities—for example, mental hospital beds—grew worse throughout the 1950s. There is no evidence that this problem of maldistribution is being automatically corrected by 'natural' market forces. One study in Michigan has indicated that $5 million a year is wasted in that State because of 'uneconomical hospitalization' and lack of co-ordinated action.[24] While 'unnatural' or governmental forces have undoubtedly brought about an improvement in the geographical distribution of doctors and medical resources in Britain since 1948, there has been little change over the past twenty years in the striking disparities in the state ratios of physicians to population in America.[6]

Other signs of consumer dissatisfaction and of the failure of corrective market forces are to be found in the growth of various forms of medico-scientific charlatanism, resort to the corner drugstore, chiropractors, naturopaths, and the steeply rising costs of malpractice insurance. In California, the young doctor has now to pay around $820 a year for such insurance—one practising doctor in four has been the target of a malpractice suit or claim. In Britain, the comparable figure is about $6. Malpractice suits are thought to be a symptom of a breakdown in doctor-patient relationships.

A nationwide study commissioned by the American Medical Association in 1958 reported that 44 per cent of all the people interviewed had had 'unfavourable experiences' with doctors, 32 per cent of them so unsatisfactory that they said they would not return to the same doctor.[6]

(IV)

The general conclusion that many students of medical care are now formulating is that the forces normally presumed in America to produce acceptable allocations of resources are singularly inoperative in the case of hospital services. Profit maximization is clearly not the force directing the behaviour of general hospitals organized as independent units under the control of self-perpetuating boards of directors. Nor is it the force which is making hospital care more and more expensive for many people. American experience does not, therefore, support Dr Lees' advocacy of transferring hospitals to private ownership on the grounds that such ownership would keep down costs, expose poor performance, redress imbalances and be more sensitive to consumer demands.

Economists in Britain like Dr Lees and Professor Jewkes have yet to learn that on both the demand and supply side the market for hospital services is to say the least unusual. Theoretical assumptions about demand have to be revised because of the almost complete consumer ignorance both of the need for and the quality of hospital care—particularly surgical treatment. Price competition in these circumstances does not exist. Patients are told to go to hospital and, in the US, to that institution at which their physician has staff privileges. Moreover, the rapid disappearance of the general practitioner means that more and more people may be losing an essential patient liberty—the advice, protection and defence which the general practitioner is in a position to give his patient. This role of standing between the patient, the hospital and over-specialization increases in importance as scientific medicine becomes more complex, more functionally divided and potentially more lethal. These developments are enlarging the need for the detached, non-specialist diagnostician—the doctor who can interpret scientific medicine and the processes of diagnosis and treatment to the patient according to the circumstances of each case, and without any functional or financial commitment to a specialized area of practice.

In thus being freer, we may suppose, to call in aid all the resources of applied medicine, institutional and community, he simultaneously widens the freedom—the area of interpreted choice—of the patient. The power of specialized authority, with its built-in professional and financial preferences for institutional care, is thus lessened. The patient has some defence against the dictates of inexplicable specialization.

In the absence of this defence deriving from a relationship with a personal, generalized doctor the patient in the United States has increasingly to resort to self-diagnosis. This has become, it is reported, a national hobby.[25] 'It is generally recognized,' said Dr Ratner, 'that America is the most over-medicated, most over-operated, and most over-inoculated country in the world.'[26] The patient has to decide, when he 'feels ill', which—if any—specialist to consult. Is he—or can he be—equipped with the requisite knowledge? Should specialists be expected to perform this generalized role and are they, in their turn, better equipped to do so than the general practitioner?

255

In the American situation, the specialist may be the answer in certain individual circumstances, but these can rarely be known or predicted in advance by the consumer. In other circumstances he may not be. If, moreover, there is a danger of the general practitioner masquerading, so to speak, as a specialist (as there undoubtedly is in the United States) the patient will understandably seek for the 'genuine' specialist. He is thus driven to self-diagnosis. Many other forces, cultural, economic and quasi-professional, also add to the attractions of the scientific 'miracle', specialism and the wonders of hospital medicine.

What we have to ask, therefore, is whether this system of medical care, beginning with patient self-diagnosis, is likely to result in better (more effective) quality of care. In considering this question, we must not forget the importance of both time and opportunity costs. Any definition of quality must take account of: (i) the time that elapses between the onset of symptoms and complete recovery, and (ii) benefits forgone by the patient during this period of illness. Dr Lees, in maintaining that there are 'no differences in principle between medical care and other goods' (p. 24), overlooks these factors and, consequently, leaves it to be assumed that, in conditions of free enterprise medicine, the processes of self-diagnosis and self-selection of the right specialist can be equated with the market choice between cabbages and cauliflowers. Moreover, if consumers are ignorant or restrictive practices also lead to 'market imperfections' these—according to Dr Lees—should be got rid of by government.

This can only mean that consumers of medical care must have as much knowledge of specialist medicine as consumers of cabbages have about vegetables. Dr Lees does not face the problem of educating consumers in medical science—let alone the annual cost of malpractice claims estimated in the United States at $45 million to $50 million[6]—nor the implications of breaking restrictive practices among an occupational group which must then, according to the logic of the market, lose its claim to be a self-controlling profession.

Another imperfection—limitation of free choice—which most observers of trends in American medical care have noted results from the pressures which are increasingly forcing resort to hospital medicine. One comes from the trend towards specialization and the fragmentation of medical practice; there are now in the United States about fifty types of physician. If this trend continues at its present pace the overwhelming majority of physicians will be specialists in twenty years.[27] Another force is expressed by the decline in home care and home visits. Only about 8 per cent of all physician-patient consultations now take place in the home. On the analogy of the market, the sick have to go to an office—or a series of offices some of which are in hospitals—or to an outpatient clinic. Is this a choice that consumers have voluntarily made?

In England and Wales, despite a relatively smaller rural population, over one-third of all such consultations under the Health Service take place in the patient's home.

Private hospital insurance, which has the approval of Dr Lees, Professor Jewkes and other British economists, is perhaps the most powerful force leading to increased hospitalization. The availability of partial prepayment of hospital bills and the absence of cover for all medical bills has resulted, according to many surveys, in unnecessary hospital stays, unnecessary diagnostic procedures, unnecessary treatments and surgical operations.[28] One nationwide survey in 1952–53 reported that 22 per cent of the operations were performed by doctors without any surgical specialization and another 27 per cent by doctors who were neither board-certified nor Fellows of the American College of Surgeons.[6] Another study from Columbia University in 1962 showed that over one-third of all hysterectomies performed were unnecessary.[29]

The imbalances and distortions created by private hospital insurance systems often contradict the principles of good medical care and consumer choice. They must inevitably flourish in market situations in which science has increased the relative ignorance and sense of helplessness among consumers. There is a 'great financial premium on organic diagnosis' because most so-called insurance contracts do not pay for mental illness. The doctor with a patient whose illness is basically mental must choose between 'making a complete diagnosis, as a result of which his patient will suffer financially, or making an incomplete diagnosis so that his patient may derive greater benefits'.[30] Dr Lees is in favour of this dichotomy. He maintains that mental health should be the responsibility of the state. He does not, however, explain why modern medical care for psychological illness is less susceptible to the superior forces of the market than medical care for physical illness—if they can, in the light of advancing knowledge, be operationally separated.

Their inability to make choices leads some consumers to demand 'their rights' written in partial prepayment contracts—X number of days in hospital, access to an expensive drug, three X-rays a year and so on. Similarly, some doctors put up their charges when they learn that consumers have already 'bought' particular units of service. A rise in the price of an appendectomy—which has been 'bought' but which may or may not be necessary—will cost the consumer nothing in the short run or until the policy comes round for renewal.[31]

Other 'commercial' costs which the consumer cannot control reside in the widespread practices between doctors of fee-splitting, rebates, payoffs, commissions and ghost surgery.[32]

In an era when science is demanding more medical teamwork, the problem grows of how to divide responsibility for the patient and how to divide fees from the patient and or his third party agent.

(V)

The cumulative result of these and other unneutral forces in the American medical marketplace in shifting the emphasis away from preventive and community medicine is leading to a cost crisis in the hospitals and in private health insurance. Professor and Mrs Somers, in their authoritative study, came to the conclusion that this problem 'appears to have reached the point where it threatens the possibility of further progress. . . . Consumer resentment could menace the survival of private health insurance.' (p. 407) The free market, which Dr Lees tells us exists in the United States, has failed to call forth an increase in supply to lower consumer costs.

Yet, in attempting to cut costs, the system has gone almost as far as it can in rejecting, cancelling and cutting-off the bad risks and their families—the old, the mentally ill, the chronically ill, the unemployed and redundant, the disabled, widows and many other physically hazardous groups.

The premium structure of voluntary carriers like Blue Cross is being 'commercialized' while the insurance companies (who are increasingly leading the field) have demonstrated their inability to cover the aged and other bad risks. The administrative and commission costs of insurance companies for individual policies rose from 42 per cent in 1948 to 52 per cent in 1958.[6] The consumer now gets less than half his dollar back in medical care.

The medical cost problems of a substantial section of the American population cannot now be solved by insurance carriers; the victory of experience-rating over community-rating has been too overwhelming. As Dr MacLean, recently retired president of the Blue Cross Association, said in 1960:

'A lifetime's experience has led me at last to conclude that the costs of care of the aged cannot be met, unaided, by the mechanisms of insurance or prepayment as they exist today. The aged simply cannot afford to buy from any of these the scope of care that is required, nor do the stern competitive realities permit any carrier, whether non-profit or commercial, to provide benefits which are adequate at a price which is feasible for any but a small proportion of the aged.'[33]

When we turn to consider the supply of doctors, all the signs point to the failure of the market. Yet Dr Lees argued—without recourse to any comparative facts—that the market would work very differently from government. It would produce more doctors—the 'whole process would be anonymous, continuous and pervasive' (p. 46). Between 1949 and 1960 the ratio of all types of practising doctors in Britain per head of the population rose by 21 per cent. In the United States it fell by 2 per cent. Even this position was only held by the use of large numbers of foreign-trained doctors, the quality of whose education is in most instances below United States standards. In 1959, one out of five of all physicians who entered practice, and about one out of three hospital interns and residents, received their medical education outside the country. Over one-half of all general practice residencies are now held by foreign graduates.

American medical education has not had to face such a serious situation since the Flexner Report in 1910. The quantity and quality of applicants to medical schools has been steadily declining, and many schools are having great difficulty in filling their first-year places with well-qualified students. The 1959 Report of the Surgeon General's Consultant Group on Medical Education shows that the United States will be confronted with a grave shortage of doctors in the decade ahead.[34] One estimate suggests that by 1975 the United States may have one doctor to 1,500 people instead of one to 1,000 today.[35] A shortage has been predicted for many years. Dr Lees' 'delicate mechanism' of market forces shows no signs of life.

(VI)

Classical supply and demand analysis may help us to understand the social institutions of very simple and primitive medical economies. But it is singularly unhelpful when applied to the immensely complicated play of forces operating in the field of modern scientific medicine. Theoretical short-cuts are no substitute for the slow and painful study of reality. In an age when we are all oppressed with the weight of facts and our own appalling ignorance such short-cuts appear to offer the prospect of a grand design and a simple choice of alternative courses of action. So Dr Lees tells us that the 'fundamental issue is whether the supply of medical care should be based on the principle of consumers' sovereignty or be made the subject of collective provision'.

This is not the issue in the United States—or in Britain. The American people are faced—and will continue to be faced in a pluralistic society—with a complex series of inter-related social, economic and ethical issues. At different levels they are about different forms of large-scale organized bigness; different degrees of freedom for doctor and patient; open and accountable power or concealed power; whether and to what extent ethical considerations should be uppermost in the principles determining the ways in which medical care is organized. These issues, as Dr Lees rightly says, lie beyond economics and derive ultimately from one's beliefs of what constitutes the good society. He then proceeds to devote his study to the economics of medical supply and demand. This is what divides us. I do not believe—either as a method of study or as a value judgment—that the economics of medical care can be considered apart from the ethical and sociological variables. In the social situation in which the doctor finds himself today, I happen to believe that the conflict between professional ethics and economic man should be reduced as far as is humanly possible. The patient will benefit—but that is the purpose of medicine. To treat him solely as a productive unit is to ignore the fact that for all people the rising level of health consciousness in modern society is one expression of a demand for an improvement in the quality of life as a whole.

How we organize rather than whether we should organize at all is the question we should ask of medical care as well as of education, social security and other social services.

In subjecting Dr Lees' thesis to the test of American experience I have had to be selective in the choice of facts and illustrations. It was necessary to draw materials from those particular sectors of medical care in which market forces are dominant or are thought to be dominant. Inevitably, the result is an unbalanced picture—a picture that omits much that is vital, excellent and dedicated in American medicine and among American doctors. For a more rounded and sympathetic account I would recommend *Doctors, Patients and Health Insurance* by Professor and Mrs Somers.

NOTES

1. Lees, D. S., *Health Through Choice*, Institute of Economic Affairs, 1961.
2. See, for example, the references to Dr Lees by the President of the American Medical Association, *New York State Journal of Medicine*, February 15, 1962.
3. See Chapter XX.
4. British Medical Association, *Report on Contract Practice, Brit. Med. J.*, Supp., July 22, 1905, p. 28.

5. Eckstein, H., *Political Quarterly*, Vol. XXVI, No. 4, 1955, p. 348.

6. Somers, H. M. and A. R., *Doctors, Patients and Health Insurance*, 1961.

7. Abel-Smith, B., *The Hospitals, 1800–1948*, 1964.

8. Jewkes, J. and S., *The Genesis of the British National Health Service*, 1961, p. 36.

9. Quoted in Carter, R., *The Doctor Business*, 1958, p. 88.

10. Kelly, D. Lowell, *Journal of Medical Education*, 1957, Pt 2, pp. 195–6.

11. Roberts, F., *The Cost of Health*, 1952.

12. Durkheim, E., *Professional Ethics and Civic Morals*, 1957 (English Edition), p. 26.

13. Péquignot, H., *Impact of Science on Society*, Vol. V, No. 4, UNESCO, 1954, p. 235.

14. For examples see Watson, G. (Ed.), *The Unservile State*, 1957; Peacock, A., *The Welfare Society*, 1961; CPC, *The Future of the Welfare State*, 1958, *The Responsible Society*, 1959, and *Principles in Practice*, 1960.

15. The principal sources of evidence for this statement on medical care in the United States are contained in references numbered 6, 16–22, 24, 27–8 and 36–45.

16. Roberts, M., '*Trends in the Supply and Demand of Medical Care*', Study Paper No. 5, Joint Economic Committee, US Congress, 1959.

17. Brewster, A. W., and Seldowitz, E., *Public Health Reports*, Vol. 77, No. 9, Washington, September 1962.

18. Gramm, S., 'The Small Scale Hospital and Optional Organization of Community Health Facilities', *Conference Papers on the Economics of Health and Medical Care*, University of Michigan, 1962.

19. Hamilton, J. A., *Patterns of Hospital Ownership and Control*, 1961, p. 95.

20. Seymour, D., *Wall Street Journal*, April 27, 1959, p. 1.

21. *Los Angeles Times*, May 21, 1961.

22. US Public Health Service, Preliminary Report, February 1962.

23. Brown, R. E., in *Principles for Planning the Future Hospital System*, US Public Health Service, Publ. No. 721, 1959.

24. Roberts, M., 'Current Trends in Organization of Health Services', *Conference Papers on the Economics of Health and Medical Care*, University of Michigan, 1962.

25. Fitts, W. T., and Fitts, B., 'Ethical Standards of the Medical Profession', *Annals of the American Academy of Political and Social Science*, January 1955, p. 25.

26. Ratner, H., *Medicine*, Centre for the Study of Democratic Institutions, 1962.

27. US Public Health Service, *Chart Book on Health Status and Health Manpower*, September 1961.

28. Hayes, J. H. (Ed.), *Factors Affecting the Cost of Hospital Care*, 1954.

29. Kaplan, M., quoting a study by Trussell, R. E., *New York Times*, May 11, 1962.

30. Poinstard, P. J., *Medical Economics*, July 7, 1958, p. 42.

31. See, in particular, Somers, H. M. and A. R., *Doctors, Patients and Health Insurance*, 1961, and Taylor, M. G., *The Administration of Health Insurance in Canada*, 1956.

32. Hawley, P. B., 'Surgeons Look at Fee-splitting', *Hospitals*, September 1952; *Annals of the American Academy of Political and Social Science*, January 1955, and State of California (see note 37).

33. MacLean, B. C., 'Group Health Insurance of America', *Health and Welfare Newsletter*, April 1960, p. 2.

34. On supply of doctors see *Physicians for a Growing America*, Report of the Surgeon General's Consultant Group on Medical Education, US Public Health Service, October 1959, and 'Meeting Health Needs by Social Action', *Annals of the American Academy of Political Science*, September 1961.
35. Silver, G. A., *The Nation*, March 18, 1961.
36. Klarman, H. E., 'Analysis of Increase in Cost of Hospital Care', *Conference Papers on the Economics of Health and Medical Care*, University of Michigan, 1962.
37. State of California, *Assembly Interim Committee Reports*, Vol. 15, No. 24, December 1960, p. 121.
38. Sheps, C. G., and Drosness, D. L., 'Prepayment of Medical Care', *New England Journal of Medicine*, February and March 1961.
39. Department of Health, Education and Welfare, *Report to Committee on Ways and Means, Hospitalization Insurance for OASDI Beneficiaries*, 1959.
40. Fulton, W. W., 'General Practice in the USA', *Brit. Med. J.*, January 28, 1961.
41. Carter, R., *The Doctor Business*, 1958.
42. Sanders, M. K. (Ed.), *The Crisis in American Medicine*, 1961.
43. Kessel, R. A., 'Price Discrimination in Medicine', *Journal of Law and Economics*, October 1958.
44. *Brit. Med. J.*, 'Drugs and the Doctor', May 20, 1961, p. 1446.
45. Hyde, D. R., and Wolff, P., 'The American Medical Association', *Yale Law Journal*, May 1954.

POSTSCRIPT TO ETHICS AND ECONOMICS OF
MEDICAL CARE, AUGUST 1967

When this article was first published in 1963 it was criticized by a number of writers. Subsequently, I had to withhold permission from the Institute of Economic Affairs who wished to reprint it with essays by Dr D. S. Lees (now Professor Lees), Professor J. Jewkes and Mrs Jewkes and Professor A. Kemp in an Occasional Paper *Monopoly or Choice in Health Services?* (1964). In deciding to include it in this volume I thought it right to draw the attention of readers to these criticisms and to provide some account of the events that followed its publication in the first number of the journal *Medical Care*.

In August 1963 I received a letter from the Institute's libel lawyer acting on behalf of the Institute and Mr Arthur Seldon. It was complained that a footnote in the article inferred that the Institute's claim to be independent of any political party or group was false. Eventually, I issued an apology (which was published in *Medical Care*) saying I had no intention of making any such imputation and withdrawing it unreservedly. The footnote in question has, therefore, been removed from the article. Otherwise, and apart from one or two corrections and changes, it is reprinted as it first appeared.

After it was published early in 1963 the editor of *Medical Care* was approached by Dr Lees and Professor Jewkes. They asked him to publish articles from them which would put another point of view and criticize my article. These requests presented some difficulties as the editor had already arranged a series of articles for future numbers and, moreover, he was reluctant to give too much space to the subject in the early days of a new journal. However, I persuaded him to offer them space for full length articles. He did so on the understanding (to which I agreed) that if, subsequently, I felt moved to reply, *Medical Care* should have the right to publish any further comment from me. At this point I should add that I received no fee for my original article and that at no time have I been paid a penny for contributions to *Medical Care*, or for consultations and advice as a member of its Editorial Board. The articles by Professor and Mrs Jewkes, Dr Lees and Professor Kemp were published in the October-December 1963 number of *Medical Care* (Vol. 1, No. 4).

In December 1963 the editor was approached by Mr Harris, General Director of the Institute, asking for permission to reprint all four articles in an Institute booklet. By then the editor had decided that *Medical Care* should reprint them in a broader symposium, and had invited other contributions from authorities on the subject as well as having asked me to write a 'winding-up' article. Mr Harris was thus informed that permission to reprint could not be given.

Later in December Mr Harris wrote to me for permission to reprint on the grounds that copyright belonged to the authors, and offered to discuss fees for reprinting. My reply was that I was already morally committed to *Medical Care*; owing to this undertaking I could not, there-fore, give permission. On January 28, 1964, Mr Harris informed me that the Institute was going ahead with its Occasional Paper reprinting in full the articles by Dr Lees, Professor Jewkes and Professor Kemp. 'In the circumstances, we shall have to fall back on the idea of reproducing such extracts from your article as are necessary to make their comments intelligible. In so doing, we have been advised that the fair dealing sec-tion of the Copyright Act permits reprinting of extracts necessary for the purposes of criticism and review.'

In March 1964 the Institute's Occasional Paper was published. It reproduced practically the whole of the section of my article dealing with the American situation; in total, it reproduced about one-half of the article. It included me as one of 'our four authors', and contained a number of misquotations, misprints and misleading statements. One made nonsense of what I had written; another implied that I had deli-berately selected the facts in order to produce an unbalanced picture.

I now add some comment on the criticisms made of my article and draw the attention of students of the subject to other books and refer-ences. I was criticized by Professor and Mrs Jewkes, Dr Lees and Pro-fessor Kemp on broadly three grounds: first, that what I had to say was based on no discernible theoretical foundation; second, that some of my facts were wrong; third, that I was wrong in believing that insurance cannot meet the medical costs problems of a substantial section of the American people.

As to the first, Dr Lees is entitled to his opinion. I have since tried to carry the discussion further in something approaching theoretical terms in some of these essays—especially Chapters XI and XII. Here and else-where I have drawn on the work of two theoretical economists, Professor K. J. Arrow and Professor Boulding of the United States.

Readers who wish to pursue further the more theoretical aspects of the subject are referred to the following materials:

Is Medical Care for Mental Health a Consumption Good?
This is an important question, more particularly because the mentally ill occupy about 40–50 per cent of all hospital beds in Britain and the USA, and take up a substantial proportion of the time of the general prac-titioner. Yet Dr Lees maintains that mental health should be the respon-sibility of the state. No theoretical explanation has been offered in sup-port of this position, nor has Dr Lees (or, to my knowledge, any other economist) demonstrated how, in the light of advancing medical know-ledge, the care of physical illness and mental illness can be operationally, administratively and financially separated in the interests of the patient. For further reading see: Avnet, H. H., *Psychiatric Insurance*, New York, 1963, and review by Forsyth, G., *Medical Care*, July-September 1963, Vol. 1, No. 3, pp. 194–6; leading article 'Pink Spot in Schizophrenia' (evidence in favour of another remarkable addition to the biochemical

theories of schizophrenia), *Brit. Med. J.*, 1, 119, 1966, and Scheff, T. J., 'Preferred Errors in Diagnosis', *Medical Care*, July-September 1964, Vol. 2, No. 3.

Is Human Blood a Consumption Good?
A brief discussion of this question is included in Chapter XII. In a forthcoming book, *The Gift Relationship*, I examine this aspect of medical care in detail.

Consumer Choice in Medical Care in the USA
In addition to other sources already cited, readers are referred to Friedman, J. W., 'The Value of Free Choice in Health Care', and Mott, F. D., 'Group Health's Answer to Our Medical Care Dilemma', both in *Medical Care*, April-June 1965, Vol. 3, No. 2.

Additional General References of Value in the Discussion of Theoretical (as well as Applied) Aspects of the Economics of Medical Care
Klarman, H. E., *The Economics of Health*, Columbia University Press, New York, 1965.
Axelrod and others, *The Economics of Health and Medical Care*, especially sections 3 and 5, University of Michigan, 1964.
Bell, C. S., *Consumer Choice in the American Economy* (especially pp. 285–9), Random House, 1967.
Arrow, K. J., 'Uncertainty and the Welfare Economics of Medical Care', *American Economic Review*, Vol. LIII, No. 5, December 1963.
Rayack, E., 'The American Medical Association and the Supply of Physicians', *Medical Care*, October-December 1964 and January-March 1965, Vol. 2, No. 4, and Vol. 3, No. 1.
Todd, J. W., 'Money and Medicine', *Lancet*, 1, 1217, 1967.
McLachlan, G., 'Non-sense and Sensibility', *Lancet*, 1, 312, 1962.
Seale, J. R., 'Reconstructing the NHS?', *Lancet*, 2, 977, 1961.
Lees, D. S., 'Welfare: Choice and the Market', *New Society*, June 3, 1965, p. 7.
Lees, D. S., *The Economic Consequences of the Professions*, Institute of Economic Affairs, 1966.
Forsyth, G., *Doctors and State Medicine*, Pitman Medical, 1966.
Powell, J. E., *A New Look at Medicine and Politics*, 1966.
Nath, S. K., 'Are Formal Welfare Criteria Required?', *Economic Journal*, LXXIV, p. 548, 1964.
Robinson, J., *Economic Philosophy*, Watts, 1962.
Reagan, M. D., *The Managed Economy*, OUP, 1963.
Scheff, T. J., *op. cit.*

To end this postscript, I deal with some of the factual criticisms of my article by Dr Lees. In support of his statement that I had given a 'grossly distorted' picture of the American medical care situation, he provided four examples.

Example 1 (The administrative and commission costs of insurance companies)

This relates to my statement that for *individual* policies 'the consumer now gets less than half his dollar back in medical care'. Dr Lees accused me of conveying a misleading impression by not providing the relevant information for *group* policies (the proportion for such policies returned in 1958 to consumers in medical care being nearly 90 per cent). I made the statement, however, in the context of a discussion of the inability of insurance companies to cover 'the aged and other bad risks'. I think it was appropriate, therefore, to instance the costs of *individual* policies—not group contracts for employed workers. Had I been dealing with the problems of group policies it would have been necessary to have included much more information. For example, it is an indisputable fact that a very heavy proportion of the administrative costs of group policies (including the work of claims administration) is generally carried by the insured employer or welfare fund and not by the insurance company. The true administrative costs are thus only shown in the published data for individual policies. For further details readers are referred to a sixty-four-page report, *Financial Experience of Health Insurance Organizations in the United States.*[1] This report, published in 1966, brings up to date earlier studies and contains a mass of data which throw light on administrative waste.

Example 2 (Comparison of hospital beds per 1,000 population in England and Wales and the USA)

Dr Lees criticized my data in certain particulars, and 'Most important of all,' he said, 'it is invalid to compare *total* beds in the USA with *staffed* beds in Britain.' I agree. But I did compare like with like. In the source quoted by Dr Lees (*Hospitals*, Guide Issue) the definition of a bed is a bed 'regularly maintained for inpatients (set up and staffed for use)'. Yet Dr Lees says '. . . there are no figures for staffed beds in the USA . . .'.

I do, however, apologize to Dr Lees for not inserting 'staffed' before the USA statistic in my article. An error in citing the period of years was due to the fact that I took the figures from the manuscript of the article in question (*Publ. Hlth. Rep.*, Wash., Vol. 77, No. 9) before publication. It was amended in proof by the authors. Again, I apologize.

For further and later information on the hospital situation in the USA see Professor Roemer's article *'Free' Enterprise in Medicine*[2] ('The US has fewer hospital beds in proportion to population than Great Britain, Sweden, France and many other countries'), *Trends*, 1964 Edition, Pt 1, published by the US Department of Health, Education and Welfare, and Harris, S. E., *The Economics of American Medicine*, Macmillan, New York.

Example 3 (Proprietary and profit-making hospitals)

Dr Lees criticized my statement about a recent spectacular growth in the number of these hospitals. Unfortunately, in his quotation he omitted my words 'in various areas'. This I had taken from the *Wall Street Journal*. For confirmation and expansion of my statement see Klarman, H. E., *op. cit.*, pp. 6–7. Professor Klarman also points out (because of the problem of distinguishing between a hospital bed and a skilled nursing-home bed in the USA) that proprietary owners operated 70 per cent of the 362,000 skilled nursing-home beds in 1962.

Example 4 (Occupancy rate of hospital beds)
Here there is disagreement about the statistics of occupancy of different categories of hospital beds. This aspect of the effectiveness of use of hospital facilities is part of the much wider problem in the USA of a general maldistribution in all sectors of medical care. This I attempted very briefly to indicate, giving a few examples of waste, maldistribution and the absence of planning. There is evidence for many areas in the USA that these problems have become more acute. I append a short list of references for further reading on these and the following issues:

(*a*) the increasing geographical maldistribution of doctors and other medical care personnel;

(*b*) large (and possibly increasing) differentials between income and ethnic groups in access to and utilization of medical care facilities;

(*c*) the inadequacies of voluntary health insurance (the introduction of Medicare in July 1966 was a bleak commentary on Dr Lees' optimism about the progress of voluntary health insurance);

(*d*) the acceleration in the rate of increase in medical care prices at a faster rate than the Consumer Price Index. A Report to the President, *Medical Care Prices*, in February 1967, indicated the magnitude of the 'rapid' and 'unprecedented' increases in 1966 in some of the medical care components'[3]

(*e*) the widening gap between the infant mortality rate for the USA and the rates for England and Wales and other countries, and the worsening differentials in various mortality and morbidity indices within the USA between white and non-white populations and between different family income groups.

References (in addition to those cited in this chapter and postscript)
Vital and Health Statistics Reports, containing data from the National Health Survey and the National Vital Statistics System published by the US Public Health Service.
Trends, Annual Reports published by the US Department of Health, Education and Welfare.
Medical Care Chart Book, Second Edition 1964, Bureau of Public Health Economics, The University of Michigan.
Social Security Bulletin, monthly report from the Social Security Administration, Department of Health, Education and Welfare.
Muller, C., 'Income and the Receipt of Medical Care', *Amer. J. Publ. Hlth.*, 1965, Vol. 55, No. 4, p. 510.
Burns, E., 'The Role of Government in Health Services', *Bulletin of the*

New York Academy of Medicine, 1965.

Medical Care Financing and Utilization, Health Economics Series No. 1, US Public Health Service, 1961.

Reed, L. S., and others, *Independent Health Insurance Plans in the United States: 1965 Survey*, Research Report No. 17, Social Security Administration, 1966.

Appraisal of Hospital Obsolescence, New York City, 1963–65, Hospital Review and Planning Council of Southern New York, Inc., 1965.

Rorie, R. A. B., 'General Practice in North America', *Lancet*, 1, 97, 1963.

Infant Mortality: A Challenge to the Nation, Children's Bureau, US Department of Health, Education and Welfare, 1966.

The Aged Population of the United States, Social Security Administration, US Department of Health, Education and Welfare, 1966.

After this postscript was written, the *Report of the National Advisory Commission on Health Manpower* was published (Vol. 1, US Government Printing Office, November 1967). The Introduction to the Report states: 'There *is* a crisis in American health care. The intuition of the average citizen has foundation in fact. He senses the contradiction of increasing employment of health manpower and decreasing personal attention to patients. *The crisis, however, is not simply one of numbers*' (italics in Report). 'The indicators of such a crisis are evident to us as Commission members and private citizens: long delays to see a physician for routine care; lengthy periods spent in the well-named "waiting room", and then hurried and sometimes impersonal attention in a limited appointment time; difficulty in obtaining care on nights and weekends, except through hospital emergency rooms; unavailability of beds in one hospital while some beds are empty in another; reduction of hospital services because of a lack of nurses; needless duplication of certain sophisticated services in the same community; uneven distribution of care, as indicated by the health statistics of the rural poor, urban ghetto dwellers, migrant workers, and other minority groups, which occasionally resemble the health statistics of a developing country; obsolete hospitals in our major cities; costs rising sharply from levels that already prohibit care for some and create major financial burdens for many more.'

The Report then proceeds to provide evidence on manpower shortages and on the maldistribution of health services and inequalities in the supply of health care.

NOTES

1. Reed, L. S., Research Report No. 12, Social Security Administration, US Department of Health, Education and Welfare, 1966. See also Professor Roemer's corrections of certain of Dr Lees' statements in his review of *Monopoly or Choice in Health Services?* in *New Society*, September 3, 1964, p. 29.
2. Roemer, M. I., *New Society*, January 9, 1964, p. 11.
3. Published by the Department of Health, Education and Welfare.

INDEX

Abel-Smith, B., 51, 138, 140
Ageing, the, 91–102
 planning of services for, 91
 population of, 93, 94, 98
 care by general medical practitioners
  of, 95–7, 101
 trends in the care of, 96–9
 problems in responsibility for care
  of, 99
 co-ordination of services for, 101
 pensions for, 200
American experience of medical care,
 251–60
Ashby, E., Sir, 18, 27, 30
Attlee, Lord, 48, 49

Ben-David, J., 28
Beveridge, Lord, 14, 134
Blindness in old age, prevention of,
 69–71, 78, 79
 see also Ageing, the
Blood transfusion services, 147
 British and New York services com-
  pared, 148–51
Boulding, K. E., 21, 22, 180
British Sociological Association, 15

Canada's health services, 73 passim
Carr-Saunders, Alexander, 17, 32
Charity Organization Society, 39, 48
Child care courses, 54
 see also London School of Economics
Children, 166
 population of, 166, 167
 endowment of, 167–9
 poverty of, 169
 plans for alleviating poverty of,
  169–72
 medical care of, 76
Class divisions,
 bias in university entrance by, 32, 33
 ethnic divisions and, 33

Dicey, A. V., 228, 229, 230, 233, 240
Diploma in Municipal Administration,
 16
Doctors,
 quality and organization of, 210–16
 medical ethics of, 224–6
 patients' conception of the role of,

222, 223
 crisis in the role of, 207
 shortage of, 209, 210, 259
 specialization of, 209
 drug therapy and, 219
 see also General medical practitioners
Donnison, David, 16, 75
Drug therapy, 218
 doctors and, 219–23
 research into, 223
 see also Doctors

Eckhard, Edith, 49
Education Act, 1944, the, 129
Education in the Welfare State, 197
 see also Universities
Emmet, Dorothy, 46
Ethnic divisions, 32, 33
 see also Classes

Family Allowances Act, 129
Family doctor, the
 see General medical practitioner, the
Family Service Departments,
 case for, 88
 arguments against establishment of,
  89
Friedman, M., 139, 153
Fulbright scholars, 54

General medical practitioners, 72, 73,
 76, 77, 207–17
 status and function of, 72
 future of, 73
 common objectives with social workers, 73
 care of the elderly by, 95–7, 101
 care of children by, 76
 concern with psychological aspects,
  108
 crisis in the role of, 207
 role in hospitals of, 209
 recent trends in work of, 216
 see also (1) Social welfare, (2) Doctors
General Medical Practitioners, the
 College of, 95, 96
Geriatric Casework Course, 54
 see also London School of Economics
Gilbert, B. B., 130
Gillie Report, 95, 97, 210, 211, 213

269

Psychiatric social workers, courses for, 53
see also London School of Economics

Raphael, M., 200–4
Reich, Charles, 44
Report on the Incidence of Blindness in England and Wales, 70
Robson, W., 228
Romano, J., 27, 209
Royal Commission on Local Government, 16
Royal Commission on Medical Education, 26

Seebohm Committee, 16, 82, 135
Shil, E., 15
Social administration,
scope of, 13
external relationships of, 15
teaching of, 16–19
problems in teaching of, 19
definition of, 20–3
Social Administration Association, 13, 14
external relationships of, 15, 16
on higher education, 17
on teaching, 17, 18
Social administrators, 14, 16, 54
Social change, 42, 43, 60, 74, 75, 139, 156, 211
Social Medical Association, 14
Social Science Department of the London School of Economics, the,
establishment of, 48–50
academic and professional status in, 49
influence at home and abroad of, 50–5
development of, 49–55
research at, 51
training of teachers at, 52–5
training courses in, 52–5
see also London School of Economics
Social Science Research Council, 23
Social Science Society, 49
Social security, 59–71
definition of, 173
relationships between programmes of, 60–2, 69
benefits and uses of, 62
classification of, 62, 63, 117

functions of, 63, 64
objectives of, 64, 65
effectiveness of, 65–7
participation, choice and rights in, 67
blindness and, 69–71
models of, 174–7
as an agent in structural change, 177–85
see also Welfare State, the
Social welfare, 74–83
problems of reform in, 81–3
possible effects of increasing wealth on, 140–64
see also Welfare State, the
Social work, schools of,
function of, 38
relationship between, 38
research by, 38–46
social policy in, 39, 42, 45
professional status in, 40, 41
social diagnosis by, 42
ethical problems of policy in, 43–5
educational role of, 45
Social work, the profession of,
education in, 15
accepted purpose of, 74
shortage in, 80, 87
criticism of, 85, 86
training for, 87
see also London School of Economics
Sorsby, Arnold, 70, 78
Sprott, W. J. H., 13

Townsend, P., 95, 134, 140

Universities,
function of, 18, 25, 28
sociology of, 25
teaching in, 26–8
balance between teaching and research in, 27
costs and distribution of, 28, 31
freedoms within, 28, 29, 31, 34 -
vocationalism in,29
class bias in admission to, 32, 33

Vivekananada, 41

Webb, Sidney and Beatrice, 48, 229, 236
Welfare, economic and social models of, 26